THE TWILIGHT LANGUAGE

For
our Parents

THE TWILIGHT LANGUAGE

Explorations in Buddhist Meditation and Symbolism

Roderick S. Bucknell
and
Martin Stuart-Fox

CURZON
PRESS

THE TWILIGHT LANGUAGE

Paperback edition

First published 1993 in the United Kingdom by
Curzon Press Ltd.
St John's Studios
Church Road
Richmond
Surrey TW9 2QA

ISBN 0 7007 0234 2

Reprinted 1994

British Library Cataloguing in Publication Data
A CIP record of this title is available on request from
The British Library

Printed and Bound in Great Britain by The Cromwell Press, Melksham, Wiltshire

CONTENTS

PLATES

See pp. 95 – 102

1 The four peripheral dhyāni Buddhas depicted around a *stūpa*. The view is from the north-east and shows Amoghasiddhi (facing north, in the no-danger *mudrā*) and Akṣobhya (facing east, in the earth-touching *mudrā*).

2 Akṣobhya (the dhyāni Buddha of the east) with his hands in the earth-touching *mudrā*.

3 Ratnasambhava (south) in the gift-bestowing *mudrā*.

4 Amitābha (west) in the meditation *mudrā*.

5 Amoghasiddhi (north) in the no-danger *mudrā*.

6 Vairocana (centre) in the Dharma-wheel *mudrā*.

7 A typical Tibetan *stūpa* or *chörten*. The *stūpa* form is considered to be composed of the traditional four geometrical shapes: the cube, sphere, cone, and hemisphere.

8 A large *stūpa* of a different style, illustrating a variant arrangement of the dhyāni Buddhas. The view is from the south-east and shows Vairocana (who properly belongs in the centre, that is, concealed inside the *stūpa*) located between Akṣobhya and Ratnasambhava. Ratnasambhava's jewel emblem, in stylized fleur-de-lis form, is visible above him on the tapering tower.

Photographs from Kathmandu and environs.

PREFACE BY R.B.

It is now some sixteen years since I first realized the importance of symbolic language in Buddhism. At the time of that initial discovery I was a *bhikkhu* (Buddhist monk), living in a quiet forest monastery near Chiangmai in northern Thailand. I had been practising, for the past year and a half, some of the best-tried techniques of Buddhist meditation and, feeling that they were too limited in scope, had begun developing different techniques which I at the time assumed to be original and unorthodox. This meditative experimentation brought some novel insights into the nature of mental processes. It also led me to rethink certain aspects of Buddhist doctrine; teachings that had seemed to make little sense now became intelligible — provided that certain key terms were understood as having a second, non-literal level of meaning, a *symbolic* meaning.

This finding encouraged me to press on with my experiments in meditation, and at the same time to study more closely the Pali canon of Theravāda Buddhism, along with modern commentators' interpretations of it. During the next year (my second as a *bhikkhu*) my meditative experiments led to extension and refinement of the techniques, and my textual studies turned up progressively more substantial evidence of symbolic language in the canon. Meanwhile, reading on related topics revealed that my findings were not original. The meditative techniques I was developing had been described by various writers decades earlier, and the importance of symbolic language in the Pali canon had been pointed out at least ten years previously by the Thai monk Buddhadasa and discussed by him in a number of lectures and publications. In addition, I learned that other branches of Buddhism explicitly acknowledge the existence of symbolic language. In the Vajrayāna tradition, now preserved mainly in Tibetan sects, it has long been recognized that certain important teachings are expressed in a form of secret symbolic language known as *saṃdhyā-bhāṣā*, 'Twilight Language'. *Mudrās* and *mantras, maṇḍalas* and *cakras*, those mysterious devices and diagrams that were so much in vogue in the pseudo-Buddhist hippie culture of the 1960s, were all examples of Twilight Language, and were therefore relevant to my developing ideas on Buddhist symbolism. I came to feel that I was confronting a vast problem in decipherment, similar to that which an archaeologist confronts when he examines a corpus of inscriptions in an unknown ancient tongue. I had gained a few hints about the nature of this symbolic language, but for the most part it remained a baffling mystery.

At about this time I began communicating my findings to my former fellow-student and travelling companion, Martin Stuart-Fox. He was in Paris at the time; but a little more than a year previously we had spent some time together when he visited me in Chiangmai, and one of our main topics of conversation had been meditation. In a series of lengthy letters I described to him the meditative techniques I was experimenting with, the apparently intentional symbolic correspondence between those techniques and certain key Buddhist teachings, and the challenging problems posed by the concept of Twilight Language. Martin expressed enthusiasm for my ideas, while at the same time criticizing some of my tentative interpretations as poorly substantiated or historically improbable. An historian, with Asia as his area of particular interest, he was able to point out chronological discrepancies entailed in the interpretations, which I, trained principally as a linguist and with a poor sense of history, had been unconscious of. Thus began a fruitful exchange of ideas which would in time lead to our agreeing to collaborate in writing this book.

I spent the third year of my monkhood in India, searching — in museums, libraries, ashrams, and Tibetan monasteries — for material relevant to my research into Buddhist symbolism. That research grew progressively wider in scope as the far-reaching ramifications of the problem gradually became apparent. On the side of symbolism the study took in material from fields as diverse as temple architecture, cosmology, and mathematical notations; and on the side of meditation it entailed numerous discussions with gurus of every religious persuasion, in addition, of course, to continued personal practice. My ideas on the nature and significance of the Twilight Language developed gradually, and I repeatedly revised and refined my tentative interpretations. In its later stages this process of finding meaning in the symbols became increasingly dependent on Martin's historical insights, particularly on his recognition of the role of macrocosm-microcosm parallelism.

It was during the summer of that year in India that I began writing the first draft of this book. At the time, I was staying near Almora, a small town in the Himalayan foothills, and the environment was particularly conducive to such work. The people with whom I was sharing the big colonial house were keen followers of Krishnamurti, whose teachings on meditation proved, on examination, to be largely in agreement with my findings; and only half a hour's walk away lived Lama Govinda, author of several books on Tibetan Buddhism, who was always happy to spend an afternoon discussing meditation and symbolism. I completed that first draft shortly after my return to Thailand, and sent it to Martin for his critical comments. He pointed out many shortcomings, but work on revising the draft had to be delayed because of various worldly problems. (These entailed, among other things, my leaving the Buddhist Sangha and returning as a layman to Australia.)

Two years later Martin and I met again in Calcutta and began a year-long field trip through India, in the course of which I wrote a second draft. Again Martin read and criticized it, but this time his criticisms and suggestions for improvement were so far-reaching and of such value that I recognized that we really ought to collaborate. The book thus became a joint work. Progress thereafter was slow because of many competing commitments; but now, a further eleven years later, the work is at last complete. In its final form the book is much less extensive than were the earlier drafts. This is because we decided to delete much material that seemed only marginally relevant; for example, the longest chapter in the second draft, entitled 'Alphabet Symbolism', has been completely deleted, as being more suitable for a specialized journal article. The result is a more compact book encompassing only the most important examples of symbolism found in the Pali canon and in the later Twilight Language of Tantric Buddhism.

A major objective in writing this book has been to offer practising meditators new lines of approach by drawing attention to possible alternative interpretations of certain Buddhist teachings. Some friends who read the nearly completed manuscript asked why we had bothered to discuss symbolism at all, since the meditative techniques to which the sybolism appears to refer are so much more important. We have two main reasons for discussing meditation and symbolism together. First, meditators with a Buddhist background are often reluctant to try out a meditative technique unless they have some convincing evidence that it was taught by the Buddha; the symbols may provide this evidence. Second, many people with an interest in Buddhism tend to take the symbols at face value; an attempt to find meaning underlying the symbols may help remove misconceptions. For both of these reasons it is appropriate to discuss symbolism as well as meditative practice, and to seek to understand the relationship between them.

Brisbane,
November, 1985

PREFACE BY M.S-F.

My interest in Asian religions and philosophies goes back to the early 1960s when I spent six months in Japan and Korea studying Zen Buddhism and Japanese art. When later I heard from Rod Bucknell that he had become a Buddhist monk, it was natural that I should visit him in Thailand, and that our discussions should centre upon Buddhist thought and meditation. The following year (1967) I spent in India pursuing my interests in early Indian history and philosophy.

When Rod later wrote to me outlining certain evidence of connections between meditative techniques and Buddhist symbolism, I was immediately impressed. During the long correspondence which ensued I acted as a critical sounding board for Rod's developing ideas. Four months of reading and meditation in southern Spain during the winter of 1969–70 enabled me to verify to my own satisfaction some of his meditative techniques, and to offer an historically-based critique of a first draft of his preliminary interpretation of Buddhist symbolism. As a result we agreed to meet again in India to pursue a further programme of joint research. This led Rod to write a much modified second draft, and me to undertake an extensive examination of the religious and philosophical presuppositions of Indian thought at the time of the Buddha.

Following discussion of the second draft, we decided to collaborate in writing a third draft which would incorporate our combined findings. At my suggestion, analysis of the more abstruse symbolism was omitted so as to focus attention on two principal objects of study: the Buddha's teachings on meditation, and the esoteric tradition that appears to have arisen from them. Emphasis has therefore been placed on the earliest Buddhist texts, and on the symbolism of the Vajrayāna. This has meant that a large part of Rod's analysis of Buddhist symbolism has still be to published, a task to which I hope he will soon be able to devote himself.

I wish to make clear that all credit for developing the introspective meditative techniques described in this book, and for the initial interpretation of aspects of Buddhist symbolism in terms of those techniques, is due to Rod Bucknell. In the early stages, my contribution was confined to criticism of Rod's original tentative interpretations, some suggested modifications, and emphasis upon methodological rigour and historical development. Subsequently my most important contribution has been to develop the argument concerning the role of magico-symbolic macrocosm-microcosm parallelism, both as an explanation for the Buddha's apparent equating of mental states with samsaric existence, and as providing a connecting theme underlying later developments.

From the point of view of Buddhist scholarship, our investigations into symbolism in Buddhism are still very incomplete. Much of the history of early Buddhist esotericism and its symbolic expression remains to be worked out. We hope, however, that this preliminary study will motivate other scholars to pursue some of the lines of investigation we have sketched out, and to correct whatever errors we may have made.

As it stands, the book is written not for scholars alone, but for a wider, less specialized readership. Consequently the use of Pali and Sanskrit technical terms in the text has been minimized, and footnoted references are for the most part to English translations of texts, or to readily accessible secondary sources. The footnotes are in any case intended for readers with more specialized interests and may be ignored by the general reader.

Brisbane,
November, 1985

ACKNOWLEDGEMENTS

Several people have, through their conversation, public speaking, or writing, deeply influenced the ideas expressed in this book. Three we would mention in particular are Buddhadasa, Krishnamurti, and Anagarika Govinda. The debt we owe to all three will be evident to any reader. We would like to thank in addition those who read earlier versions of our manuscript: Ross Reat, Elisabeth and David Stuart-Fox, and Greg Tutko. Their criticisms and comments were of great value, though not always acted on. Finally we would like to thank Mary Kooyman, who so patiently typed the final draft from our often barely legible manuscript.

CHAPTER I

MEDITATION AND SYMBOLISM

The past two decades have seen, particularly in the more affluent Western nations, a rapid growth of interest in Eastern techniques of meditation. Many thousands of Westerners, from all age groups and all walks of life, now regularly practise methods of mental development which previously were little known outside the Hindu and Buddhist communities of south and east Asia.

This interest in meditation reflects a growing recognition of the centrality of consciousness, both in the life of the individual and in the evolution of the human species. While man's understanding of his physical environment is increasing at an astonishing rate, his understanding of his own mind remains slight. Meditation provides, its proponents claim, a means for redressing this imbalance, a means whereby an individual can gain insight into his own nature, develop supernormal mental powers, or simply attain tranquillity and detachment amid the stresses of modern life.

Meditation has become more than a matter of personal experimentation by individual seekers. It has become as well an area of systematic research by psychologists, physiologists, and others. Within psychology there has developed a new and admittedly still controversial branch, transpersonal psychology, which, since it recognizes the reality and importance of 'ego-transcending' states of consciousness, is particularly concerned with the subjective side of meditative practice.[1] Meditation, until recently one of the most mysterious aspects of Eastern religious practice, is rapidly coming to be recognized throughout the world as a subject for serious scientific and scholarly study.

However, any serious attempt, whether by trained researchers or by individual seekers, to investigate the how and why of meditation soon reveals a mass of controversy and confusion. The meditative techniques presently being practised are, outwardly at least, very diverse. For example, the 'mindfulness of breathing' (*ānāpānasati*)[2] practised in many Buddhist communities, the *kōan* meditation of Zen, and the visualization of deities prescribed by some Tibetan and Hindu gurus appear to have little in common. Equally diverse are the effects claimed for the different practices: trance-like states (*jhānas*), a sudden breakthrough into a new mode of consciousness (*satori*), supernormal powers such as clairvoyance, even enlightenment, *nirvāṇa*, or oneness with Brahman. Regarding the relative merits of these techniques and effects, practising meditators hold a variety of views. Some insist that only their own chosen method is 'correct'; others maintain that all methods are equally valid, being simply different paths to a single ultimate goal; and a few paradoxically declare that there is no method of practice and no goal, that all the meditator should do is 'be aware'.[3]

The jargon of meditation is often unclearly defined and loosely used. Meditation masters commonly employ specialized terms such as *samādhi* and *jhāna*, or refer to unfamiliar concepts such as 'opening the *cakras*' and 'arousing the *kuṇḍalinī*', without first making clear what they understand by them. Scholars writing on meditation are often guilty of a similar fault, freely using Sanskrit or Pali terms without adequate explanation. Often one gains the impression that few authorities, whether meditation masters or scholars, are at all clear in their own minds about some of the most important terms they use.

Anyone who expresses curiosity about the effects of meditation or questions meditators about their practice is likely to be rebuked for adopting a wrong approach. He will be told that the only way to find out about meditation is to practise oneself, and that no amount of intellectual discussion can ever take the place of actual experience. But this confronts the inquirer with a dilemma, because even if he does intend to take up meditation practice, he is hardly in a position to decide which of the many meditative techniques to adopt unless he has some prior knowledge to guide him. The decision to embark on a meditation course is one that cannot be taken lightly. Some gurus warn that their course of practice calls for a lifetime of unremitting effort — perhaps even several lifetimes! Before making such a commitment, the aspiring meditator will need to have considerable confidence in the efficacy of his chosen technique. It therefore seems essential that any decision to begin practising meditation be based on a preliminary intellectual appraisal of the different techniques.

But for an aspiring meditator or a research psychologist to be in a position to make such an evaluation, he would need to have access to clear and comprehensive accounts of the various available techniques and resulting mental states, written by people with adequate first-hand experience of them. Ideally such accounts would include an assessment of the efficacy of each technique in producing its claimed mental or 'spiritual' effect, so that comparisons could be made.

Such a body of literature on meditation does not yet exist; indeed the suggestion that competent meditators should produce such detailed accounts of their experiences would probably be rejected by most meditation masters, and by many psychologists as well. Meditation masters would reject it on the grounds that knowledge of meditative techniques must be gained not by reading books but by practising under an experienced guru, who will reveal his method step by step. It is for this reason that a meditation master usually says little to lay people about his methods, and urges his students not to discuss their experiences with anyone but himself. This objection of course begs the question, since it again tells the would-be meditator that he must embark on the course of practice with little or no prior knowledge of what it will entail and where it will lead.

Many psychologists would reject the idea of experienced meditators producing adequate accounts of their inner experiences on familiar anti-introspectionist grounds: inner mental experiences are beyond the reach of scientific observation, an investigator cannot effectively observe his own mental states, etc. But such objections carry less weight now than they did a few decades ago. There has recently been a marked movement back toward the pre-behaviourist position that the proper object of psychological investigation is, after all, mental phenomena as they may be introspectively observed, rather than their physiological correlates. (For example, research into mental imagery has come to rely increasingly on observation of purely mental phenomena by trained introspecting subjects.)[4] The emergence of the transpersonal perspective in psychology has led to the publication of several first-person descriptions of meditative experiences covering a limited range of meditation techniques.[5] It remains true, however, that most published psychological studies of meditation report what the psychologist has observed in his meditating subjects. The psychologist still usually approaches meditation from the outside rather than from the inside; only rarely does he practise meditation himself and report on his own inner experiences.

Psychologists' scepticism about the possibility of meditators making accurate inner observations may in time be shown to be unjustified. A major claim made for some forms of meditation is that they bring to the meditator an ability to perceive with exceptional clarity everything that is happening in his own mental world. With this claim goes an admonition against speculation on related philosophical problems, for example on the old question whether such observation is even in principle possible; if the meditator will simply put the method into practice, he will find — the texts claim — that he does in fact attain the promised insights. The available scant descriptions of *satori* and other meditative attainments stress that they are very different from ordinary perception and knowing. It would therefore seem premature for psychologists to rule out the possibility that an experimenter practising meditation himself could gain supernormally clear insight into, and understanding of his own inner experiences.

The Buddhist Path

At present, in the absence of any adequate comparative assessment of meditative techniques, arguments in favour of this or that method are often supported by citing textual evidence that it was practised and taught by some great master in the distant past. The problem of finding out about meditation is therefore commonly approached through the texts of early Hinduism and Buddhism. But this approach raises further problems. Both Hinduism and Buddhism, as products of centuries of growth and accretion, are very heterogeneous. Hinduism is particularly complex because it is not based on the teachings of a single original founder. The Hindu meditative tradition probably had a multiple origin somewhere in the prehistory of the non-Aryan cultures of north India, and though certain branches of it have been codified at different times, it has always been many-sided and diffuse.

On the other hand, Buddhism, though now split into numerous schools, did have a single, definite beginning. Buddhism in its various forms derives from the teachings imparted some 2,500 years ago by one man, the Buddha, Gotama Sākyamuni. Indeed Buddhism can be said to have originated from the unique experience which Gotama underwent on a certain night, when, according to his own account, he attained his spiritual goal, enlightenment and *nirvāṇa*. Gotama's teachings as they have come down to us are for the most part a description of the course of practice whereby others may attain that same goal. Consequently there is, beneath the diversity of Buddhism, a unity which one approaches more and more closely the further one traces back the different strands.[6] Buddhism lays great emphasis on meditation, and has developed a massive literature on the subject.

The aspiring meditator might therefore expect to find in the Buddhist scriptures ample information on the basis of which he could decide which technique to adopt; and the Western-trained psychologist might expect to glean there some idea of the materials and methods of traditional oriental research into the mind.

A preliminary survey appears to confirm these expectations. The Buddhist texts contain numerous accounts of Gotama's course of practice leading from ignorance and bondage, to enlightenment and liberation. Of such accounts the best known and most highly esteemed is the 'Noble Eightfold Path',[7] a graded series of eight stages, namely: right view, right aspiration, right speech, right action, right livelihood, right effort, right mindfulness, and right concentration. Of these eight stages the first five deal with the intellectual and moral basis which must be established before meditation can be undertaken, and the last three are concerned with meditative practices.

The first of the eight stages, right view (or right understanding), is the basic intellectual understanding of the purpose and value of the path which the aspirant needs before committing himself to its practice.[8] (The would-be meditator, consulting gurus and reading books on meditation, may recognize that he is already in the process of developing this first stage.) The second stage, right aspiration, consists in a firm resolve by the aspirant to follow the path until he has achieved enlightenment. The next three stages, right speech, action, and livelihood, embrace certain rules of moral conduct which the aspirant takes upon himself as a foundation for the meditative practice that will follow. Right effort consists in a conscious striving to eliminate 'unwholesome' thoughts, that is, thoughts based on greed, pride, hatred, anger, and so on, and to cultivate 'wholesome' thoughts in their place. Right mindfulness (*sammā sati*) is a very comprehensive practice, in which the meditator develops 'bare attention' to every movement and posture of his body, every feeling, and every activity of his mind. Finally, right concentration (*sammā samādhi*) is the developing of proficiency in the *jhānas*, stages of progressively deeper concentration, usually given as four in number. This path of practice is described in outline in a number of the earliest *suttas*[9] (supposedly Gotama's original discourses), and is explicated in minute detail in the post-canonical manuals. Furthermore, it is practised by many Buddhist monks at the present day, so that the aspiring meditator should have little difficulty finding teachers prepared to guide him through even its more advanced stages.

The Eightfold Path as described gives an impression of orderliness and completeness. However, closer study of the texts indicates that it is not after all a complete account of Gotama's course of practice. A number of *suttas* describe a Tenfold Path.[10] This differs from the Eightfold Path in having two further stages following right concentration, namely right insight or knowledge or wisdom (*sammā ñāṇa*) and right liberation (*sammā vimutti*). These two extra stages are nowhere described, nor is any explanation given for their frequent omission. The tenth stage, right liberation, is presumably to be equated with the final goal, *nirvāṇa*. However, the ninth stage, right insight, which appears from its position in the list to be of crucial importance, remains unaccounted for.

In the Pali Tipiṭaka (the canon of Theravāda Buddhism) meditative practices are divided into two broad categories: practices leading to mental tranquillity (*samatha*) and practices leading to insight (*vipassanā*).[11] Tranquillity meditation, the more basic form, consists in stilling the mind through concentration; insight meditation, the more advanced form, brings the meditator progressively to a full realization of 'the true nature of things'. It is stated that tranquillity meditation, though valuable as a foundation for insight meditation, is not indispensable, and may be bypassed by exceptionally gifted meditators.[12] Thus the essence of the course of meditation is the developing of special powers of insight, while the practice of concentration serves as a valuable but not indispensable preparation and foundation for this. The Eightfold Path, stopping short at right concentration, therefore appears to be incomplete. If right liberation (*nirvāṇa*) is to be attained, right concentration must be followed by right insight.

The nature of right insight can be clarified to some extent by comparing the Tenfold Path with other lists of stages to be found

Table 1. Correspondences between latter portions of Tenfold Path and Footprints of a Buddha.

Tenfold Path	Footprints of a Buddha
7. right mindfulness	4. mindfulness
8. right concentration	5-8. the four *jhānas*
9. right insight	9-11. the three knowledges
10. right liberation	12. liberation

in the Tipiṭaka. Particularly useful in this respect is a list of twelve stages, of which the last eight are referred to figuratively as the 'Footprints' of a Buddha.[13] This list generally agrees closely with the Tenfold Path; however, toward the end of the series the correspondence is as shown in Table 1. In the Tenfold Path, right insight (*sammā ñāṇa*) comes between right concentration (i.e. the *jhānas*) and right liberation; and in the 'Footprint' series, the three knowledges (each of which bears a name ending in *-ñāṇa*, see below) come between the *jhānas* and liberation. Clearly, then, right insight is to be equated with the three knowledges.

The three knowledges (*vijjās*) are listed as:

1. recollection of one's former existences in *saṃsāra* (*pubbenivāsānussati-ñāṇa*);
2. knowledge of the death and rebirth of beings according to their *karmas* (*sattānaṃ cutūpapāta-ñāṇa*);
3. knowledge of the destruction of the cankers (*āsavakkhaya-ñāṇa*).

The aspiring meditator who turns to the Buddhist texts for guidance may well be disconcerted at this finding: once he has mastered the *jhānas*, he must practise recollecting his former existences and so on. That this is indeed the Buddhist course of practice is made clear at many places in the Tipiṭaka. In particular, it is indicated by Gotama's account of his own enlightenment (as given, for example, in the *Bhayabherava-sutta*).[14] In that account Gotama describes how, having perfected the four *jhānas*, he then developed the three knowledges. The perfection of the third knowledge, equated with enlightenment, was immediately followed by the long sought-for liberation. The three knowledges are therefore clearly crucial stages in the Buddhist course of meditative practice.

According to the texts, Gotama attained these three knowledges in succession during a single evening of meditation beneath the Bodhi Tree (at Gayā in north India). The canonical description of his experience is as follows:

> Thus with the mind composed, quite purified, quite clarified, without blemish, without defilement, grown soft and workable, fixed, immovable, I directed my mind to the knowledge and recollection of former habitations: I remembered a variety of former habitations, thus: one birth, two births, three. . . four. . . five . . . ten. . . twenty. . . thirty. . . forty. . . fifty . . a hundred . . a thousand. . . a hundred thousand births, and many an eon of integration and many an eon of disintegration and many an eon of integration-disintegration; such a one

was I by name, having such and such a clan, such and such a colour, so was I nourished, such and such pleasant and painful experiences were mine, so did the span of life end. Passing from this, I came to be in another state where such a one was I by name, . . . so did the span of life end. Passing from this, I arose here. Thus I remember divers former habitations in all their modes and detail. This, brahman, was the first knowledge attained by me in the first watch of the night; ignorance was dispelled, knowledge arose, darkness was dispelled, light arose, even as I abided diligent, ardent, self-resolute.

Then . . . I directed my mind to the knowledge of the passing hence and the arising of beings. With the purified *deva*-vision surpassing that of men I see beings as they pass hence or come to be; I comprehend that beings are mean, excellent, comely, ugly, well-going, ill-going, according to the consequences of their deeds, and I think: Indeed these worthy beings who were possessed of wrong conduct . . . at the breaking up of the body after dying, have arisen in a sorrowful state, a bad bourn, the abyss, Niraya Hell. But these worthy beings who were possessed of good conduct . . . after dying, have arisen in a good bourn, a heaven world. Thus with the purified *deva*-vision surpassing that of men do I see beings as they pass hence, as they arise . . . according to the consequences of their deeds. This, brahman, was the second knowledge attained by me in the middle watch of the night . . .

Then . . . I directed my mind to the knowledge of the destruction of the cankers. I understood as it really is: This is anguish, this is the arising of anguish, this is the stopping of anguish, this is the course leading to the stopping of anguish. I understood as it really is: These are the cankers, this is the arising of the cankers, this is the stopping of the cankers, this is the course leading to the stopping of the cankers. Knowing this thus, seeing thus, my mind was freed from the canker of sense-pleasures, and my mind was freed from the canker of becoming, and my mind was freed from the canker of ignorance. In freedom the knowledge came to be: I am freed; and I comprehended: Destroyed is birth, brought to a close is the Brahma-faring, done is what was to be done, there is no more of being such or such. This, brahman, was the third knowledge attained by me in the last watch of the night; ignorance was dispelled, knowledge arose, darkness was dispelled, light arose even as I abided diligent, ardent, self-resolute.[15]

This description, purporting to be Gotama's own account of how he attained enlightenment, is repeated a number of times in the Tipiṭaka. It is also repeated, with appropriate grammatical changes, as an exhortation to others to do likewise, or as a description of how the well-disciplined monk practises the higher stages of meditation. For example: 'With his mind composed . . . fixed, immovable, he [the monk] directs his mind to the knowledge and recollection of former habitations . . .'[16] The introductory phrase describes the condition of a mind established in right concentration; the remainder describes the attainment of the three knowledges.

It is not immediately evident why right insight and right liberation should have been omitted from most descriptions of the Path. One possible explanation is that these two stages are particularly difficult and so were taught only to the most advanced meditators. Right effort, mindfulness, and concentration, though not easy to practise, present no insuperable problems; but recollection of one's former existences and the other two knowledges appear, on the face of it, truly superhuman attainments, even if one accepts on faith the doctrine of rebirth which they presuppose.

A second possible explanation is that the three knowledges are perhaps to be understood as *fruits* of the perfecting of earlier stages, rather than as active practices. Perhaps the knowledges will arise spontaneously once right concentration and the rest have been perfected, in which case there is no need to do more than list them. But such an explanation is ruled out by the wording of the available descriptions of the knowledges. Gotama's statement, 'I directed my mind to the knowledge and recollection of former habitations . . .' indicates an active mental exercise. And discussions of the knowledges to be found in post-canonical manuals such as the *Visuddhimagga* (The Path of Purity), indicate that the authors understood recollection of former existences etc. as calling for considerable conscious effort on the part of the meditator.[17] It therefore appears that the three knowledges are active practices to which the meditator must devote his energies once he has perfected the *jhānas*.

For a meditator who is ready to move on to the practice of right insight, the Tipiṭaka account is inadequate as a practical guide.[18] It tells the meditator to recollect his former existences without indicating how he should go about it. Now we would not expect to find in the Tipiṭaka a full description of right liberation, *nirvāṇa*. Gotama maintained that the aspirant should not waste time asking about the nature of the goal, but should concern himself instead with the path leading to that goal. We would, however, expect a clear and adequate description of the stages on this path; and indeed, up to and including right concentration, the textual account is generally sufficient as a guide for a practising meditator. But for some reason the crucial next stage, right insight, is described not only inadequately, but in terms that leave one wondering whether it was even meant to be taken literally.

The texts do give some further details about what happened on the night of Gotama's enlightenment. They tell, for example, how Māra (the Buddhist counterpart of Satan), armed with weapons and accompanied by his three seductive daughters, attempted to distract the meditating Gotama; and of how Gotama repulsed them by calling on the earth to bear witness to the merit he had acquired in former existences.[19] But such anecdotes, though they possibly have a concealed meaning, are of no immediate help to the meditator seeking practical guidance on how to achieve the goal to which all Buddhists aspire — to replicate Gotama's experience of enlightenment.

Symbolism in the Tipiṭaka

The failure of the earliest surviving Buddhist scriptures to provide an adequate account of the meditative path to enlightenment not only comes as a disappointment to the aspiring meditator; it also poses problems for the scholar. Why are the most advanced meditative techniques described so cryptically? Did Gotama, despite claims to the contrary, deliberately hold something back? Or was his description perhaps couched in symbolic language which made sense only to initiates or to monks who had already made considerable progress in meditation? For the Buddhist scholar, as well as for the meditator, these are important and far-reaching questions.

To suggest that Gotama deliberately held something back, or that he described his path of meditative practice in symbolic language intelligible only to the select few, is to suggest the existence of an esoteric transmission in Buddhism. This raises a question long debated by Buddhist scholars and meditators: Was there, in addition to the overt teaching recorded in the Tipiṭaka, a special teaching on advanced meditative techniques which adept masters passed on only to certain selected students considered fit to receive it? The historical and textual evidence for and against an esoteric transmission in Buddhism will be considered fully in Chapter II; here discussion is limited to the evidence provided by examples of seemingly symbolic language.

The question of symbolic language in the Tipiṭaka has recently attracted much attention among Buddhists, mainly as a result of the writings of the Thai monk-scholar-meditator, Buddhadasa Bhikkhu. Buddhadasa points out that certain aspects of Buddhist teaching are unintelligible, or at least lacking in useful content, unless they are assumed to be symbolic.[20] He cites, as an obvious and uncontroversial example, the account of the attempt by Māra and his daughters to distract Gotama in his meditations. It is widely recognized by practising Buddhists, unsophisticated laymen and scholarly monks alike, that Māra is a purely symbolic figure, a personification of 'unwholesome thoughts'. The same is true of Māra's daughters, the symbolism being in this case quite explicit, since the names of the three, Taṇhā, Arati, and Rati, are Pali terms meaning 'Craving', 'Discontent', and 'Desire'. The story of Māra and his daughters is therefore a symbolic account of events in the mind of the meditator; it symbolizes the arising of distracting thoughts, or as Buddhadasa puts it, 'any mental state opposed to the good and wholesome, opposed to spiritual progress'.[21] Buddhadasa goes on to interpret in similar fashion many otherwise unintelligible aspects of Buddhist doctrine. For example, he identifies the various hells and heavens of the Buddhist cosmology with states of consciousness, some of them familiar, everyday states, others supernormal states such as the *jhānas*, which may be attained in the course of meditation practice.[22] (He does not, however, suggest that the three knowledges might be interpreted in this way.)

The essence of Buddhadasa's position is that certain aspects of Gotama's teaching as we find it in the Tipiṭaka are couched in a kind of symbolic language. This he terms Dharma Language, as opposed to Everyday Language. In this symbolic Dharma Language mental states and processes are represented by physical objects, places, and events. Buddhadasa claims that many serious misunderstandings of Buddhist doctrine have arisen through people's failure to recognize Dharma Language as such, and interpret it accordingly.

Though Buddhadasa does not press his argument so far, it is clear that this notion of a disguised symbolic language provides a possible explanation for the inadequacy of the Tipiṭaka account of advanced meditative techniques: perhaps the necessary information is there after all, but concealed in symbolic language.

Symbolism in the Tantras

In the Tipiṭaka the existence of such symbolic language can be inferred; however, in certain texts of later Buddhism it is explicitly acknowledged. The *tantras*, a class of texts which begin to appear in the Vajrayāna school of Buddhism about a thousand years after Gotama's death, frequently refer to a Twilight Language (*saṃdhyā-bhāṣā*) or Intentional Language (*saṃdhā-bhāṣā*), a purposely created mode of communication having a concealed meaning. (There is some disagreement about which of the two terms is correct. We adopt here the more widely accepted 'Twilight Language'.)[23] For example, the *Hevajra-tantra* speaks of 'the Twilight Language, that great convention of the *yoginīs*, which the *śrāvakas* [disciples] and others cannot unriddle'.[24]

Scholars researching Tantric Buddhism have long recognized the existence of the Twilight Language. In his introduction to the *Tibetan Book of the Dead*, a text rich in symbolism, W. Y. Evans-Wentz wrote:

> Some of the more learned *lamas*, . . . have believed that since very early times there has been a secret international symbol-code in common use among the initiates, which affords a key to the meaning of such occult doctrines as are still jealously guarded by religious fraternities in India, as in Tibet, and in China, Mongolia, and Japan.[25]

More explicitly, B. Bhattacharyya says, in his *Introduction to Buddhist Esoterism*:

> They wrote in a language which was designated by them as the Sandhyabhasa, or the twilight language, meaning thereby that the contents may be explained either by the light of day or by the darkness of night. The songs composed by the Mahasiddhas were all written in this language, which had always a hidden or a mystic meaning.[26]

The Lama Anagarika Govinda, who has written extensively on the Twilight Language, describes it as follows:

> Their works . . . are written in a kind of symbolical language, which was known in India as *Sandhyabhasa*. This Sanskrit term means literally 'twilight language' and indicates that its words bear a double meaning, in accordance with whether they are understood in their ordinary or in their mystic sense.[27]

Mircea Eliade, referring in particular to the use of sexual symbolism, describes the Twilight Language as 'a secret, dark, ambiguous language in which a state of consciousness is expressed by an erotic term'.[28] It is widely accepted that the symbols of the Twilight Language do, as Eliade suggests, refer to states of consciousness. Generally it is explained that the Twilight Language was created by *siddhas*, adept masters of psychic power in an esoteric Buddhist tradition, partly to ensure against misuse of meditative practices and powers by the uninitiated or ignorant, and partly to provide themselves with a means of describing supernormal experiences for which ordinary language was inadequate.[29]

A well-known and relatively simple example of Twilight Lanugage is the popular *mantra Oṃ Maṇi Padme Hūṃ Hrīḥ* (often abbreviated by omitting the final *Hrīḥ*) — see Fig. 1. This is usually translated — inaccurately, we shall see later — as '*Oṃ!* The jewel is in the lotus. *Hūṃ! Hrīḥ!*' The jewel and the lotus are taken as symbols, and the *mantra* is therefore interpreted as meaning '*Nirvāṇa* is in *saṃsāra*', 'The Buddha is in the world', or something similar.[30] Thus the *mantra* is recognized as having, in addition to its obvious and trivial meaning, a secret symbolic meaning known only to those initiates who possess the key to the symbolism.

A more complex example of Twilight Language is the *maṇḍala* of the dhyāni Buddhas (see Figs. 2, 3). This is a diagram often portrayed in Vajrayāna art, which occupies an important place in certain Tibetan rituals, and which is found throughout the geographical range of Vajrayāna Buddhism, from Tibet to Indonesia and Japan. Essentially the *maṇḍala* is a cross-shaped framework of five cells, each of which contains a definite grouping of symbolic objects, usually dominated by a dhyāni Buddha, or Buddha of meditation.[31] Each dhyāni Buddha is identified by a characteristic *mudrā* or hand-pose, an emblem, a colour, and a *bīja* or mantric syllable. (The *mudrās*, barely visible in Fig. 2, are clearly shown in Plates 1 to 6.) In addition each dhyāni Buddha is accompanied by a female consort and a *vāhana* or animal mount, and is considered to correspond to a certain kind of supernormal wisdom, a certain element (earth, water, fire, air, or space), and a certain *skandha* or 'component of existence'. For example, the eastern cell of the *maṇḍala* is presided over by the dhyāni Buddha Akṣobhya, whose principal identifying characteristic is his earth-touching *mudrā*, the right hand placed with palm against the leg and finger-tips touching the ground — see Plates 1 and 2. Akṣobhya is coloured blue and his emblem is a *vajra*, a mythological weapon originally identified with the lightning-bolts hurled by the Vedic storm-god, Indra. His *bīja* is *Hūṃ*, his consort is the goddess Locanā, and his *vāhana* is an elephant. He 'corresponds to' or 'is associated with' the Mirror-like Wisdom, the water element, and the *skandha* of form (*rūpa*).[32] Not all of these details are necessarily present in every representation of the *maṇḍala*. In some simpler representations only a few sets of symbols are shown, for example only the dhyāni Buddhas with their *mudrās*, or only the *bījas*. The complexity of the *maṇḍala* is sometimes limited by the medium used. Much detail can be shown when the *maṇḍala* is painted in colour on a wall-scroll or a temple ceiling; greater simplicity is necessary when it is engraved on a metal plaque, carved from stone, or traced in coloured powders, as is done in certain Tibetan rituals.

The *maṇḍala* is explicitly connected with meditation; however, the nature of the connection is disputed. Many regard the *maṇḍala* as an object of meditation. They gaze at or visualize each of its cells in turn, beginning with the eastern cell, moving around clockwise until the northern cell is reached, then finally moving to the central cell. However, some authorities maintain that this view is incorrect, the *maṇḍala* being not an object of meditation but rather a symbolic map of the meditative path.[33] Thus the eastern cell, the first encountered by the meditator, is taken as a symbolic representation of the first stage of the meditation, and each of the objects it contains as denoting some aspect of that first stage. For example, the dhyāni Buddha Akṣobhya represents, according to Govinda, 'the first step of the unfoldment of Buddha-knowledge',[34] and according to Rambach, 'the first stage on the road to salvation'.[35] If this view is correct — and it is certainly in keeping with the nature of the Twilight Language in general — then perhaps the *maṇḍala* contains within its complex structure the missing information about the most advanced stages in Buddhist meditation.

The *maṇḍala* contains all the components of the *mantra Oṃ Maṇi Padme Hūṃ Hrīḥ*: *Oṃ* is in the central cell as the *bīja* of the dhyāni Buddha Vairocana, the jewel (*maṇi*) is in the southern cell as the emblem of Ratnasambhava, and so on. This kind of interconnectedness is characteristic of the Twilight Language; certain symbols recur again and again in different contexts, producing a network of cross-references.

A further example of this interconnectedness is to be found in the *Tibetan Book of the Dead* (*Bar-do thos-grol*). That text describes a series of visions allegedly seen by a dying person on successive days. The first five visions are based on the *maṇḍala* cells, as is clear from the following excerpt, describing the vision of the fourth day:

Fig. 1. The *mantra Oṃ Maṇi Padme Hūṃ Hrīḥ*. The first six syllables are read clockwise from the top petal; the final *Hrīh* (often omitted from the *mantra*) is in the centre. From ceiling decoration of 'Potala' Temple, Chengde, China. Original size approx. 50 × 60 cm. Drawing by Amanda Yorke.

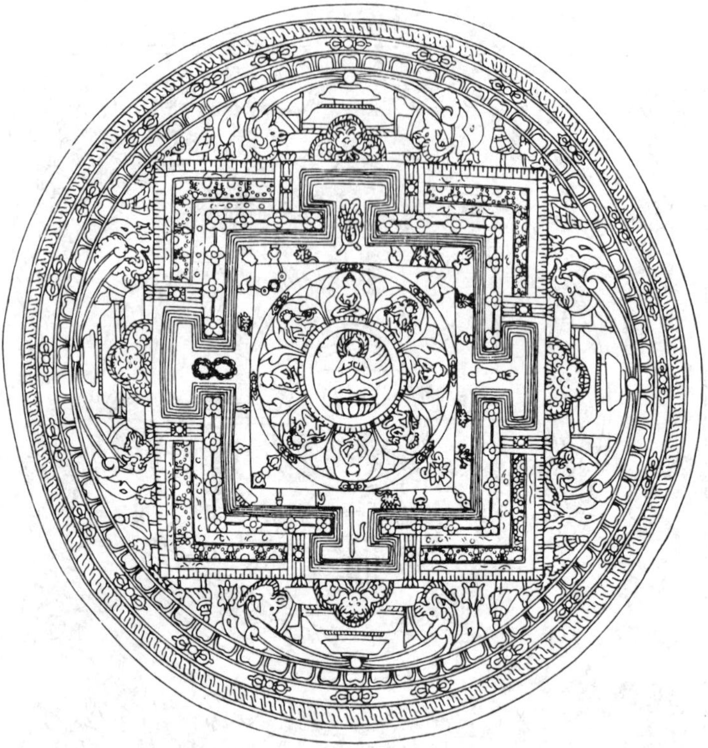

Fig. 2. A much elaborated form of the dhyāni Buddha *maṇḍala*. The *maṇḍala* proper is the lotus-shaped central portion in which are located the five dhyāni Buddhas and four of their female consorts. From a brass plaque at Svayambhu Stupa, Kathmandu. Original size approx. 50 cm diameter. Drawing by Amanda Yorke.

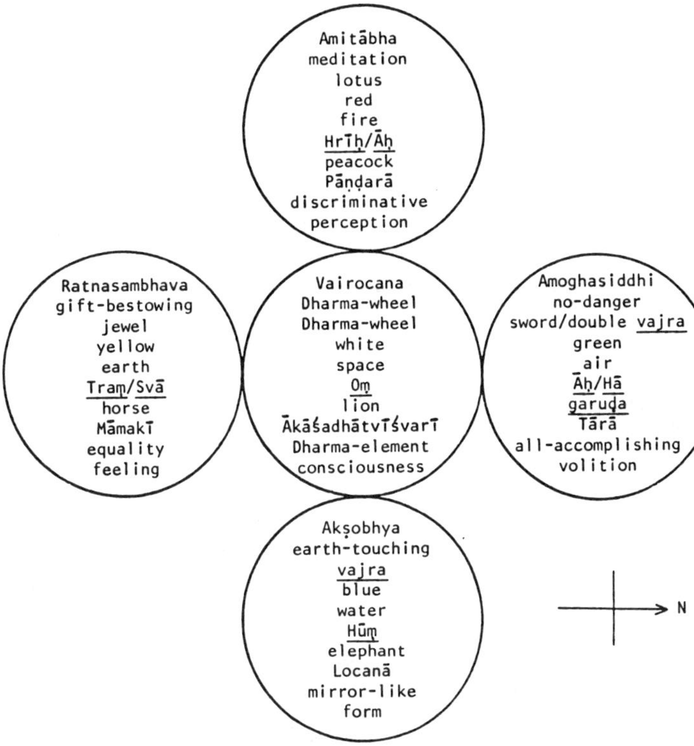

Fig. 3. Key to the dhyāni Buddha *maṇḍala* oriented, like Fig. 2, with the northern cell to the right. Listed in each cell are: the dhyāni Buddha, his *mudrā*, emblem, colour, element, *bīja, vāhana,* female consort, wisdom, and *skandha.* Each cell is of the same colour as its dhyāni Buddha, except the central and eastern cells, which are blue and white respectively.

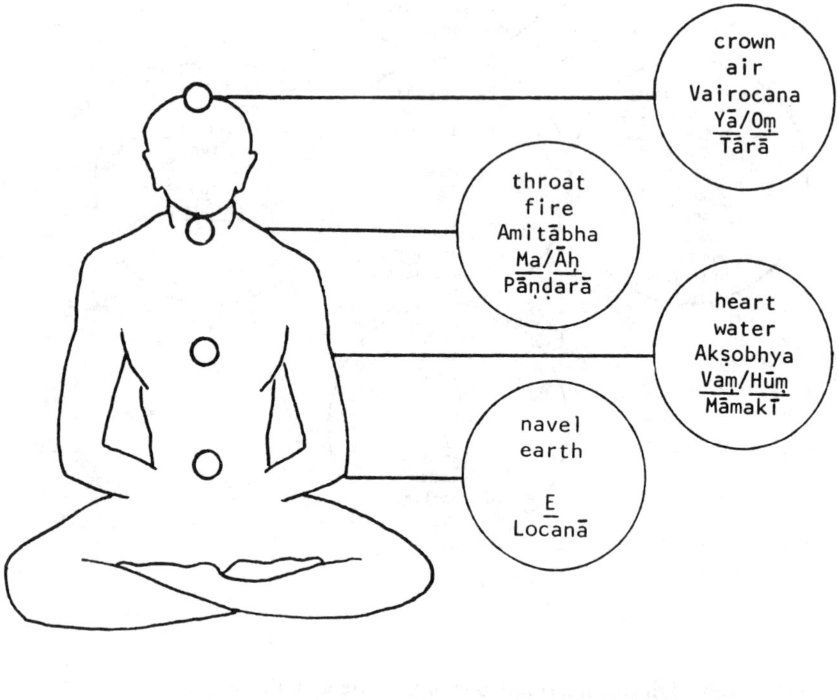

Fig. 4. The *cakra* system. Drawing by Amanda Yorke.

> On the fourth day, a red light, the purified element of fire, will shine, and at the same time Blessed Amitābha will appear before you from the red western Realm, The Blissful. His body is red in colour, he holds a lotus in his hand and sits on a peacock throne, embracing his consort Pāṇḍaravāsinī . . . The red light of the skandha of perception in its basic purity, the wisdom of discrimination, brilliant red, adorned with discs of light, luminous and clear, sharp and bright, will come from the heart of Amitābha and his consort and pierce your heart so that your eyes cannot bear to look at it.[36]

This vision is clearly based on the western cell of the *maṇḍala* (cf. Fig. 3). An understanding of the *maṇḍala* would therefore probably lead to an understanding of this section of the *Tibetan Book of the Dead* as well. Evans-Wentz, while accepting the common view that this text is a breviary for the dying, maintains in his commentary that much of its content is symbolic.[37] Govinda goes further, claiming that the *Tibetan Book of the Dead* is not intended for the dying at all, but for the living. He sees it as 'a key to the innermost recesses of the human mind'; however, he fails to explain how this key might be used.[38]

Another complex example of Twilight Language is the system of *cakras*, the 'centres of psychic energy' which are said to be located at certain points along the spinal column — see Fig. 4. The following description, given by Dasgupta in his *Introduction to Tantric Buddhism*, demonstrates that the *cakras* are indirectly connected with the *maṇḍala*.

> The four *Cakras* are associated with the four *Mudras*, . . . which are again associated with the goddesses *Locana, Mamaki, Pandara* and *Tara* respectively, who again in their turn are the presiding goddesses over the elements . . . earth, water, fire and air; these are again represented by the syllables *'e', vam, ma* and *ya*. . . . Thus the *Nirmana-cakra* in the navel region stands for the element of earth, represented by the syllable 'e' and presided over by the goddess *Locana*. . . .[39]

Like the *maṇḍala*, the *cakras* are explicitly linked with meditation: each one is identified with a certain level of meditative achievement. The meditator, contemplating each *cakra* in turn, progresses upwards through the series at his own pace until he reaches the crown *cakra*, which corresponds to the culmination of the practice. Depending on the kind of practice followed, this culmination may be one of the lower *siddhis* (psychic powers) such as the ability to generate inner heat, or it may be the highest of all *siddhis*, enlightenment.

The Problem of Interpretation

How the Twilight Language of the *tantras* originated is a problem that Buddhist scholars have yet to confront. It may be that the Twilight Language developed out of the Dharma Language of the Tipiṭaka recognized by Buddhadasa. Evidence of a connection can be found in certain symbolic cross-references, the best example of which is provided by the *mudrās* (hand-poses). It has long been recognized that certain of the *mudrās* of the dhyāni Buddhas refer to events surrounding Gotama's enlightenment. For example, the meditation *mudrā* (which identified the dhyāni Buddha Amitābha) refers to Māra's attack on the meditating Gotama; and the earth-touching *mudrā* (Akṣobhya) refers to Gotama's repulsing of Māra by calling on the earth to bear witness to the merit he had acquired in former existences.[40] If Māra's attack represents the arising of distracting thoughts in the mind of the meditator, then the dhyāni Buddha Amitābha is linked symbolically to the same mental event. Such interconnections have generally been overlooked by those who have attempted to assign specific meanings to the symbols of the Twilight Language.

This leads to the question: How might one go about discovering the meaning of the Twilight Language? If, as suggested, the mythological events surrounding Gotama's enlightenment, and the complex structure of the *maṇḍala* and *cakras*, are symbols denoting advanced stages on the meditative path, how might one set about deciphering those symbols and identifying the meditative stages in question?

To interpret the meaning of Māra's daughters is relatively simple. Anyone who has attempted the basic techniques of meditation will be familiar with the problem posed by distracting thoughts, so will readily recognize the symbolic significance of these seductive sirens. Interpreting a symbol is simple if one is familiar with the referent, the entity symbolized. However, if the referent is some totally unfamiliar meditative technique or supernormal state of consciousness, it is difficult to see how any amount of rational analysis of the symbols could ever reveal the nature of that technique or state.

One possible approach would be to consider the distinguishing feature which a symbol and its referent may be expected to have in common. For example, if the sword held by the dhyāni Buddha Amoghasiddhi symbolizes some meditative technique or mental state, then that technique or state may be expected to be in some important respect sword-like, to have some distinguishing feature in common with a sword — rather than with, say, a jewel or a lotus. The point is, however, that a person would be able to perceive this symbolic correspondence only if he was already familiar with that sword-like technique or state. So analysis of the *maṇḍala* or the *cakras* or the Buddha legend, however systematic and thorough, cannot be expected to reveal previously unknown meditative techniques on the path to enlightenment. It cannot be expected to do more than indicate whether or not certain already known meditative techniques are likely to be stages on that path.

Some researchers into the Twilight Language disregard meditation altogether. Adopting a purely scholarly approach, they combine historical and philological analysis in an attempt to arrive at useful conclusions concerning the nature and development of esoteric Buddhism.[41] Other investigators do take account of meditation, but their interpretations are purely intuitive — or so one must assume in the absence of any explanation of how the interpretations are arrived at.[42] These two approaches throw little light on Gotama's teachings on meditation mainly because they are methodologically back to front.[43] No amount of scholarly analysis and no amount of intuitive speculation can be expected to reveal which meditative technique or mental state a symbol represents, unless the investigator himself is already familiar with that technique or state. The symbols can do no more than indicate whether or not one is on the right meditative track. But for a practising meditator, an indication whether or not he is on the right track could be of great value. Perhaps, then, the symbols of the Twilight Language could prove useful as landmarks by which meditators could chart their progress.

In the following chapters an attempt is made to elucidate the advanced stages of Buddhist meditation by seeking correlations between, on the one hand, meditative techniques, and on the other, the symbolic language of the Tipiṭaka and certain symbols found in the *tantras*. In accordance with the principles outlined above, meditative practices are discussed fully before making any attempt at interpretation. Following an introductory discussion of historical questions (Chapter II), certain important meditative techniques and associated states of consciousness are described from the point of view of a practising meditator (Chapters III, IV). These meditative techniques and states are then compared with certain seemingly symbolic teachings in the Tipiṭaka and with some of the more explicit symbols of Tantric Buddhism for evidence of systematic correspondences (Chapters V, VI, VII). This leads to a suggested interpretation of the three knowledges and of the *maṇḍala* and *cakras* in terms of advanced meditative practices. Some doctrinal and historical implications of this interpretation are then examined and evaluated (Chapter VIII). In conclusion (Chapter IX) the present-day relevance of our findings is briefly discussed.

We attempt throughout to bring together two different approaches to the problem: on the one hand the meditative-descriptive approach, based on experience in practical meditation; and on the other hand the historical-scholarly approach, based on an examination of the corpus of Buddhist texts, in particular the Pali Tipiṭaka. We reject without apology the 'mystical' approach, which would regard the symbols as somehow eternal and outside the flow of history, or would assign meanings to them on the basis of intuition alone.

Our principal concern is to discover what information on meditative techniques may be contained in the symbols of the Twilight Language. The first step to that end must be to assess, on the available historical, textual, and other evidence, the likelihood that there did exist an esoteric meditative tradition in Buddhism, for which the Twilight Language might have served as a secret means of communication. We therefore turn now to an examination of this and related historical questions, in order to provide a basis for the discussion of meditation and symbolism to follow.

CHAPTER II

THE TWILIGHT LANGUAGE IN HISTORICAL CONTEXT

The Twilight Language of Tantric Buddhism is claimed to be a secret symbolic representation of Gotama's teachings on advanced meditation. This claim assumes that there existed in early Buddhism an esoteric meditative tradition. We therefore begin our investigation into possible relationships between Buddhist meditation and symbolism by addressing the question whether such an esoteric tradition is likely to have existed. What evidence is there that Gotama or his immediate disciples propagated an esoteric teaching on meditation? We shall approach this question by considering the historical context within which Gotama lived and taught. Against the historical background of early Buddhism we shall examine how knowledge of meditation was traditionally communicated in India, how Gotama himself acquired knowledge and guidance from his early gurus when he embarked on his spiritual quest, and how he passed on his own teachings to the monks of the order he founded.

Gotama the Śramaṇa

In abandoning his princely life and retiring to the forest, Gotama became a *śramaṇa*, one of the many wandering mendicant yogis practising in north India in the sixth century B.C. He thus joined an ancient tradition of yogic practice, involving austerities, breath control, concentration exercises, and other techniques, a heterodox tradition which questioned the two basic tenets of orthodox Brahmanism, namely the authority of the Vedas and the efficacy of Brahmanical rituals.[1]

Within the *śramaṇa* tradition, knowledge was passed on — as it still is at the present day — through series of guru-disciple relationships. Any *śramaṇa* known to be particularly strict in his austerities or saintly in his bearing, would become recognized as a guru, and attract about him a circle of lay followers and aspiring yogis. The lay followers came to offer food and other necessities, to seek moral advice, or to listen to uplifting discourses on spiritual topics; the aspiring yogis came as *śiṣyas*, practising disciples. No *śiṣya* expected that his chosen guru would immediately provide explicit verbal instructions on how to follow in his footsteps. The guru might teach entirely by example; and if he did give verbal teaching, he gave it only gradually, over a long period. A close and trusting personal relationship had to be developed, through which the disciple's progress could be guided in accordance with his particular personality, talents, and needs. What had to be imparted was not intellectual knowledge but a kind of direct experience, the realization of a truth through living it. Consequently the relationship might last many years, as the disciple was led gradually through the sequence of stages which the master had already traversed. Some disciples would move through the stages more rapidly than others. Some would in time feel they had learned all they could from one guru, and leave in search of another who might lead them further. And some, having learned as much as they considered of value from all the gurus known to them, would go off to practise their austerities or meditation alone, perhaps later to become gurus in their turn.[2]

Gotama began his spiritual career as a typical *śramaṇa*. The Tipiṭaka account tells that he practised under some of the best-known teachers of his day, and acquired from them various yogic skills, including mastery of the *jhānas*.[3] Gotama was conversant with, and generally sceptical of, the various speculative philosophical and religious systems of his time. He rejected many of the current views; however, he did accept certain basic tenets, including the widely-held notion of *saṃsāra*, the concept of an ever-repeated cycle of death and rebirth conditioned by *karma*. Indeed the notion of *saṃsāra* dominated Gotama's world-view. In common with many of his fellows *śramaṇas*, Gotama saw as his goal the attainment of *nirvāṇa*, liberation from the cycle of rebirth with its inherent suffering (*dukkha*). It was not long before he realized this could not be achieved by the methods his gurus were teaching. He therefore went off to practise on his own account.

After six years of painful struggle, Gotama realized that the way to liberation from *saṃsāra* lay not in austerities and self-mortification, but in contemplating his own mental states:

> Monks, it is as if in the last month of the hot weather when all the corn is stored at the confines of a village a cowherd might be looking after the cows; while he is at the root of a tree or in the open he

> remembers there is something to be done, and thinks: Those are the cows. Even so, monks, remembering there is something to be done, did I think: Those are mental states. Monks, unsluggish energy was stirred up in me, unmuddled mindfulness was set up, the body was tranquil, impassible, the mind composed, one-pointed. . . .[4]

Gotama meditated all night beneath the Bodhi Tree. Having attained the four *jhānas*, he developed in succession the three knowledges; and on attaining the third knowledge, he realized: 'I am freed, . . . destroyed is birth, . . . done is what was to be done.' He had become *buddha*, awakened or enlightened, and had thereby attained *nirvāṇa*, liberation from *saṃsāra*.

After due consideration, Gotama decided to teach others his unique path to liberation. The first to hear his teaching were five yogis who had accompanied him in his earlier ascetic practices. One discourse was sufficient to convince the five and they immediately became his disciples. Thereafter the number of his disciples quickly grew. Gotama organized them into a formal order of monks, the beginning of the Buddhist Sangha, and drew up a code of monastic discipline, the beginning of the Vinaya.

Throughout the next forty-five years Gotama taught in many situations and to a wide variety of audiences. His listeners ranged from beggars to kings, and from newly-ordained novices to monks at advanced stages of spiritual development. To simple lay-people he usually spoke about right speech, action, and livelihood, while to members of the Sangha he more often taught the more advanced stages of the path. Sometimes he taught individuals, sometimes large gatherings. His discourses were always received with joy and appreciation. Several *suttas* even state that some of his listeners attained enlightenment on hearing a single discourse, so lucid and effective was his presentation — though this should perhaps be seen as pious hagiography rather than a record of fact.

Gotama and his following of monks moved about constantly, staying only a few days in any place, living on alms-food, and sleeping under trees or in caves. An exception was made, however, for the three months of the annual rainy season. That period was always spent in places where adequate shelter was available, usually a properly constructed retreat donated by some wealthy patron. But whether on the move or in temporary residence, the monks spent most of their time practising meditation or reflecting on the teaching. Even necessary daily tasks, such as going into the villages to receive alms-food, and washing or mending robes, were performed with right mindfulness, and thus incorporated into the meditation practice. Discussion of the teaching was limited to questions immediately relevant to the task of attaining enlightenment and *nirvāṇa*; speculation on cosmology or abstruse metaphysical points was discouraged as unprofitable.[5] These conditions were conducive to rapid progress; many monks passed through the recognized stages of development to become *arahants*, enlightened and liberated beings whose attainment differed from that of Gotama only in having been facilitated by instruction from an already enlightened teacher. These most advanced monks became teachers in their turn, some of them undertaking missionary work in distant places.

The Development of the Tipiṭaka

In his final days Gotama was asked who should succeed him as leader of the Sangha. But he refused to appoint a successor, declaring that the function of leader would thenceforth be fulfilled by the Vinaya (the monastic discipline that he had laid down) and the Dharma (his teaching).[6]

After Gotama's death the monks convened and discussed how best to preserve his teaching. It was recognized that of his closest followers Upāli had the best knowledge of the Vinaya rules, while Ānanda best remembered the *suttas* — this despite a tradition that Ānanda had been relatively slow in practising the teachings which those *suttas* contained.[7] So in the presence of the assembled monks, Upāli recited from memory the monastic rules, while Ānanda recited a large number of Gotama's discourses on Dharma. The monks then committed this mass of material to memory. (There is no definite evidence of a writing system in India at this time.) Some monks memorized the Vinaya-piṭaka, the collection of monastic rules, others the Sutta-piṭaka, the corpus of discourses. Thus began an oral transmission which was to be, for the next five centuries, the only canonical record of Gotama's teaching.

The task of preserving the oral tradition during those first five centuries must have placed heavy demands on the time and mental energy of the monks, even though the total corpus was not at first as bulky as it would later become. Through communal chanting, older monks taught the codified Vinaya and *suttas* to novices, and at the same time constantly refreshed their own memories. However, not all monks became *vinayadharas* or *suttantikas*;

some became *ābhidhammikas*, experts in explicating the Dharma, and others again became *jhāyins*, specialists in the practice of meditation. There was thus a division of labour: the *vinayadharas* and *suttantikas* memorized the teaching, the *ābhidhammikas* analysed and explicated it, and the *jhāyins* put it into effect.[8] The *jhāyins* were originally the dominant group; however, they appear to have steadily decreased in relative numerical strength as time passed, while the other groups, especially the *ābhidhammikas*, steadily increased — a trend which Gotama himself is said to have foretold.

During the first few centuries after Gotama's death, conditions within the Sangha changed considerably. As Buddhism grew in popularity, monks acquired high status in the eyes of the community and their material living conditions became increasingly comfortable and secure. No longer did monks necessarily live as homeless mendicants, wandering for nine months of the year; increasingly they became established permanently in comfortable monasteries, with an assured supply of alms-food and other necessities provided by devout lay followers. This trend was greatly accelerated in the third century B.C., when, under the generous patronage of the emperor Aśoka, Buddhism received an unprecedented level of material support. The result was a great increase in the number of monks — with, we may safely assume, a corresponding decline in the genuineness of their commitment to the quest for enlightenment.[9]

As time passed, the canon grew steadily in bulk. The increasing complexity of the large monastic communities necessitated more and more elaborate rules of conduct with commentaries to explain them, all of which had to be memorized. The ever-increasing remoteness from Gotama and his original teaching caused the monks to spend more and more time in doctrinal discussion, not only among themselves but also with the followers of other schools, such as the Jainas, the Ājīvakas, and the adherents of the various Brahmanical sects which would later become Hinduism.[10] These activities encouraged the learned *ābhidhammika* monks in their attempts to summarize, systematize, and explicate the contents of the *suttas*. Numerous lists of doctrinal terms were drawn up, seeming inconsistencies in the Dharma were explained — or explained away — and a sometimes spurious order and symmetry was imposed on the doctrinal material.[11] These attempts at summary and exegesis were also committed to memory, to become the Abhidhamma-piṭaka, a third branch of the canon, alongside the Vinaya- and Sutta-piṭakas. There is evidence, however, that much of what passed as *sutta* was actually *abhidhamma*, the commentators having frequently placed their own summaries and explanations in the mouth of the founder.[12]

During the first five centuries of Buddhism sectarian differences developed within the Sangha, another trend that Gotama is said to have foretold. Disagreements on points of discipline and doctrine led to the formation of a number of distinct schools, later grouped in two major divisions — the Hīnayāna or 'Lesser Tradition', and the Mahāyāna or 'Great Tradition'. This was in part a consequence of difficulties in communication across the great distances separating different monastic communities, for already by the time of Aśoka, Buddhism had spread southward as far as the island of Lanka, and north-west as far as Bactria and central Asia. The diverse climatic conditions prevailing in this vast territory led some monastic communities to revise the Vinaya rules relating to food, dress, and shelter; and given the fallibility of the human memory and the practice of inserting explicatory material into the *suttas*, it is not surprising that the memorized canon came to differ somewhat from one region to another. What is remarkable is that basic texts differ as little as they do, especially as the principal sectarian division also had a linguistic component. The Theravādins, the major school of the Hīnayāna, attempted to preserve the canon in Pali, a dialect closely similar to that in which Gotama had originally taught; Mahāyāna schools converted it, sometimes not altogether accurately, into classical Sanskrit.

Around the first century B.C. the various Buddhist schools began writing down their different versions of the canon. Only one of these written versions has been preserved essentially intact down to the present day, namely the Pali Tipiṭaka of the Theravāda. Most of the canonical literature of the other early schools has been lost, though some of it is indirectly preserved in Chinese and Tibetan translations. However, even the Pali Tipiṭaka, which is the textual foundation of the variety of Buddhism now practised in Sri Lanka and Southeast Asia, cannot be taken as a complete and accurate record of what Gotama taught. Although it is the nearest thing we have to such a record, it must be recognized as the canon of just one school among several. As such it may well include material that is specifically Theravādin, material designed to define and support the position of the Theravāda in its disputes with other schools.

The Élite Meditative Tradition

It has always been claimed by the Theravādins that Gotama taught his followers everything they needed to know, holding back nothing that would assist them in their pursuit of *nirvāṇa*; and further that this teaching is recorded in its entirety in the Pali canon. The principal textual support for this claim is a passage in the *Mahāparinibbāna-sutta*, which in Rhys Davids' often-cited translation reads:

> I have preached the truth without making any distinction between exoteric and esoteric doctrine; for in respect of the truths, Ānanda, the Tathāgata has no such thing as the closed fist of a teacher, who keeps some things back.[13]

Gotama is said to have spoken these words shortly before his death in order to allay fears expressed by Ānanda about the future of the Dharma and Sangha. From the passage as quoted it does seem that Gotama denies having initiated an esoteric tradition. The key phrase 'without making any distinction between exoteric and esoteric doctrine' is actually a very free rendering of the Pali *anantaraṃ abāhiraṃ katvā*. A strictly literal translation would be 'making no inner and no outer', and this is the rendering preferred by F. L. Woodward in his translation of the same passage.[14] However, the commentary explains that the import of the phrase is 'without omitting anything or excluding anyone'.[15] This does appear to justify the free translation of Rhys Davids and to support the Theravāda claim that the passage denies the existence of an esoteric transmission.

The force of the Theravāda claim is weakened, however, by a statement in a section of the Saṃyutta-nikāya entitled 'The *Siṃsapā* Grove'.[16] There it is related that Gotama on one occasion picked up a handful of *siṃsapā* leaves and asked the monks which were more, the leaves in his hand or those in the trees overhead. When the monks indicated the latter, Gotama declared: 'Just so, monks, much more in number are those things I have found out, but not revealed; very few are the things I have revealed.' This statement does not in itself imply the existence of an esoteric tradition, because the things withheld were apparently withheld from *all* monks without distiuction. Nevertheless, it does appear to be at odds with Gotama's assurance that he had taught the Dharma 'without omitting anything'. If these two statements are to be reconciled, it must be assumed that both are subject to an implicit qualification: Gotama did not omit anything that was relevant to the central task of attaining enlightenment; whatever he did withhold was irrelevant and non-essential.

But in that case it would seem that one ought to read a similar implicit qualification into the second half of Gotama's claim, his statement that he taught the Dharma 'without excluding anyone'. It is unlikely that Gotama imparted his entire teaching to anyone and everyone who came to him for instruction. For example, he would hardly have taught advanced meditation to busy householders who had neither the ability nor the opportunity to practise it. Even within the Sangha there was a wide range of intellectual and meditative competence. Some monks, such as Sāriputta, progressed rapidly; others, like Ānanda, progressed slowly. Gotama would clearly have taken such differences into account in teaching. And in fact it is apparent from the Tipiṭaka that he did tailor his discourses to suit his audience.

We conclude, then, that Gotama's claim to have taught the Dharma 'without omitting anything or excluding anyone' is subject to two implicit qualifications: He taught without omitting anything *that was essential to the attaining of enlightenment*, and he taught without excluding anyone *who had the ability to understand and apply his teaching.*

Strong support for this conclusion comes from the traditional mode of teaching commonly used in India at the time and still widespread at the present day. As mentioned in Chapter I, present-day Buddhist meditation masters usually impart their teaching step by step to individual students in private. The student must complete each stage in the course of meditative practice before receiving his instructions for the next stage; and he is urged to refrain from discussing the details of his practice and attainments with other students. This policy is based on two main premises: first, if the student knew in advance what the next stage was to be, he would tend to anticipate and so be distracted from his current practice; and second, the teacher cannot decide how to lead into the next stage until he has heard the student's report on progress made and difficulties encountered.

This relationship between a present-day meditation master and each of his students closely resembles that which has always existed in India between guru and *śiṣya*. There are no grounds for supposing that the relationship between Gotama and the more advanced of his immediate disciples was significantly different. Gotama was a typical *śramaṇa* and clearly a very competent teacher of meditation. Except perhaps in the most elementary stages, he would have instructed each student in a series of private sessions, revealing each stage in the practice only as the student became ready for it. As is evident from the Tipiṭaka, broad summaries of the entire course of practice were sometimes outlined by Gotama in his public discourses; however, details of the highest stages in that course were never so freely imparted. These would only have been taught step by step and in private, a method of teaching which in the sixth century B.C. in north India both lay people and monks would have expected and taken for granted.

It is therefore inherently probable that Gotama taught in two different ways, at two different levels.[17] From the Sutta-piṭaka we know that he gave general instruction on basic principles of Dharma and broad outlines of meditation procedures in public discourses to lay people and monks; and from the known practices of *śramaṇas* and meditation masters throughout the ages, combined with the previously noted lack of textual information on the practice of 'right insight', we may infer that he gave detailed instruction on advanced meditation during private meetings with individual monks. Like present-day meditation masters, he probably would have urged his students to avoid discussing their practices and attainments with unqualified people. Gotama did not have 'the closed fist of a teacher, who keeps some things back'; he revealed everything to those capable of applying it. But he would almost certainly have imparted his higher teachings by means of the rather secretive person-to-person method of instruction, which was, and still is, considered the only satisfactory way of teaching advanced meditation.

Although Gotama's death marked the beginning of a period of great change in the Sangha, it would hardly have had any substantial effect on the method of instruction. The *suttas* tell that many monks who had attained enlightenment engaged in active teaching well before Gotama's death.[18] It is therefore unlikely that any sudden break was made in the traditional method of teaching. Instruction in advanced meditation would almost certainly have continued in the time-honoured manner.

Not all monks possessed a natural aptitude for meditation. Those who did continued to learn from their *arahant* teachers; those whose temperaments inclined them more to a devotional or intellectual approach busied themselves with memorizing or debating the founder's public but more superficial teachings, or with elaborating the philosophical principles implicit in them. That the Sutta-pitaka contains little information on the most advanced stages in meditation is therefore not surprising. The *suttas* are supposedly those discourses which Ānanda heard and later remembered,[19] and Ānanda could hardly have known what Gotama said in his many private sessions with individual advanced meditators. The monks who dedicated themselves to memorizing the *suttas* were probably the ones least gifted as meditators, because any monk who properly understood and applied Gotama's teaching would have seen little value in memorizing it. It is therefore inherently likely that the memorized material that became the Sutta-piṭaka, contained only the public, more elementary component of Gotama's teaching. The more advanced component would not have been memorized and chanted in public; it would have been passed on in private in the usual Indian fashion, through chains of guru-disciple relationships.

There is therefore good reason for supposing that Gotama initiated what may be called an élite meditative tradition, a tradition in which monks who had mastered the most advanced meditative techniques taught them in private to a few chosen students. Such a transmission is naturally unlikely to have left tangible historical traces which might provide direct evidence of its existence. However, indirect evidence, most importantly our knowledge of practices prevailing among *śramaṇas* in the sixth century B.C. and among meditation masters at the present day, is enough to indicate that such a method of transmission probably did exist.

The existence of the *jhāyin* category in the later classification of monks indicates that some kind of specialized meditative tradition continued through the first few centuries of Buddhism. The *jhāyins* were probably, in part at least, a continuation of the original élite meditative tradition. Their steady decline numerically is as might be expected, because such a meditative élite would have been constantly threatened by hostile influences. In the first centuries after Gotama's death the threat came from the rise of popular devotional Buddhism with its need for monks to minister to the lay community, from the massive influx of less dedicated monks into the Sangha at the time of Aśoka, from the monastic training which encouraged monks to become memorizers, and from the constant trend towards scholasticism.[20] Later when the widespread revival of Hinduism challenged the social status of the Sangha, forcing monks to spend much time and energy defending Buddhism against its detractors,[21] the meditative tradition would have again suffered.[22]

The Vajrayāna and the Twilight Language

Around the second or third century A.D. there developed from within the Mahāyāna, the school known as the Vajrayāna, the 'Diamond Tradition'.[23] The Vajrayāna, later to become established as the dominant form of Buddhism in Tibet, represented a reaction against two aspects of the Mahāyāna: its philosophical and doctrinal speculations, and its emphasis on the accumulation of merit. In opposition to these scholastic and popular pursuits, the Vajrayāna was concerned with the immediate quest for enlightenment by means of meditative practices taught secretly by adept masters to their disciples.

The Vajrayāna claimed to teach a path to enlightenment more rapid — but also more dangerous — than that presented in the Tipiṭaka.[24] This path was said to represent the 'third turning of the Dharma-wheel' — the first and second being the Hīnayāna and Mahāyāna[25] — and was set down in a class of texts known as *tantras*. The *tantras* contain the first recognizable examples of Twilight Language, including descriptions of the *cakras* and the *maṇḍala* of the dhyāni Buddhas, with their associated elements, colours, *bījas* and so on. They contain also a lavish admixture of sexual symbolism, which has come to be thought of, rightly or wrongly, as the hallmark of the Tantric tradition. The earliest extant *tantra* that describes the dhyāni Buddhas is the *Guhyasamāja-tantra*, usually dated around the fifth century A.D.[26] It is certain of these early *tantras* that first mention explicitly the *saṃdhā-bhāṣā*, 'Twilight Language' (or *saṃdhā-bhāṣā*, 'Intentional Language'), and give hints of its important hidden meaning.[27]

Authorities on the Vajrayāna have consistently maintained that the Twilight Language of the *tantras* was a code used in a secret meditative transmission, whereby the means for attaining enlightenment were revealed to initiated disciples.[28] This view is in keeping with our earlier conclusion that information on the most advanced meditation practices was not recorded in the Tipiṭaka but was transmitted through a secretive, élite tradition. It suggests that that tradition may have continued unbroken during the millennium between Gotama's death and the composing of the *tantras*: while the mainstream monastic communities were occupied with memorizing and openly transmitting the teachings contained in the Tipiṭaka, small numbers of monks in the élite tradition were practising and secretly transmitting the advanced techniques of meditation.[29] Viewed in this way, the Vajrayāna would represent a surfacing of the hitherto hidden élite transmission which Gotama had initiated.

How the Twilight Language might have developed within that tradition is unclear. We have noted that a simple form of symbolic language — Buddhadasa's Dharma Language — is found in the Tipiṭaka, and have suggested that this may be linked historically with the elaborate symbolism of the *maṇḍala* and *cakras*. But any such historical connection could be only tenuous, because most components of the Twilight Language are demonstrably far removed in time from Gotama. For example, the dhyāni Buddhas, though individually much older than the *Guhyasamāja-tantra* which first describes them as a set, cannot go further back than the first century A.D., when the first Buddha images were produced.[30] The description of the *maṇḍala* and *cakras* given in Chapter I refers to an already comparatively developed form of the Twilight Language. For example, the set of five dhyāni Buddhas shown in Figs. 2 and 3 evolved out of an earlier set of three, namely Amitābha, Akṣobhya, and Vairocana.[31] The set of four *cakras* shown in Fig. 4 also developed from an earlier set of three; and if one traces the subsequent development of the system through the later Buddhist Tantric tradition into its Hindu derivative, one finds the number of *cakras* increasing progressively to five, six, seven, and even more. The trend is always towards great complexity. So while some of its most primitive components may perhaps go back to the time of Gotama, the Twilight Language is in the main a later development. If the Twilight Language was, as claimed, a mode of communication used by successive generations of *siddhas*, adept teachers in the élite meditative tradition, then it must have been, for the most part, developed by those *siddhas* themselves, centuries after Gotama's death.

There are several possible reasons why such a cryptic mode of communication should have been developed, why meditative techniques or attainments should have been denoted by dhyāni Buddhas, *bījas*, and so on. One possibility is that the Twilight Language was devised to ensure that knowledge about advanced practices would remain concealed from all but those known to be capable of applying those practices effectively. A system in which meditative techniques were represented by sets of symbols would have made it possible for the initiated to discuss techniques freely, even in the presence of people from whom those techniques had to be concealed. Another possibility is that the Twilight Language was intended to supplement and illustrate the instructions given by gurus, each symbol suggesting in vivid graphic form some essential characteristic of the technique to be practised. Or it may be that the Twilight Language was created to ensure against loss of the precious teaching, as Buddhism and its meditative tradition declined in India; it would then have served the function of a coded inscription which would survive beyond any breaks in the line of oral transmission and facilitate rediscovery at a later time. Finally, the Twilight Language may perhaps have been merely another of the many digressions from the path of meditation which have characterized the development of Buddhism; it may have been nothing more than a scholarly elaboration like the Abhidhamma, an attempt to reconcile teachings on meditation with then current Indian ideas on symbolic parallelism.[32]

A more systematic attempt to account for the motives behind the creation of the Twilight Language must wait until after the symbolism itself has been examined and interpreted. For the present it is sufficient to have demonstrated that there is likely to have existed in early Buddhism an élite tradition within which knowledge of advanced meditative practices was passed on secretively from adept masters to selected worthy pupils.[33] We can now turn to the problem of interpreting the symbols used within that élite tradition, beginning with an examination of their most likely referents, Buddhist meditative practices.

CHAPTER III

CONCENTRATION

As foreshadowed in Chapter I, our search for possible correspondences between Buddhist symbolism and meditation begins with an examination of the various meditative techniques and associated mental states to which the symbols might refer. This undertaking presents some daunting practical problems, of which the most obvious is its sheer magnitude. In the *Visuddhi-magga*, written by the Theravāda monk Buddhaghosa in the fifth century A.D., no fewer than forty 'subjects of meditation' are listed;[1] and if to these are added the more recent Theravāda practices and the various techniques employed in Tibetan Buddhism and Zen, the number to be considered seems impossibly large. Most Buddhists assume that even a monk practising continuously under optimum conditions may take years to master the technique of his choice. It would seem, then, that no one could hope, in a reasonable space of time, to practise the entire range of meditative techniques, let alone become sufficiently proficient in them to be qualified to appraise their relative merits.

Another problem is that the meditation practices we are most concerned to elucidate, in particular the techniques associated with the three knowledges, are the very ones that are least adequately described in the texts and least understood by present-day meditation masters. How one might go about investigating such techniques is hard to foresee. Any attempt to formulate in advance a practical methodology would almost certainly be futile. We shall therefore heed Gotama's advice on the futility of speculation. Instead of theorizing on how one might investigate little-known techniques of advanced meditation, we shall simply begin by investigating the best-known techniques, and see where that investigation leads.

Mindfulness of Breathing

Of all Buddhist meditative techniques the best authenticated and most widely practised is mindfulness of breathing (*ānāpānasati*).

Its importance is recognized by many authorities on meditation, for example, Vajirañāṇa: 'Mindfulness in regard to Breathing . . . is first and foremost in the field of mental training in Buddhism',[2] and Singhathon: 'Mindfulness of Breathing takes the highest place among the various subjects of Buddhist meditation.'[3] Textual evidence indicates that mindfulness of breathing is, as Vajirañāṇa puts it, 'the Buddha's meditation'.[4] According to the *Mahāsaccaka-sutta* and its commentary, Gotama attained the first *jhāna* while still a child by practising mindfulness of breathing;[5] and according to the commentary on the *Bhayabherava-sutta* it was by practising this same technique that he attained the fourth *jhāna* before going on to develop the three knowledges.[6] Gotama frequently urged his monks to practise mindfulness of breathing, declaring this technique to be 'of great fruit, of great advantage'.[7] Mindfulness of breathing is described in outline in a number of *suttas*, and explained in detail in the *Visuddhi-magga* and many later manuals on meditation.[8] Throughout the history of Buddhism, it has probably been the most widely practised of all techniques, and at the present day it is still one of the most popular, despite competition from other, better publicized methods. For these reasons mindfulness of breathing is taken as the starting point of this investigation into Buddhist meditative practices.

In the *Ānāpānasati-sutta* and elsewhere the first steps in the practice of mindfulness of breathing are described as follows:

> Herein, monks, a monk who is forest-gone or gone to the root of a tree or gone to an empty place, sits down cross-legged, holding his back erect, arousing mindfulness in front of him. Mindful he breathes in, mindful he breathes out. Whether he is breathing in a long (breath) he comprehends, 'I am breathing in a long (breath)'; or whether he is breathing out a long (breath), he comprehends, 'I am breathing out a long (breath)'; or whether he is breathing in a short (breath) he comprehends, 'I am breathing in a short (breath)'; or whether he is breathing out a short (breath) he comprehends, 'I am breathing out a short (breath)'.[9]

The *sutta* goes on to describe how the meditator, practising in this way, passes through a series of stages: 'experiencing the whole body', 'tranquillizing the activity of body', 'experiencing rapture', 'experiencing joy', and so on up to 'beholding stopping' and 'beholding casting away'.

However, for anyone actually wishing to practise mindfulness of breathing, the *sutta* account is inadequate. For example, it fails to make clear what is meant by 'arousing mindfulness in front of him'. These shortcomings have been made good in the *Visuddhimagga* and other manuals, though it is uncertain how accurately even the earliest of such works reflect Gotama's original teaching.

The manuals describe the basic steps in *ānāpānasati* as follows.[10] The meditator, having found a quiet spot in which to practise, seats himself in the cross-legged 'lotus posture', with his hands resting in his lap, his back and neck held erect but not stiff, and his eyes closed. He then concentrates his attention on the slight tactile sensation experienced at the rim of the right nostril as the breath passes in and out. Resolutely excluding all other sense impressions and suppressing all thoughts, he observes attentively the sensation at the nostril throughout the in and out-breathing phases. Whenever his attention wanders he brings it back, gently but firmly, and resumes concentrating on his breathing. Given favourable conditions, the meditator eventually finds — after weeks or even months of constant effort — that he is able to keep his attention fixed on the breathing for several minutes together. This condition, in which thought has been brought to a standstill and attention remains fixed on the chosen object, is called mental onepointedness (*cittass' ekaggatā*). It is an important and fundamental meditative attainment.

The manuals go on to describe how the meditator may consolidate and further develop the onepointed condition; however, we shall pause at this point to examine more closely the practical details of the early stages. The practice consists in attempting to keep attention fixed on the fine tactile sensation produced by the breath at the rim of the nostril. The actual experience of this practice usually proceeds more or less as follows.[11]

The meditator, attempting to keep his attention focused on his breathing, soon discovers that this is extremely difficult to do. His mind wanders repeatedly. After only a few seconds he realizes that instead of concentrating on the breathing, he is thinking about something totally unrelated to the practice, such as the tasty meal he had the previous evening, or the letter he has to post. As soon as he becomes conscious of having digressed, he returns attention to the object of concentration, only to find, a few seconds later, that the same thing has happened again; his mind has again wandered to some irrelevant topic — the arrangement of the furniture in his living-room and how it might be altered, or the possibility that his car is developing serious mechanical trouble, or the meditation master's habit of rocking his body slowly to and fro as he talks. Again and again he concentrates his attention on the sensation at the right nostril, and every time it wanders. The thoughts that arise seem to become more trivial and irrelevant as time passes. Yet these trivial and irrelevant thoughts are found irresistibly attractive, while the concentration practice, consisting as it does in rejecting every form of mental diversion, becomes increasingly boring. Time passes slowly, and the meditator easily finds excuses for cutting short the period of practice. And mental restlessness is not the only problem. The meditator also finds himself afflicted by various unpleasant physical sensations, such as body pains, drowsiness, and attacks of itching, which make concentration all the more difficult.

Repeatedly returning attention to his breathing, and repeatedly finding it has wandered again, the meditator soon realizes that his mind is remarkably difficult to discipline. This discovery, interesting at first, soon becomes exasperating. As he struggles with his mind in this way, the meditator is likely to become increasingly disheartened, perhaps to the point of being ready to abandon the meditation course completely. However, the meditation master assures his distressed student that all meditators have similar experiences. The mind is like a wild forest monkey. Gotama once said: 'Just as a monkey, brethren, faring through the woods, through the great forest catches hold of a bough, letting it go seizes another, even so that which we call thought, mind, consciousness, that arises as one thing, ceases as another, both by night and by day.'[12] This fact is not realized until one tries to tie down the monkey mind with the rope of mindfulness.

If the meditator finds the practice particularly difficult, he may be advised to adopt one of several devices to facilitate concentration. The most popular device is to count mentally in time with the breathing, for example, to count from one to five on the in-breath, and from five back to one on the out-breath. Occupied with inwardly saying the numbers, the mind is prevented from straying, and will then remain fixed on the breathing when the counting is later abandoned. Or the meditator may obtain the same effect by mentally repeating some *mantra*-like formula, such as *Namo Buddhassa*.

The meditation master makes light of the body pains, attacks of itching, and so on, explaining them as a side-effect of the meditator's developing concentration. Every meditator has the same experience; as concentration develops, minor aches and irritations that would normally go unnoticed, are perceived with great clarity. The meditator must regard them not as an excuse for giving up the practice, but as a sign that he is making progress.

Thus reassured, the meditator presses on with his practice, and eventually the day comes when he is able to sit with attention fixed onepointedly on his breathing for minutes together.

Mental Onepointedness

Once attained, the condition of prolonged mental onepointedness is one of great pleasure and contentment. No bodily discomfort is felt because all attention is on that one sensitive area, the rim of the right nostril. With his mind empty of thoughts, the meditator knows no boredom, since he now has no sense of time. Previously he had seized on any excuse to interrupt or postpone the practice; now he enjoys the practice so much that he is reluctant to break off even for meals.

On opening his eyes and rising from his seat after a prolonged period of onepointedness, the meditator finds that a remarkable change has come about. Things now have a quality they had lacked before; trees, rocks, and clouds all seem full of freshness, beauty, and meaning. The meditator finds he has lost all sense of selfhood, all sense of being a separate 'I'; instead he has become 'one with all things'. Also his mind seems to have been 'purified', freed of restlessness, desire, and other 'negative' qualities. Many a meditator has happily interpreted these effects as a sure sign that he is already well on the way to *nirvāṇa*! When the condition wears off, as it always does after a time, the meditator returns to his practice with renewed enthusiasm and confidence.

Probably few meditators seek an explanation for these effects, and indeed the mechanism of the process is not likely to become apparent until more advanced practices have been mastered. (Details are discussed in the next chapter; here only a brief summary is offered.) Normally the mind is almost continuously engaged in thinking, planning, daydreaming, reminiscing, . . . Sequences of mental imagery and verbalizing arise, one after the other, almost incessantly, throughout the entire waking day. These thought sequences normally go unnoticed; they are so much a part of our lives that we are rarely aware of their existence. Like an endless television programme, the flow of thought goes on and on, forming a largely unnoticed background to our more obvious sensory experiences. The attempt to concentrate, to stop this thinking activity of the mind, makes the meditator acutely conscious of its existence, perhaps for the first time in his life. Thus concentration practice, by temporarily stopping the movement of thought, provides the first insights into the nature of that movement.

Normally when we are engaged in any activity, our attention is divided. We assume that we have all attention on what we are doing; in fact, however, we are being more or less distracted by our own thoughts. For example, when driving a car, we take for granted that we are concentrating on the road and traffic; however, in reality we have part of our attention on the mental television show, the endless sequence of mental imagery and inner speech — which is probably a major cause of traffic accidents. Anyone who has acquired some facility in concentration can verify that almost all daily activities are carried on in this half-attentive fashion, with, in most cases, a corresponding loss in efficiency. The effect can be observed best when one is engaged in some rather mechanical task. For example, when one is typing from a prepared copy, speed and accuracy remain high as long as there is no thought, as long as all attention is on the task itself; but as soon as some word in the text, or some irrelevant sensory stimulus, sets in motion a train of thought, one's fingers begin striking the wrong keys. Proficiency in concentration would therefore be a valuable asset in many everyday activities.

It is not only meditators who experience mental one-pointedness, the state of temporary freedom from thought. Anyone may gain a taste of it under certain favourable conditions. The flow of thought sometimes stops temporarily when one becomes totally engrossed in sensory input. This may happen, for example, when one is gazing at a magnificent sunset, or listening attentively to a great orchestral performance, or skiing at high speed down a steep and difficult slope. In such circumstances 'time stands still'; the experience has a strangely magical quality; one seems to have gone beyond the normal humdrum level of consciousness. The condition is always short-lived, however; the flow of thought soon resumes and the magic is lost. As soon as one makes some mental comment about the magnificent sunset, or recalls that it is almost time for dinner, the spell is broken; as soon as one mentally compares the performance of the orchestra with earlier performances, the effect is ruined just as effectively as if the person in the next seat had audibly made the same critical comments.

Normally we see things through a veil of mental imagery and hear them against the background of our own mental chatter. Consequently our view of the world is partly obscured; we see and hear things unclearly. The sharpness and clarity of perception which is attained following mastery of mindfulness of breathing, or which comes unbidden on certain rare occasions, is therefore experienced as something wonderful and precious.

The veiling effect of thought and the possibility of eliminating it are often mentioned by present-day masters of meditation. For example, Krishnamurti says:

> When you look at a tree, you never look at it except with the image you have of that tree. Your eyes see through the image of knowledge, of remembrance . . .[13]

Krishnamurti points out that this 'image of knowledge' interferes with and distorts our perception of the sense object. He urges us to eliminate mental imagery and verbalizing and thus eliminate the interference and distortion:

> If one wants to see a thing clearly, one's mind must be very quiet, without all the prejudices, the chattering, the dialogue, the images, the pictures — all that must be put aside to look.[14]
>
> One of the most difficult things is . . . to look at anything without the image of that thing, to look at a cloud without the previous associations with regard to that cloud, to see a flower without the image, the memories, the associations concerning that flower.[15]

Robert S. De Ropp, known for his studies of altered states of consciousness, gives the following description of perception freed from the veil of thought:

> The eye rests on the objects of sight, not naming them, not desiring, passing no judgments. The shapes of buildings, the texture of trees and grass, of clouds and earth, take on a meaning so new, so fresh and so exciting that they seem on the point of relating their innermost secrets . . . All, without a single exception, take a new meaning when the doors of perception are cleansed, when the wandering thoughts are silenced, when simple direct awareness takes the place of day-dreams, and our 'thought-ridden nature' . . . throws off the burden of a useless cerebration leaving consciousness open to receive the sensory messages derived from physical realities.[16]

The effect of removing the veil of imagery and verbalizing has also been well described by Roger Walsh, one of the few psychologists to take up meditation seriously:

> Sensitivity and clarity frequently seem enhanced following a meditation sitting or retreat. Thus, for example, at these times it seems that I can discriminate visual forms and outlines more clearly . . . The experience feels like having a faint but discernable veil removed from my eyes, and that the veil is comprised of hundreds of subtle thoughts and feelings. Each one of these thoughts and feelings seems to act as a competing stimulus or 'noise', which thus reduces sensitivity to any one object. Thus after meditation any specific stimulus appears stronger and clearer . . .[17]

To anyone who has used mind-altering drugs, particularly cannabis, the above descriptions of the condition of mental one-pointedness will seem familiar. The great clarity of sensory perception that follows successful concentration practice is identical in nature with an often-remarked characteristic of the 'high' experience. A person under the influence of cannabis is likely to see colours and textures with remarkable vividness, to hear clearly the faintest, most distant sounds, or to find himself 'grooving' for long periods on the changing shapes of a cloud or the patterning of a leaf. He discovers that things which formerly were tiresomely mundane are now fresh and remarkable, as if he were seeing them for the first time in his life. Inward observation would reveal that this characteristic of the cannabis experience is due simply to prolonged cessation of the flow of thought, which normally gets in the way of sense perception. The mind has ceased applying names to sense objects or referring the present experience back to earlier, related experiences. The result is the *jamais vu* effect, the same sense of freshness and newness as is experienced by the meditator who has mastered concentration.

On the basis of reports by drug users, Krishnamurti acknowledges that cannabis can induce the thought-free experience and thus eliminate interference with sensory perception. However, he points out that this effect is temporary and artificial, and by implication an unsatisfactory substitute for the genuine meditative experience.[18] Similarly De Ropp, while recognizing the role of drugs in this connection, maintains that genuine freedom from the veil of thought can be achieved only by hard practice:

> Only by work, by a steady, unremitting effort can he [the aspirant] learn to stop the wheel of the imagination, to halt that flood of inner conversations, arguments, mere chatter, with which the roof brain, by its useless overactivity, floods the awareness from dawn to dust . . . Stop thoughts![19]

Recognition of the transience and artificiality of drug-induced thought-free states has led many former drug users to take up meditation.

As described in the manuals, and as currently practised, mindfulness of breathing does not stop with the attainment of simple onepointedness. The meditator who has succeeded in halting the mental wandering can, through further prolonged concentration, deepen the state of onepointedness and thereby bring about various changes in his perception of the meditation object. In the details of its content — the actual colours, shapes, sounds, etc. involved — this process varies from one meditator to another; however, in its essential nature it is always the same. The following description is typical.

As the meditator continues to sit for long periods with eyes shut and attention fixed on the sensation at the rim of his nostril, that sensation increases steadily in vividness. Consciousness of other bodily sensations diminishes, until the crescent-shaped zone of sensitivity at the nostril seems to be all that exists. At this point the concentration object is likely to undergo a transformation. By a kind of synaesthesia the tactile sensation is replaced by a vivid visual image or *nimitta*, depicting a large, glowing crescent suspended in the midst of a black nothingness.[20]

This *nimitta* is now taken as the object of concentration. In each meditation session, the meditator begins in the usual way by concentrating on his breathing; but as soon as the *nimitta* arises, he concentrates on that instead. As the days pass, the *nimitta* becomes more and more vivid, and may change in shape or colour. Eventually there comes a time when, in the midst of this practice, the *nimitta* suddenly vanishes. Thus deprived of his only content of consciousness, the meditator is as if suddenly plunged into an infinite black vacuum — a strange and sometimes alarming experience. Like all the other states attained in the course of the concentration practice, this state of total mental emptiness comes to an end sooner or later, and the meditator returns to normal consciousness. The practice thereafter consists in progressively prolonging this state of emptiness, which can be done by making a firm resolution to that effect at the beginning of each meditation session.

The development of these deeper states of concentration is often accompanied by various remarkable side-effects. At times the meditator may feel his body suffused with delightful feelings of warmth or of coolness; or he may feel as if he has become weightless and is floating a short distance above the seat; or he may inwardly see his body radiating a wonderful coloured aura or surrounded by a circle of flames.[21] On returning to normal consciousness after one of these experiences, the meditator is likely to conclude that he has developed the power of levitation or is acquiring a halo, and may become elated at this seeming evidence of spiritual progress. However, the meditation master quickly dispels such illusions. The feeling of weightlessness and other effects are, like the body pains and attacks of itching, simply incidental consequences of the developing power of concentration. They have no real value. Far from cultivating them, the meditator must pass them by, merely acknowledging their existence and returning to the prescribed meditation practice. Some meditators, lacking proper guidance from an experienced teacher, do encourage these remarkable side-effects of concentration. However, most meditation masters consider that such people are deluded, that they have strayed from the path to enlightenment into an attractive side-alley which leads nowhere.

Regarding the development of the *nimitta* and the subsequent plunge into total mental emptiness, meditation masters are in disagreement. Some encourage their students to proceed in this direction, identifying the plunge into emptiness as 'entry into *jhāna*', and therefore as a valuable preparation for the attainment of enlightenment. Others (as will be seen in the next chapter) condemn this deepest form of concentration as yet another blind alley, comparable to 'levitation' and 'haloes'. Most agree, however, that the earlier stages in mindfulness of breathing are a valuable, if not indispensable practice for the aspirant on the Buddhist path.

Other Concentration Techniques

Mindfulness of breathing is only one in a long list of seemingly diverse techniques available to Buddhist meditators. However, experimentation reveals that the appearance of variety is misleading. In many cases the actual mental exercises involved and the mental effects produced prove to be identical with those described for mindfulness of breathing. This may be illustrated by the case of *kasiṇa-bhāvanā*, a technique mentioned briefly in the Tipiṭaka and described in detail in the *Visuddhi-magga* but rarely practised at the present day.[22] In this technique the meditator gazes at a series of ten different discs. The first four discs are composed of the 'elements' earth, water, fire, and air, the next four are of materials in the traditional four colours: blue, yellow, red, and white; and the ninth and tenth are composed of space and either light or consciousness. The meditator begins with the earth *kasiṇa*, a disc of earth 'of the size of a tray or of a pot-lid', which he has carefully prepared by smearing clay over a wooden frame. Having set up his earth *kasiṇa* in a suitable place, he sits and gazes at it for long periods, repeating to himself 'earth, earth, . . .' and dwelling on the properties of the earth element. In time he succeeds in excluding all extraneous sense impressions and all thoughts, until he is conscious of nothing but the disc of earth. With further concentration, the visual experience of the disc is replaced by a *nimitta*, a mental replica which is clearly seen when the eyes are shut. This *nimitta* then undergoes the same series of transformations as in the case of mindfulness of breathing.

Any meditator who has mastered the practice of concentration can verify that the nature of the onepointed condition is independent of the concentration object used, and of the sense modality involved. Admittedly, gazing at a disc of earth is a different experience from focusing attention on the tactile sensation at the nostril, and different again from listening attentively to the ticking of a clock or to an inwardly chanted *mantra*; in the initial stages each of these practices does have its own characteristic quality. But the actual mental exercise involved is identical in all cases: the meditator attempts to stop the usual movement of thought by keeping attention fixed on the chosen object. In the advanced stages, when the original meditation object has been replaced by an inwardly experienced *nimitta*, all difference is obliterated. A decision on which concentration object to use can therefore be based entirely on the meditator's personal preferences or on considerations of practical convenience. For a meditator who finds auditory objects easiest to concentrate on, the best choice may be the ticking of a clock or a *mantra*; one who prefers a visual object may do better to gaze at a *kasiṇa* disc or a Buddha image. The popularity of mindfulness of breathing is probably due to certain practical advantages inherent in this technique. Since one must always breathe, concentration on breathing can be practised anywhere and at any time; it requires no equipment, unlike concentration on a *kasiṇa* disc or a ticking clock. Also, concentrating on the breathing produces no physical strain, unlike gazing at discs, which can tire the eyes. Nevertheless, in essence the practice is always the same regardless of what concentration object is used. It consists of fixing attention on the chosen object until the movement of thought is stopped and onepointedness is attained.

This discussion of meditation techniques began as an examination of mindfulness of breathing as described in the texts and as currently practised. It has now broadened in scope to embrace a number of techniques which, though superficially diverse, all reduce to one and the same mental exercise, namely concentration. A distinction has thus been drawn between the superficial, outward form of a meditation technique and the actual mental exercise it entails. It may seem that it would therefore be appropriate at this point to draw up a list of all the techniques which come under the heading of 'concentration'. However, to do that would be misleading. Just as it can sometimes be shown that several superficially different techniques entail one and the same mental exercise, so too it can sometimes be shown that a nominally unitary technique is in fact interpreted and taught so differently by different masters, that it entails several essentially distinct mental exercises. An example of the latter case is 'Burmese *vipassanā*'. This technique was originally intended as a means for attaining insight — for example, insight into the 'three characteristics (transience, suffering, and non-selfhood) — and it is still widely used as such.[23] However, as currently taught by many meditation masters, Burmese *vipassanā* has become a typical exercise in concentration, whose culmination is 'entry into *jhāna*'.[24] Similar changes in the application of meditation techniques have probably occurred throughout the long history of Buddhism. Some of the many techniques which now serve as means for attaining onepointedness may have originally served quite different ends. The *kasiṇa* technique is almost certainly in this category; otherwise why should ten different discs be used to attain the very same state of deep concentration? (The original purpose of the *kasiṇas* is discussed in Chapter VII.)

These uncertainties are, however, of no concern at this early stage in our examination of meditation techniques, the purpose here being to identify and describe actual mental exercises. It is clear that Gotama did teach and attach great importance to concentration as a basic meditation exercise; for this there is abundant canonical evidence. Right concentration is the eighth stage of the Noble Path. It is equated with proficiency in the four *jhānas*, states of progressively deepening concentration characterized, above all, by the mental factor onepointedness (*ekaggatā*). And in almost every account of the three knowledges, which culminate in enlightenment, practice of the *jhānas* is mentioned as a meditative prerequisite.[25]

Concentration also figures prominently in non-Buddhist traditions, for example Jainism and various schools of Hinduism. In Hindu yoga, concentration is all-important, judging by Patañjali's definition: 'Yoga is the cessation of the movements of the mind'.[26] Since attainment of the deepest stages of onepointedness demonstrably induces a slowing of the body's metabolic processes, it is probable that some of the remarkable physiological feats performed by adept yogis — prolonged breath-holding, etc. — depend on proficiency in concentration. Concentration has also been practised in non-Indian religious traditions. It is probable that some of the remarkable experiences described by Christian mystics were actually side-effects of concentration, practised unknowingly during devotional exercises. A devotee kneeling in a quiet chapel and gazing fixedly for long periods at an icon, chanting, or praying might well attain the state of mental onepointedness. Should this state become so profound as to yield one of the side-effects familiar to Buddhist meditators — heightened sensory perception, a sense of having been purified, even auras or feelings of weightlessness — the devotee would naturally interpret this in Christian terms. This may well be the explanation for mystics' reports of visitations by the Holy Spirit, and similar experiences.

As noted earlier, Buddhist meditative practice is recognized as having two major divisions: tranquillity meditation (*samatha*) and insight meditation (*vipassanā*).[27] The various degrees of concentration — ranging from the temporary state of freedom from thought which comes unbidden when one is absorbed in a sunset, to the prolonged state of total mental emptiness which can be attained after months of intensive practice — all belong under the heading of tranquillity meditation. As such, concentration is, in the overall scheme of Buddhist meditation, a relatively elementary practice, serving as a foundation and preparation for the practice of insight meditation.

CHAPTER IV

INSIGHT MEDITATION

Many present-day meditation masters teach only concentration, apparently convinced that this is all there is to meditation. If asked where insight fits into their scheme, they usually answer that insight will come of its own accord once concentration has been mastered. Some explain this by likening the mind to a deep pool of water, whose surface is constantly ruffled by the wind, so that one cannot see what lies beneath. Just as the sand, pebbles, and crabs at the bottom of the pool become visible once the surface movement subsides, so — it is said — the mind's hidden deeper layers will be perceived once the superficial activity has been stilled through concentration practice.

Limitations of Concentration Practice

Despite such assurances, the meditator who has developed the ability to sit for long periods 'in *jhāna*' may well ask himself how this state of total mental emptiness and immobility could possibly yield insight. Such doubts about the value of prolonged deep concentration are to some extent supported by the canonical account of enlightenment. As noted in Chapter I, the first of the three knowledges, said to follow the perfecting of the *jhānas*, is described in the Tipiṭaka, and more particularly in the *Visuddhimagga*, as a systematic recalling of past events. This would seem to imply some form of image-like mental content, and therefore a departure from the state of mental onepointedness. It appears, then, that the deeply concentrated condition, though no doubt necessary as a *preparation* for insight meditation, has to be relinquished as insight meditation is actually put into practice.

Some of the great masters of the past have warned that concentration practice is of limited value. For example, Hui Neng, the sixth Chinese patriarch of Zen, says in his *Platform Sūtra*: 'To concentrate the mind and to contemplate it until it is still is a disease and not *dhyāna* [Zen]. To restrain the body by sitting up for a long time — of what benefit is this towards the Dharma?'[1]

He goes on to say that the meditator who has succeeded in suppressing thoughts must allow them to arise naturally once again. However, he does not make clear what, if anything, the meditator should then do with those thoughts.

Some present-day authorities also play down the value of concentration. For example, Buddhadasa states that concentration is merely a preliminary exercise, a kind of mental limbering-up, whose function is to render the mind 'flexible, manageable, . . . fit for work, ready to *know*'. The real goal of meditation, he says, is insight attained through introspective observation and investigation. As a foundation for that practice one requires only a relatively shallow level of concentration. Buddhadasa therefore condemns deep concentration, in which the meditator 'sits rigidly like a stone image, quite devoid of awareness':

> Sitting in deep concentration like that one is in no position to investigate anything. A deeply concentrated mind cannot practise introspection at all. It is in a state of unawareness and is of no use for insight. *Deep concentration is a major obstacle to insight practice.*[2]

Buddhadasa declares that a meditator who has attained these states of deep concentration must abandon them and return to shallower levels, thus allowing his mind to become flexible and capable of taking up the real practice, which is introspection.[3] He fails, however, to give explicit instructions on how to carry out this practice of introspection.

Assuming that the meditator has mastered the deepest stages of concentration, and that he has learned how to return from them to shallower levels in which the mind is 'fit for work, ready to know' — what should he do then? What is the nature of this 'work' whereby the mind will come to know? Let us consider the situation of a meditator who has 'emerged from *jhāna*' and returned to the threshold of normal consciousness. His mind, which had been empty of thoughts, approaches again its normal condition; thought sequences begin to arise; ruffles begin appearing on the surface of the pool. If the meditator is convinced of the value of the onepointed condition, or at least firmly committed to practising it, he suppresses these intruding thoughts each time they arise. If at any time he realizes that his mind, instead of remaining fixed on the chosen concentration object, is following some train of thought, he immediately cuts off that train of thought and directs his attention back to the concentration object.

The meditator's mind therefore alternates between two contrasting conditions: (1) It is attentive and the flow of thought is stopped; (2) It is inattentive and the flow of thought goes on as usual. The practice is such that the meditator never discovers what takes place during the periods of inattention; he never learns anything about the thought sequences themselves, or how they are made up; he never finds out *how* the mind wanders.

If, however, the meditator's interest in meditation derives from a wish to understand the mind rather than to control it, to attain insight rather than tranquillity, then he may come to see the practice he is engaged in as limiting. If he is sufficiently curious about the unseen processes that take place when the mind is *not* onepointed, then he may, once the novelty of onepointedness has worn off, begin to feel a need for a meditative practice that will reveal those processes rather than suppressing them.

Retracing

For a meditator in this situation the Tipiṭaka and the classical treatises on meditation are of little practical help. However, some guidance can be obtained from certain present-day manuals. A preliminary outline for a technique is given by Ernest Wood in his book *Mind and Memory Training*. It is presented not as a formal meditative procedure but as an account of an experience most people are more or less familiar with, namely the experience of suddenly realizing, while working on some task, that one is thinking of a totally unrelated matter, and of then introspectively reconstructing how this mental digression came about. Wood gives the following example:

> I start by thinking about a cat. A few minutes later I find myself thinking about a very strikingly designed iron bridge that spans the river Indus between the towns of Sukkur and Rohri. I might imagine . . . that my mind had leaped from the idea of the cat to the idea of the bridge, that it had merely casually forgotten the first thing and merely casually thought of the other. But if I take the trouble to recall what has happened and to study the matter I shall find that there was an unbroken chain of images leading from the first to the last . . .
>
> I thought of a cat, then of a cat lying on a hearth-rug before a fire . . ., then of the hearth-rug without the cat, then of the hearth-rug being made in a factory that I know very well, which was near the river Indus, and then of a scene further up the river where the great bridge already mentioned rises into the air.[4]

This example is typical; however, the description is incomplete, since it fails to explain how, in practice, one should 'recall what has happened'. More satisfactory in this respect is the following account given by Christmas Humphreys in his manual *Concentration and Meditation*:

> To take a simple example, one may begin to concentrate on an orange. Before one is aware of it, the mind has leapt from orange to fruit in general, from fruit to the need of buying some for lunch, from this to the theatre which the people coming to lunch are taking one to see, from this to tickets one promised to pick up on the way, and thence the best way of arriving at the theatre and the proper time to leave the house in order to get there in time. With a start you realize how far you have travelled from the orange, *but instead of returning direct* to the orange and beginning again, *force the attention to travel back the way it came.* From planning times and routes return to tickets, and thence to visitors, lunch, fruit and the need for it, and so back to the orange sitting in front of you. This habit of thought recalling is a valuable exercise in itself, and much may be learnt from it.[5]

Any meditator who experiments with retracing thought sequences can verify Humphreys' claim that it is 'a valuable exercise'. Yet this exercise is apparently little known. Those meditators who do practise retracing appear to have discovered it independently of their teachers. An example is to be found among the written reports that were submitted by student participants in a two-week meditation workshop conducted at Oberlin College (in Ohio, USA) in 1968.[6] One of the students found himself frequently digressing from the concentration object (the breathing) and going off on 'mental tangents'; so he decided to 'trace the links within the mental tangents back to their trigger points (e.g. sound of toilet flushing, twitching in the eyelid), some of which seemed ridiculous . . .'[7] He found this exercise far more interesting than the mindfulness of breathing which he had been told to practise: 'My fascination with tracing the thought processes was so overpowering that I wasn't paying much attention to breathing.'[8]

The effects of retracing and its value as a meditative practice will be discussed shortly. First, however, some practical details must be clarified. In any particular meditation session retracing of thought sequences can be practised as a sequel to conventional concentration practice. As always, the meditator attempts to keep his attention fixed on the chosen object. However, when he realizes that his attention has wandered, he does not return to the object directly; instead he returns by the devious way he came, retracing his mental steps one by one. The starting point to which he thus returns may prove to be the concentration object itself (as in Humphreys' example of the orange), or it may turn out to be some extraneous sense impression (as in the Oberlin College student's example of the flushing toilet or twitching eyelid). The meditator then directs his attention again to the concentration object and repeats the process. The retracing procedure is therefore a cycle of three stages:

Stage 1: Attention is concentrated on some chosen object.
Stage 2: A short sequence of thoughts arises.
Stage 3: That sequence is retraced to its source.

In this cycle concentration (Stage 1) fulfils several useful functions. Most importantly it provides a degree of control over the otherwise overwhelming flood of thought. Having stopped thought completely, the meditator can then, by judiciously relaxing the intensity of his concentration, allow short thought sequences to arise, which he can retrace before they get out of hand. The discipline of concentration prevents thought sequences from running on at such speed and to such lengths that they become impossible to retrace effectively. Also, concentration provides sufficient mental control to overcome a major difficulty inherent in the retracing procedure, namely a tendency for a new thought sequence to begin before the original one has been retraced all the way to its source.

Again, concentration is important in providing a blank background against which thoughts will stand out conspicuously and be readily recognized for what they are. Concentration produces mental stillness; the arising of thoughts out of that stillness can be observed with exceptional clarity. This last-mentioned function of concentraiton is often stressed by Krishnamurti in his talks on meditation:

> And it is only in silence that you can observe the beginning of thought . . . it is only when you are completely quiet . . . that you will begin to see, out of that silence, how thought takes shape.[9]

In these ways the onepointed condition facilitates observation of the thinking process with which it contrasts. Thus concentration, though perhaps not entirely indispensable, is nevertheless a valuable part of the retracing procedure. To be able to practise retracing effectively, one requires only a relatively shallow level of concentration. Deep concentration, in which thought is stopped for long periods, does have its place, as a means of subduing a particularly turbulent mind, thus preparing it for a session of retracing; however, for the actual practice of retracing, concentration must be shallow enough to break down intermittently. A meditator who has become proficient in concentration and wishes to move on to retracing may even find it necessary to stimulate the arising of thoughts by intentionally exposing himself to varied sensory input.

The meditator practising retracing need not sit in the formal meditative posture or keep his eyes shut. He may instead combine the retracing practice with some simple physical activity. This has several advantages. It eliminates the physical fatigue that comes with prolonged sitting; it provides the mind with a variety of external stimuli which can act as 'triggers', setting in motion a diversity of thought sequences; and it serves as a step towards the ideal situation in which meditation, far from being incompatible with everyday activities, will become part of those activities, practised throughout the entire day. A suitable procedure is to walk slowly along a quiet path with attention focused on some chosen sensory experience (such as the tactile sensation in the soles of the feet or the changing visual pattern that passes before the eyes), and to retrace each thought sequence that arises. With practice the meditator soon becomes able to retrace even long sequences rapidly. As his power of attention develops he may retrace scores of thought sequences in the course of an hour-long session.

The following is a typical example of the mental processes involved in this practice. The meditator, walking slowly along his garden path and attempting to keep attention fixed on his visual sensations, suddenly realizes that he is instead thinking about a tasty slice of rye bread and Camembert cheese which formed part of his lunch a few hours earlier. He thereupon retraces the thought sequence back to its source, and thus reconstructs the course of mental events. If asked to describe the experience as reconstructed, he might do so as follows: 'My attention was distracted by the sound of the neighbour's small dog barking. That made me think of the dog himself, and then of his small white kennel, which I have often seen in the neighbour's back yard. Then I thought of a beehive belonging to a friend of mine, probably because it resembles the kennel in appearance; and that reminded me of the friend himself, whom I had seen a few hours earlier when we had lunch together. Then I thought of the lunch itself and so of the bread and cheese.' (We shall see later that this is in fact a very imprecise way of describing the experience.)

Once he has become proficient in retracing, the meditator may introduce a modification into the procedure, whereby he can get a closer look at the structure of thought sequences. Having retraced a thought sequence, he then recalls one particular thought from that sequence. For example, in the case of the sequence described above, the meditator may arbitrarily cause the thought of the neighbour's dog to arise again. On doing so, he sees a faint picture of the dog, apparently superimposed on his view of the path in front of him. It is as if a photographic transparency or slide depicting the dog were projected on to the path. The meditator thus sees each 'thought' as a *mental image*, a faint replica of an earlier sense impression. Seen in this way, the image quickly vanishes. The meditator may then call it forth again a few times over, thereby reinforcing the insight. He thus comes to realize that where he would normally say 'I thought of the neighbour's dog', it would be more accurate to say 'There arose a mental image of the neighbour's dog.'

The analogy between the arising of an image and the projecting of a photographic slide is very apt. Just as a projected slide is a frozen replica of a past situation, so each image is (with certain exceptions) a re-presentation of a past sensory experience. At some time in the past the meditator had the experience referred to as 'seeing the dog'; later, when the dog is nowhere in sight, he has the experience referred to as 'remembering the dog' or 'thinking of the dog'. This second experience, the arising in his consciousness of a visual image of the dog, differs from the original one only in being less vivid and of shorter duration. Thus in most cases, though not all, the arising of an image amounts to a faint and transient re-presentation of an earlier sensory experience. Past experiences are somehow stored in that vast slide collection called the memory, to be brought out at certain times and projected one by one into the present moment. Normally they arise not by haphazard but in more or less coherent sequences. Thus the image sequence that led from a dog to a cheese sandwich is now seen by the meditator as resembling a 'slide show' based on a small selection of images from his personal collection.[10]

Turning his gaze in different directions and calling forth different images, the meditator observes repeatedly how images appear as if projected on to whatever is in the field of vision. For example, looking at the tree at the bottom of his garden, and calling forth the image of the friend with whom he had lunch, he observes how the image appears as if superimposed on his visual perception of the tree. Through this practice the meditator comes to realize how, under normal circumstances, thought interferes with and blurs sensory perception. In these ways, retracing, whether of entire thought sequences or of single images, reveals the nature of the veil of imagery — in contrast to concentration practice, which merely temporarily *removes* that veil.

Though faint and insubstantial compared with sense impressions, images are often remarkably realistic. Sometimes they are so realistic as to evoke strong emotional responses with overt physical manifestations. The image of a deceased loved one may bring tears to the eyes; the image of one's enemy may evoke anger, with clenching of the fists or even more violent reactions. When such emotively charged images arise, we tend to react to them as if we were back in the original situation. We do not perceive the image of the deceased loved one *as an image*, a transient mental phenomenon; we perceive it *as the person it depicts*, and we react accordingly.

The practice of retracing changes this situation. Retracing enables one to see beyond the content of the image to the image itself as a neutral mental phenomenon. This effect may be likened to that of switching on the light in a darkened room in which someone is watching television. A person watching a well-presented drama on television may become so absorbed in it that he forgets completely who and where he is. He becomes emotionally involved in the action, loving the heroine, admiring the hero, hating or fearing the villain, and so on. He forgets completely that he is sitting in his own living-room watching moving patterns of light on a glass screen. However, it may happen that through some cause — for example a distracting sound or an uncomfortable posture — he suddenly becomes conscious again of his real situation. He then sees his emotional involvement in the drama as inappropriate. Retracing thought sequences produces a similar effect, revealing the mental television show for what it is. Through retracing, the things in which one was so involved are seen to be actually the contents of images, insubstantial and transient mental phenomena. Seen in this way, they lose their power to evoke emotional responses. The meditator who has just retraced sees his images *as images*, and thus automatically becomes emotionally detached from their contents. He then sees that becoming emotionally involved in images is as inappropriate as running away from a photograph of a snake. The insight is only temporary, however. The flow of thought soon resumes and the meditator becomes as much as ever involved in its contents — at least until the next time he retraces.

Repeated application of the retracing procedure reveals greater complexity than the above simple account would suggest. The meditator in time discovers the existence of images in sense modalities other than vision. Auditory images — replays of sounds heard in the past — are common; gustatory, olfactory, and other images are relatively rare, but when they do occur are sometimes very realistic. An important special case of auditory imagery is mental verbalizing, 'inner speech'. Often the mind names or comments on the contents of visual images. The resemblance to a 'slide show' is then even closer, since the pictures being flashed on the screen (visual images) are now found to be accompanied by a running commentary (inner speech). Sometimes the relative prominence of the visual and auditory components is reversed, so that the effect is more that of a lecture only occasionally illustrated by slides. Inner speech commonly takes the form of imaginary conversations, in each of which some particular person is taken to be the hearer. A meditator fluent in more than one language may observe that in these mental conversations the language switches to suit the supposed hearer: if the supposed hearer is an English-speaker, the conversation is in English; if a Chinese-speaker, in Chinese; and so on.

Another necessary qualification is that not all images are simply re-presentations of previous sense experiences. Some images are modified versions of sense experiences, as when one visualizes what one's living-room would look like with the piano shifted into a new position. Other images are diagrammatic constructs, as when one visualizes the layout of a geometrical problem or the map of an intended journey. Such manipulated or creative images are found to make up only a small fraction of total imagery, though their very novelty and their occasional practical or artistic value may make them exceptionally conspicuous.

Creative imagery is utilized in certain Mahāyāna meditative techniques. The Tibetans have a practice in which the meditator must visualize a deity or demon, complete with identifying symbols and other attributes. The meditator, instructed to visualize a certain demon, builds up an image of it, which he consolidates over a period of days or weeks. He dwells on it constantly until he can visualize the demon instantly and finds it genuinely terrifying. But there comes a time when the meditator suddenly no longer finds the demon terrifying. Instead of a demon he sees *a mental image of a demon*, an insubstantial phenomenon, powerless to evoke terror or any other response. The meditator has seen beyond the content of the image to the image itself; and having seen one image in this way, he can quickly learn to see all images in the same way.[11]

Another version of this technique is to be found in the *kōan* practice, which is characteristic of the Rinzai school of Zen. A *kōan* is a special kind of problem which the meditator is required to solve. But the problem has no solution in the conventional sense, and the real purpose of the exercise is not to find a rational solution, but rather to bring about a certain transformation in consciousness. Of the hundreds of *kōans* in use, the following are some of the best known examples:

'A full-grown goose is imprisoned inside a large, narrow-necked bottle. Get the goose out without harming it or breaking the bottle.'

'A cow came in through the window. Its head, body, and legs passed through without difficulty, but its tail could not pass through. Why?'

'You know the sound of two hands clapping. But what is the sound of *one* hand clapping?'[12]

The meditator struggles for days and weeks to find the answer to his *kōan*. Told to extricate the goose from the bottle, he thinks of every possible method — greasing the neck of the bottle, heating the neck to make it expand, starving the goose until it is thin enough to pass through — all of which the master rejects as unacceptable. Finally the day comes when the meditator suddenly shouts exultantly: 'The goose is out!' He has not solved the *kōan* according to conventional ideas of problem-solving, but in the course of grappling with it he has broken through into a new dimension of consciousness.

The meditator's breakthrough (*satori*) consists in suddenly realizing that what he has been agonizing over for so long is not a goose in a bottle at all, but a mental image. The same may happen with the cow coming in through the window, and — with the addition of an auditory component — the clapping hand(s). The meditator's efforts to solve his *kōan* necessarily entail repeatedly calling up the appropriate constructed image and focusing all attention on it. The practice is therefore ultimately a special case of retracing, and in due course is bound to have the same effect: the image is seen *as an image* rather than as whatever it depicts.[13]

In Western psychology and philosophy, interest in the nature of thought-sequences has provoked debate and research since the time of Aristotle. Research has been done on problems such as the nature of images as faint replicas of sense experience, and the relative prominence of visual imagery and inner speech. Recent research in this area has generally employed a method of reporting by untrained introspecting subjects in a laboratory situation, combined with various forms of objective testing and measurement. The findings arrived at generally agree with the account given above. For example, it has been demonstrated in various well-designed experiments that a visual image is, for the person experiencing it, indistinguishable from a faint visual perception.[14] Also data have been accumulated which indicate that visual imagery is a universal phenomenon; anyone who denies having visual images has simply not learned to recognize them as such.[15]

Earlier research was based on introspective observation, by the psychologist himself, of his own mental processes. For example, the nineteenth-century psychologist Francis Galton used the following technique:

> My method consists in allowing the mind to play freely for a very brief period, until a couple or so of ideas have passed through it, and then, while the traces or echoes of those ideas are still lingering in the brain, to turn the attention upon them with a sudden and complete awakening; to arrest, to scrutinise them, and to record their exact appearance. . . . On several occasions . . . I walked leisurely along Pall Mall, a distance of 450 yards, during which time I scrutinised with attention every successive object that caught my eyes, and I allowed my attention to rest on it until one or two thoughts had arisen through direct association with that object; then I took very brief mental note of them, and passed on to the next object.[16]

Clearly Galton's method is essentially identical with the retracing practice described above.

Given that retracing of thought sequences is so valuable as a means for gaining insight into the mind, it is pertinent to ask whether retracing was among the meditative practices taught by Gotama. On superficial examination the answer appears to be 'No'. As far as can be discovered, the Pali Tipiṭaka contains no overt reference to retracing. Certain Mahāyāna texts possibly do mention it, but the references are obscure and difficult to interpret with any certainty. For example, in the *Yoga of the Six Doctrines* the meditator is told: '. . . by the retrospective observation process . . . place thyself in the state of the Clear Light'.[17] And the *Śūraṅgama Sūtra* speaks of 'returning intellect to its source', and states: '. . . by the attainment of the "turning about" in the deepest seat of consciousness self-realization of Noble Wisdom is fully entered into'.[18] These could be seen as references to retracing;

however, they are open to other interpretations and hardly suffice to demonstrate that retracing was among the meditative practices taught by Gotama.

This lack of explicit textual references to retracing is hard to reconcile with the demonstrable value of the practice as a means to insight. It raises the question whether retracing was perhaps taught and practised within the élite meditative tradition and referred to only obliquely in the symbolism of the Twilight Language. This question will be taken up in the next chapter. First, however, it is necessary to complete our discussion of insight meditation practices.

Awareness

We began this chapter with a critique of concentration, examining the situation of a meditator who has mastered concentration, has perceived its limitations as a means to insight, and is seeking a practice that will take him further. Now we shall undertake a similar critique of retracing. We shall examine critically the scope and value of retracing and consider what options are open to a meditator who has mastered this practice and feels a need to go beyond it.

The beginner is likely to be impressed by the efficacy of retracing as a means to insight into the mind. However, as he becomes more proficient, and as the novelty wears off, he may come to realize that retracing has certain inherent defects. Its most obvious defect is that it cannot be readily applied in all situations. Retracing can be practised without difficulty only if the activities one is engaged in are simple and mechanical; as soon as one turns to tasks that are at all mentally demanding, problems arise. It is of course always possible — and indeed advantageous from a meditator's point of view — to pause in whatever one is doing and retrace. But to pause repeatedly and retrace when delivering a lecture, working on a mathematical problem, or even simply carrying on a conversation, would obviously interfere with the activity in hand.

Another defect of retracing is that it reveals only a small fraction of the totality of thought. The practice consists in dissecting out occasional fragmentary thought sequences and reversing them. For example, in the case of the thought sequence cited earlier, the meditator cuts short his train of thought when it reaches the image of bread and cheese, and retraces. He thereby discovers the nature of the mental processes that led up to the arising of that image, but in so doing he denies himself the possibility of knowing what might have followed next, had the train of thought been allowed to carry on unimpeded.

To overcome these defects would require a meditative practice which could be applied in all situations, and which would reveal, as fully as retracing does, the true nature of images without interfering with the flow of thought. The ideal would be a practice whereby the meditator could insightfully watch thoughts *as they arise*, a practice whereby he could see all images as images and recognize the inner voice as the inner voice continuously and simultaneously *while thought is going on*, rather than fragmentarily and retrospectively after thought has been stopped.

Such a meditative practice does exist. It has been advocated by some of the great masters of the past, and is taught and practised by a limited number of people at the present day. We cited earlier an extract from the written report of a student participant in a meditation workshop at Oberlin College, who independently discovered retracing. That same student went on to develop a further practice which he described as follows:

> Today I made the discovery that it is literally possible to sit back and watch the thoughts come and go just as it is possible to watch breath movements rise and fall . . . There was a feeling of what I will have to call detachment . . . in sitting back and watching the breathing and flickering thoughts without working at maintaining concentration on the breathing or tracing back the thoughts.[19]

The last sentence contains a summary of the different practices which this meditator successively applied: (1) 'concentration on the breathing', (2) 'tracing back the thoughts', and (3) 'watching the breathing and flickering thoughts'. Having mastered first concentration and then retracing, he developed the technique of watching thoughts as they arise. This third practice he likened to 'being above myself and looking down'.[20]

Anyone who has developed, even if only briefly and imperfectly, the ability to watch thoughts as they arise, will recognize the above account as a description of that experience. Unfortunately, the account fails to indicate by what means this special ability to watch thoughts was acquired.

In his *Concentration and Meditation* Christmas Humphreys has a section entitled 'On Watching Thoughts', in which he gives the following instructions:

> Merely note that the thought of this or the desire for that is now arising in the mind, is passing before the mind, is passing from the mind, and watch the unceasing process calmly and dispassionately. Note how the thoughts flow past in an unbroken succession, each the outcome of the last, but only two being linked before one's mental vision at a time.[21]

The practice described is again that of watching thoughts as they arise. And as before, the author gives no indication *how* that ability may be acquired; although presented in the form of instructions to a practising meditator, the description is of no practical help except in telling the meditator what he must ultimately achieve.

One of the strongest advocates of the practice of watching thoughts is Krishnamurti. He says:

> Observe what your mind is doing. Don't try to control it, don't say it should not jump from one thought to another, from one interest to another, but just be aware of how your mind is jumping. Don't do anything about it, but watch it as from the banks of a river you watch the water flow by.[22]

Krishnamurti advises the meditator:

> Be attentive to every movement of the mind wherever it wanders . . . Meditation is to be aware of every thought . . . just to watch it and move with it.[23]

This condition, in which one watches thoughts and is 'attentive to every movement of the mind', is referred to by Krishnamurti — and by several other advocates of the practice — as *awareness*. We shall adopt the same term. Awareness, then, is a condition in which the movements of the mind are seen clearly without being impeded, a condition in which one knows from moment to moment what the mind is doing without interfering with it. Krishnamurti repeatedly claims that this is the only real meditation, this is ultimately what meditation is all about.[24]

Another authority who considers the practice of awareness or watching thoughts to be the only real meditation is the Thai master Dhiravamsa, who formerly taught under the name Sobhana Dhammasuddhi. He urges his students to '*Be aware* of the thinking process':

If you become completely aware of the mind, you will see how it operates.

The practice of meditation is to make us aware, from moment to moment, 'seeing' everything which arises and goes on within us.

Look at the mind and its mental processes . . . Let all thoughts flow into your mind. Your duty is just to look at them objectively, to see them as they are. Our task is to *look at* the mind.

Your memories and thoughts will be like an unceasing stream welling up within you . . . Let them come. Do not try to exorcise them . . . Simply be aware of them, understand them for what they are.[25]

Elsewhere Dhiravamsa identifies the essence of meditation as 'actual awareness in life — the constant movement of awareness'. He says:

If you practise awareness everything will be revealed . . . Everything is within you, and all that must be done is to look at it, to be constantly aware of yourself in all situations.[26]

Dhiravamsa often speaks of awareness as inner observation of the activities of the 'me':

If we leave the 'me' alone we can then watch it in its activities — thoughts, perceptions, feelings. If we can see these processes as they are, and how they arise and disappear, we shall be able to understand the whole structure of the 'me' through its activities.

Let the 'me' do what it wants to do, but notice what it is doing.[27]

Certain Tibetan masters teaching in the West also stress the importance of awareness. For example Tarthang Tülku says:

When we learn how to recognize thoughts, we begin to develop awareness.

So, in meditation watch your thoughts closely.

Simply watch them . . . Simply watch the flow of mental images pass through your mind.

The mind simply observes its own natural process.[28]

The reports of western researchers with firsthand knowledge of the meditative tradition in Tibet itself confirm that awareness was regarded there as the highest meditative practice. David-Neel found that two distinct practices were recognized. The first, applied by all meditators without distinction, consisted in 'training which tends to develop a perfect concentration of mind'; the second, reserved for the most advanced meditators, consisted in 'observing with great attention the workings of the mind without attempting to stop it'.[29] This second practice is described by David-Neel as follows:

> Seated in a quite place, the disciple refrains as far as he can from consciously pointing his thoughts in a definite direction. He marks the spontaneous arising of ideas, memories, desires, etc., and considers how, superseded by new ones, they sink into the dark recesses of the mind . . .
>
> During that exercise, he avoids making reflections about the spectacle which he beholds, looking passively at the continual, swift, flowing stream of thoughts and mental images . . .[30]

Elsewhere David-Neel states:

> It suffices to allow the current of existence to flow freely without attempting to prevent or guide it, watching it like an interested spectator, . . . always detached . . .[31]

The seventeenth-century Tibetan master Padma Karpo appears to have taught awareness. His *Manual of the Spontaneous Great Symbol* contains the following instructions:

> Let these thoughts now do whatever they want, not cutting them off at all, yet not falling under their spell. And thus contemplate, setting out the mind itself as its own sentinel.
>
> Thus you feel your thoughts occur, but you yourself neither cut them off nor react to them in any way . . .
>
> Now you know how to leave every thought and passion entirely alone, not cutting it off at all, yet not falling under its spell . . . Try simply to recognize every thought for what it is . . . By just recognizing the thought, the imposition of a construct, you are freed from it spontaneously . . .[32]

Here the meditator is told to refrain from cutting off thoughts — apparently an admonition to give up the practice of concentration — and equally to avoid falling under the spell of thoughts, that is, to avoid reverting to the usual everyday condition in which one becomes deluded by and emotionally involved in the contents of images. What the meditator must do is 'recognize every thought for what it is', that is practise awareness. Padmo Karpo further describes this practice as follows:

> The *yogin* then looketh on, mentally unperturbed, at the interminable flow of thoughts as though he were tranquilly resting on the shore of a river watching the water flow past.
>
> Whatever thoughts, or concepts, or obscuring . . . passions arise are neither to be abandoned nor allowed to control one; they are to be allowed to arise without one's trying to direct . . . them. If one do no more than merely to recognize them as soon as they arise, and persist in so doing, they will come to be realized . . . in their true . . . form through not being abandoned.[33]

The above quotations describe a practice that consists in watching thoughts continuously, while remaining detached from them and fully aware of their true nature. This fits the ideal practice suggested earlier. The quotations represent several independent lines of investigation by individual meditators, most of whom belong to various traditions within present-day Buddhism. The question whether this practice of awareness or watching thoughts goes back to the time of Gotama will be considered later. First the nature of the practice itself will be examined in more detail.

The meditator practising awareness observes thoughts insightfully as they arise unhindered. This insightful observation broadly resembles that employed in the practice of retracing, but lacks its disruptive effect. In awareness the observation is sufficiently subtle for it in no way to interfere with the normal flow of thought. The meditator establishes a delicate state of balance, in which the flow of thought coexists with a refined form of the same insightful scrutiny that applies in retracing.

How this state of balance may be attained is not made clear in any of the available accounts of awareness. There exists no description of a technique whereby awareness may be developed, indeed some authorities explicitly deny the possibility of such a technique. For example, Dhiravamsa says: 'Awareness *itself* is the doing, the practice, the acting — there is no technique for being aware.'[34] Krishnamurti, too, is emphatic that there is no technique for generating awareness. There is, he declares, no step-by-step progression towards awareness; either one is aware or one is not; the awareness itself is the technique:

> The first step is the last step . . . The first step is to perceive, perceive what you are thinking . . . Now that perception is the final step, and when you have perceived, you leave it, forget it, because the next minute you have to perceive anew, which again is the final step.[35]

In effect the meditator is simply told, 'Be aware' or 'Watch thoughts', without being given any advice on how to go about it.

In rejecting the possibility of a technique or method for becoming aware, Krishnamurti rejects even formalized concentration practice, calling it a favourite gimmick of gurus, and 'a most stupid, ugly thing'.[36] No doubt some people do manage to develop awareness without having provided themselves with even this most elementary foundation; that would be in keeping with the principle that particularly gifted meditators can bypass tranquillity meditation (*samatha*) and proceed directly to insight meditation (*vipassanā*). But the suggestion that the more elementary practices are valueless is an exaggeration. For the average meditator both concentration and retracing are valuable stepping-stones to awareness. Furthermore, for a meditator who has mastered concentration and retracing but has not yet discovered how to develop awareness, there exists a practice whereby the transition can be effected. This transitional practice will now be described.

Observation of Linking

As outlined earlier, the practice of retracing entails two essentially identical but quantitatively different exercises. In the first, an entire image sequence is caused to arise again in reverse order; in the second, an individual image from that sequence is caused to arise again several times over. Now there is a third variant of retracing which yields its own particular kind of insight, and at the same time serves as the first step in the transition to awareness. It is based on *pairs* of successive images. Having retraced a complete image sequence, the meditator then causes any particular pair of consecutive images from that sequence to arise again in succession several times over. Suppose, for example, that the thought sequence is the one described earlier: dog, kennel, beehive, friend, lunch, bread-and-cheese. The meditator, having retraced this sequence, then causes the image of the dog and the image of its kennel to arise again alternately several times. Then he does the same with the image of the kennel and that of the beehive; and so on with successive pairs to the end.

This practice yields insight into the nature of the link between each image and the next. Among other things it reveals the 'laws of association' of classical psychology.[37] For example, the image of the dog is followed by the image of the kennel because dog and kennel have often been seen together ('contiguity in experience'); and the image of the kennel is followed by the image of the beehive because the two objects are similar in appearance ('similarity'). Of particular interest are the linking processes that occur towards the end of the sequence, those whereby the image of the friend is replaced by the image of the lunch as seen set out on the friend's kitchen table a few hours earlier, and that in its turn is replaced by the image of the slice of bread liberally spread with a favourite cheese. The meditator perceives that in these linking processes the guiding factor is an interest in food.

Frequent repetition of this practice reveals that the pattern just described is typical. Every image sequence tends to veer in the direction of more emotively charged images; beginning with neutral images it soon leads to images carrying some form of emotive charge, images depicting past situations towards which one had reacted emotionally. In the earlier part of a thought sequence it is the rule that successive images are linked according to contiguity in experience and so on; in the later part it is the rule that images are linked according to a special cause-and-effect principle involving emotive factors, a principle which is soon recognized by the meditator to be of paramount importance in the formation of his thought-habits, and which therefore becomes the main object of his introspective scrutiny.

To illustrate we consider another sample thought sequence, which the meditator, after retracing, might loosely describe as follows: 'Walking slowly along the path, I happened to notice a discarded cigarette butt. This reminded me of the ashtray on my desk at the office. That made me think of an important and troublesome contract on which I have been working for the past few days, and then of a meeting I had yesterday with the boss in connection with that contract. I then thought — as I have done many times today — of the dressing-down which the boss gave me during that meeting, in which he accused me of "downright carelessness". It was at that point that I remembered the meditation practice, and retraced.'

This experience consists of a sequence of images depicting the following: the ashtray; the desk covered with various papers, pens, and other objects, including the file relating to the troublesome contract; the meeting with the boss; and finally the boss's flushed face — this last visual image accompanied by a replay of the boss's words 'downright carelessness'.

On examining successive pairs of images in the manner described above, the meditator readily perceives why the image sequence proceeded as it did. The contract had been a cause of much worry over the past few days; of all the objects on his desk, the file relating to the contract was the one with which he was emotionally most involved. Had his major preoccupation over the past few days been not the contract but, say, the recent death of his father, then the image of his desk would probably have been followed not by an image depicting the contract file, but by one depicting the sentimentally much-valued pen given him by his father. This same process becomes apparent again and again when pairs of images are examined: of the various contents of an image, one particular detail is 'selected' to become the theme of the next image; and the detail thus selected is the one that is the most emotively charged, the one to which one has in the past reacted with the strongest emotional response. Further examples of this process are provided by the next two links in the sample image sequence, whereby the image of the contract file is replaced by the image depicting the meeting with the boss, and that in its turn is replaced by the image depicting the boss's flushed face as he utters the words 'downright carelessness'. Of the incidents associated with the contract, the one in which there had been the greatest emotional involvement was yesterday's meeting with the boss; and of the incidents that had taken place during that meeting the words 'downright carelessness' had evoked the strongest response. The meditator perceives that, in thought sequences involving emotively charged images, it is the most emotively charged detail of content in any given image that determines which image shall follow it. This is why thought sequences tend to veer away from neutral images and towards emotively highly-charged images.[38]

As he further examines the offending images, the meditator may come to realize that the emotive charge inhering in the image of his boss's face is a consequence of his earlier emotional reaction to two things: (1) his actual encounter with the boss; and (2) his subsequent memories of that encounter. This is found to be a general principle: The emotive charge inhering in the content of an image is a reflection of emotional involvement in (1) the original sensory experience of which the image is a representation; and (2) earlier occurrences of the image itself. Ultimately, then, the process of linking is determined by earlier emotional involvement in sensory input and in imagery.

The practice of examining pairs of images that yields this insight has two distinct phases. In the first phase, the original order of the two images is reversed, as in ordinary retracing; for example, the meditator goes back from the image of the contract file to the image of the ashtray which originally preceded it. In the second phase there is a return to the original order; the image of the ashtray is allowed to yield place to the image of the file, as in the original image sequence. As he practises, the meditator becomes conscious of an important difference between these two phases, a difference which, however, is not easy to describe. It is as if the second phase, in which linking proceeds in the original forward direction, entailed less 'mental effort' than the first, in which linking is made to occur in reverse. In the switch from the first phase to the second one must, as it were, reduce the strength of the insightful scrutiny of the images; otherwise the forward linking cannot take place. The meditator in time becomes sensitive to this difference between the two phases; he acquires the ability to 'tone down' his scrutiny of images just sufficiently to permit linking to take place.[39] In other words, he acquires the ability to watch insightfully the transition from each image to the next.

Having learned to do this with any particular pair of consecutive images chosen from the given image sequence, the meditator can then extend the process to cover the entire sequence. Proceeding image by image, link by link, he moves on until he reaches the last image of the sequence. The meditator now finds that the practice can be streamlined, reduced to its bare essentials. The backward-linking phase can be dispensed with, so that only the forward-linking process is observed, and that once only for each image pair. The technique is perfected when the meditator is able to move rapidly through a complete sequence, from the first image to the last, causing each image to arise once only, while insightfully observing each linking process. For this practice we shall adopt the term *observation of linking*.

To recapitulate, the successive steps in observation of linking are as follows: After an image sequence has been retraced, two consecutive images from that sequence are caused to arise again alternately several times over. The same is done with successive pairs throughout the sequence. Particular attention is paid to the forward-linking process, that in which the two images arise in their original order, and in time this alone is practised. (Thus each pair of images is caused to arise once only rather than several times over.) The practice is thereby reduced to observation of the forward-linking process, from the first image through to the last in each sequence.

The transition from this to awareness entails a simple, but nevertheless important modification. Instead of retracing and going through the above series of steps, the meditator applies the final step directly to each image sequence as it arises. Instead of reconstituting each sequence, in order to watch it insightfully on its second occurrence, he watches each sequence insightfully from the outset, his mind in that finely-tuned state of tension which permits insight to coexist with the normal flow of thought. All the insights associated with the earlier practices, are now experienced simultaneously and continuously in a state of alertness and emotional detachment. This is awareness, the state of being fully conscious of thought *as it happens*.

Characteristics of Awareness

No matter how one tries to maintain it, awareness always breaks down after a time and has to be re-established. The beginner has difficulty maintaining, even for a minute at a time, the required state of balance between the normal flow of thought and the insightful scrutiny of it. What usually happens is that insight cuts out, with the result that thoughts again run on unobserved. Realizing he has lost awareness in this way, the meditator may re-establish it by passing again through the sequence of stages: concentration, retracing, observation of linking. However, as he becomes more experienced, he may find he can dispense with this preparatory practice, and establish awareness directly. Realizing at any moment during his daily activities that his thoughts are running on unchecked, the meditator can, provided he has already developed the necessary skill, immediately re-establish awareness, that is, he can immediately resume insightfully watching his thoughts.

It seems theoretically possible that awareness could be maintained continuously throughout one's entire waking day. In practice, however, a day in the life of an experienced meditator typically consists of brief periods of awareness separated by long periods of unawareness. The meditator who has lapsed into unawareness may, at certain moments, suddenly remember that he ought to be practising awareness. He can then re-establish awareness directly, without concerning himself about the period of unawareness that has just passed. That period may as well be written off; the meditator recognizes that what is past does not matter; the important thing is to be aware, as from the present moment. As Krishnamurti says: 'When you are not aware, do not bother. Begin again. . . .'[40] And Tarthang: 'We can lose contact with awareness, and then gradually forget — yet awareness is accessible in every instant — we have one chance, then another chance. . . .'[41]

Because awareness moves with the flow of thought, it can be practised in virtually any situation. One can be aware not only while sitting in formal meditation, or engaged in simple mechanical activities; one can also be aware while engaged in the most mentally demanding tasks, such as serious reading or problem-solving. Unlike retracing, awareness in no way interferes with such activities. On the contrary, it can improve efficiency by revealing immediately any tendency to digress. Unlike retracing, awareness is compatible with every kind of thought sequence. In addition, awareness can ride smoothly over all discontinuities, including sudden switches to new topics, temporary lapses of memory, and so on.

Watching his mind in this way throughout the daily round, the meditator gains valuable insights into the nature and mechanism of thought processes. He also learns a great deal about his thought habits; he becomes familiar with his own inner world. The meditator may, for example, discover that a surprisingly large part of his mental life is taken up with unproductive thoughts on 'trivial' topics, such as food, sex, or what he would do if he were in politics. He comes to see his 'hang-ups' and psychological problems of every kind clearly, in their totality, and thereby resolves them. In this respect the practice of awareness resembles psycho-analysis: what was 'unconscious' becomes 'conscious' and is thereby rendered innocuous.

Awareness can coexist with imagery of every kind, but, like retracing, it is incompatible with any form of emotional involvement in that imagery. Awareness implies detachment. When seen under the spotlight of awareness, images which might otherwise evoke anger or embarrassment, desire or guilt, are merely found slightly amusing. Watching with awareness the antics of one's mind, one is often moved to smile. As Krishnamurti says: 'Just watch your mind. It is great fun.'[42] 'It is really very interesting, far more interesting than any film.'[43]

When there is awareness, mental events are neither condemned nor approved; they are simply seen for what they are. Images when seen *as images* are not judged; they are no longer seen as 'good' or 'bad'. Here once again it is Krishnamurti who best describes the situation:

> . . . Perceive what you are thinking, . . . perceive it without any condemnation, justification, without wishing it to be different. Just perceive it as it is. . . .[44]
>
> If there is an awareness of how thought begins then there is no need to control thought. We spend a great deal of time and waste a great deal of energy . . . trying to control our thoughts — 'This is a good thought, I must think about it a lot. This is an ugly thought, I must suppress it.' . . . But if there is an awareness of the beginning of thought, then there is no contradiction in thought.[45]

The contradiction referred to is the contradiction between the kind of thoughts we *in fact have* and the kind of thoughts we have been led to believe we *ought to have*, the contradiction between what *is* and what we feel *ought to be*. With awareness this contradiction ceases to exist because thoughts are no longer judged acceptable or unacceptable. The contradiction between what we are, and what we feel we ought to be or would like to be, is often a source of much guilt and frustration. Awareness resolves the problem by eliminating the contradiction. For example, a person who knows he is conceited but feels he ought not to be is in a state of conflict: on the one hand he enjoys and cultivates the conceited ideas he has, and on the other he condemns those ideas as undesirable and attempts to eradicate them. However, with awareness, the same person simply sees his conceited thoughts for what they are, acknowledges them as part of the present reality, and does no more than perhaps smile at the pettiness and pretension of them. The conceited thoughts are therefore neither encouraged nor condemned; they are simply allowed to arise and pass away under the spotlight of awareness, and as a result they cease to be a problem.

Awareness therefore brings a range of benefits: unobscured insight into the nature of thought-processes, genuine understanding of one's mental habits, emotional detachment from the contents of thought, freedom from the painful conflict that normally comes with the realization that one's thoughts are not what they ought to be — to name only the most obvious ones.

A written account of awareness can go only a small way towards conveying an appreciation of the nature of the experience itself. To have awareness is to be fully conscious of the activities of one's own mind, fully conscious of the very essence of the life-process. This is something quite different from the *knowledge* which a psychologist may have *about* the nature of mental processes. Awareness is totally unlike knowledge. It is immediate experience, not memory of earlier experience. As such it does not accumulate. At any moment either one is aware or one is not; and if one is not aware, it is as if one had never been aware. Naturally, one may have a memory of what awareness was like, knowledge about it and about what it reveals; but dwelling on that memory or knowledge is no substitute for the experience itself. Realizing at any moment that one is not aware, one can do no better than re-establish awareness immediately; and each experience of awareness is a totally new experience, not something that adds on to previous experiences.

The Nature of the Self

We have spoken of the practice of awareness as 'watching thoughts'. But it is to the point to ask: What is the nature of that watching? Who or what is it that watches?

One tends to conceive of the meditator practising awareness as an onlooker watching as the parade of thoughts moves past, which raises a host of psychological and philosophical questions. In fact, however, watching image sequences with awareness is not at all like watching a street parade. The meditator practising awareness finds it self-evidently inappropriate to ask who it is that is watching the image sequences. He knows, through direct experience, that both the supposed watcher of the images *and* the supposed process of watching them are nothing other than the images themselves. Awareness is not at all a matter of X watching Y, though it may be convenient to speak of it loosely in those terms. When there is awareness, the images, which had formerly been indistinct and deceptive like shadowy forms at dusk, become instead distinct and unmistakable images, like objects in broad daylight. No one watches the images; the images arise and pass away, and that is all. The 'watcher of the images' and the 'process of watching the images' are one and the same as the images themselves.

Normally we say '*I* think', '*my* mind', and so on; but as soon as there is awareness, this feeling of 'I' and 'my' with respect to mental events evaporates. No longer can one accurately say '*I* think'; one can only say 'There is thought' or 'Thought is going on'. The 'I', which under normal circumstances seems to be doing the thinking, is found to be nothing other than the thoughts themselves. The meditator who has awareness realizes that the supposed thinker of the thoughts *is* the thoughts. As the images flash past and the inner voice chatters on, he realizes: 'I am *this*!'

As soon as awareness breaks down there is a return to the feeling of I-ness, of a thinker separate from the thoughts. I-ness is coexistent with the normal failure to recognize mental contents for what they are, failure to recognize images as images. In effect, I-ness is identical with unawareness, with the state of delusion regarding the nature of thought.

Here again a distinction has to be drawn between knowledge and experience. It is one thing to acknowledge, on the basis of a logical argument or a memory of previous meditative experiences, that the supposed thinker or watcher of the thoughts *is* those thoughts: it is a quite different thing to live that fact from moment to moment during a period of awareness. Perhaps the closest one can come to this insight, short of actually attaining awareness, is in the experience of total absorption in sensory perceptions described earlier in connection with concentration practice. The state of total freedom from imagery and verbalizing, however attained — through concentration practice, through total absorption in music or a beautiful sunset, or through taking cannabis — is characterized by a feeling that the 'self', the 'I', has lost its identity. People often describe the experience in retrospect by saying: 'I *became* the sunset', or 'I *was* the breathing'. This amounts to saying that in the state of one-pointedness there is no 'I' or 'self' other than the totality of sensory perceptions. There is no 'I' experiencing the perceptions; rather the 'I' *is* the perceptions. In awareness this insight is broadened to include thought as well. The 'I' or 'self' is found to be identical with the totality of consciousness. The 'I' *is* that totality of consciousness, and not, as one had formerly assumed, a separate experiencer or watcher of it. Awareness brings the recognition that the perceiver is the perception, the thinker is the thought.

This identity of the thinker with the thought, of the watcher with the mental events he appears to be watching, is often mentioned by those familiar with awareness. For example, Padma Karpo writes: 'You are beginning to see that your introspection is finding nothing there at all, that the watched and the watcher are both the same.'[46] Similarly Tarthang says:

> The thought is not separate from the 'watcher'.
>
> There is no self to watch anything. There is only watching, only the process.
>
> Letting go of all thoughts and images, letting them go wherever they will, reveals there is nothing behind, no independent watcher. . . .[47]

Krishnamurti rightly attaches great importance to this insight that 'the observer *is* the observed', 'the observer, the thinker, *is* the thought'. He finds in it the resolution of the conflict between what we in fact think and what we have been conditioned to believe we ought to think:

> But what takes place when the observer is aware that the observer is the observed? . . . The observer has always said, 'I must do something about these images, I must suppress them or give them a different shape' . . . But when the observer realizes that the thing about which he is acting is *himself*, then there is no conflict between himself and the image. He *is that*.[48]

This can, then, be added to the list of benefits inherent in awareness: awareness reveals the ultimate falseness of the notion of 'I, the thinker', 'I, the watcher', 'I, the self', distinct from the continuity of consciousness.

We have described a course of meditative practice culminating in awareness, a course which forms an integrated whole, with each stage a preparation and foundation for the next.[49] This course includes some well-attested Buddhist techniques but excludes others. For example, 'meditation on loving-kindness', recommended in the Tipiṭaka and the *Visuddhi-magga*, has no place in the course. It is not included because it has little bearing on the central objective, the developing of awareness.[50] The contents of this chapter and the preceding one are therefore not intended even to approximate the ideal comprehensive treatment of meditation which we suggested in Chapter I ought to be produced for the benefit of aspiring meditators. Rather it is a description of one particular course of practice which has proved effective in the attainment of one particular meditative goal.

One familiar Buddhist practice of which we have said little is mindfulness (*sati*). Many meditators and scholars assume that mindfulness is an insight practice, a suitable sequel to concentration. This view appears, however, to be not entirely correct. The various lists of stages given in the texts consistently put mindfulness *before* concentration. For example, in the Noble Eightfold Path right mindfulness (*sammā sati*) is the seventh stage while right concentration (*sammā samādhi*) is the eighth; and in several different listings of five or seven 'powers' (*bala*), the final stages are always mindfulness, concentration, insight (*sati, samādhi, paññā*).[51] This indicates that mindfulness precedes concentration rather than following it. The textual account of *ānāpāna-sati* (mindfulness of breathing) indicates the same. It begins: 'Herein, monks, a monk . . . sits down cross-legged, holding his back erect, arousing mindfulness in front of him. Mindful he breaths in . . .'[52] These facts appear to indicate that mindfulness is a prerequisite to the practice of concentration.

As practised by most monks, mindfulness consists in continuous attentiveness to all bodily sensations experienced in the course of the daily round, often facilitated by performing all actions in exaggerated slow motion. This practice entails suppression of thoughts, and is in effect a shallow form of concentration. Many textual references to mindfulness as a stage in the monk's progress (as for example in the 'footprints' of a Buddha) indicate that this attentiveness to bodily sensations and movements is indeed what is meant by the stage *sati* which precedes *jhāna* practice.[53]

On the other hand, more detailed accounts of mindfulness, for example that given in the *Mahāsatipaṭṭhāna-sutta*, list many additional practices, grouped in four broad categories: mindfulness of the body, of feelings, of *citta* (mind?), and of *dhammas* (mental states?).[54] Under mindfulness of the body are listed the preliminary stages in *ānāpāna-sati* and the above-noted practice of attending to bodily sensations, followed by meditations on the body as made up of various impure components, as analysable into the four elements, and as subject to decomposition after death. Mindfulness of feelings consists in recognizing feelings, physical and mental, as pleasant, painful, or neutral. Mindfulness of *citta* and mindfulness of *dhammas* both consist in recognizing various mental factors, as set out in well-known stereotyped lists: the 'three unskilful roots', the 'five hindrances', the 'seven factors of enlightenment', and others.

Of these four categories of mindfulness, the first and second are clearly associated with the development of the *jhānas*. Mindfulness of the body (in particular of the breathing, as in *ānāpāna-sati*) is instrumental in the attainment of the first and second *jhānas*, and mindfulness of feelings becomes important in the attainment of the third and fourth *jhānas*, which entails the development and subsequent elimination of pleasurable feeling (*sukha*). The remaining two categories, mindfulness of *citta* and mindfulness of *dhammas*, appear from the *sutta* description to be possibly instrumental in attaining insight. However, if this is so, it is of little practical value to the meditator since the texts give no instructions on how these higher forms of mindfulness should actually be developed. This problem, and the role of the different categories of mindfulness, will be dealt with in the chapters to follow, particularly in Chapter VIII, which examines doctrinal questions.

The meditation course that we have described includes a series of three insight techniques: retracing, observation of linking, and awareness. Unlike concentration, which precedes them in the course, these three insight practices are neither widely applied at the present day nor overtly described in the Buddhist texts. The following three chapters will bring us back to the question first posed in a general way in Chapter I: Were these advanced practices taught in the élite meditation tradition and referred to cryptically in the symbols of the Twilight Language? We shall begin our examination of this question by turning to the record of Gotama's teaching on enlightenment as preserved in the Pali canon.

CHAPTER V

THE THREE KNOWLEDGES

In Chapter I we identified certain problems concerning Gotama's teachings on meditation, which are summed up in the question: What form of practice should follow once concentration has been perfected? This question arises out of several considerations, most importantly the following.

First, the Buddhist texts recognize meditation practices as falling into two categories: tranquillity meditation (*samatha*), that is concentration or *jhāna* practice, a relatively elementary and not altogether essential form of practice; and insight meditation (*vipassanā*), a more advanced form of practice which is indispensable if liberation is to be attained. In the texts tranquillity meditation is fairly fully explained, but insight meditation is left quite unclear.

Second, in several *suttas* the course of Buddhist practice is summarized in the Tenfold Path, whose last three stages are right concentration, right insight, and right liberation. However, detailed expositions of the Path stop short at right concentration, i.e. they deal only with the Eightfold Path.[1] Thus, while the texts state that right concentration must be followed by right insight, they fail to explain how this right insight is to be developed.

Third, Gotama states in his accounts of his enlightenment that, having practised the *jhānas*, he developed in succession three supernormal knowledges or *vijjās*: knowledge of his former existences in *saṃsāra*, knowledge of the death and rebirth of beings according to their *karmas*, and knowledge of the destruction of the cankers (*āsavas*). (See pp. 7 – 8 above.) The attainment of these was followed immediately by the long-sought-for liberation. Gotama also exhorts his monks to follow the same course of practice, mastering first the *jhānas* and then the three knowledges. However, he gives no instructions on how, in practice, the three knowledges are to be attained.

As pointed out in Chapter I, comparison of different accounts of Gotama's course of practice indicates that insight meditation (*vipassanā*) is to be equated with right insight (the ninth stage of the Tenfold Path) and with the three knowledges (*vijjās*). A possible approach to the problem of discovering the nature of the meditative practice that should follow concentration is therefore to examine Gotama's teaching on the three knowledges. This we now do, against the background of our discussion of meditative practices.

The Buddha as a 'Threefold-Knowledge Man'

According to the canonical accounts, Gotama attained the three knowledges in succession, one in each of the three watches of the night. In the first watch he attained the 'former-habitations-recollection-knowledge' (*pubbe-nivās-ānussati-ñāṇa*), in the second watch the 'beings' falling-arising-knowledge' (*sattānaṃ cut'-ūpapāta-ñāṇa*), and in the third watch the 'canker-destruction-knowledge' (*āsava-kkhaya-ñāṇa*).

Possession of these three knowledges, in particular the third, is the mark of an *arahant* or enlightened being. Gotama states this explicitly in the *Tevijjā-Vacchagotta-sutta*, which records a conversation between himself and a *śramaṇa* named Vaccha. The *sutta* begins with a request by Vaccha for confirmation of reports he has heard about Gotama's enlightenment:

> Reverend sir, I have heard: 'The recluse Gotama is all-knowing, all-seeing; he claims all-embracing knowledge-and-vision, saying: "Whether I am walking or standing still or asleep or awake, knowledge-and-vision is permanently and continuously before me." '

Gotama replies that whoever made that statement was misrepresenting him. Vaccha then asks what is the true nature of Gotama's enlightenment, to which Gotama replies:

> The recluse Gotama is a threefold-knowledge man . . . For I, Vaccha, whenever I please recollect a variety of former habitations, that is to say one birth, two births, . . . thus do I recollect divers former habitations in all their modes and details. And I, Vaccha, whenever I please . . . see beings as they pass hence and come to be . . . according to the consequences of deeds; and I, Vaccha, by the destruction of the cankers [*āsava*], having realized here and now by my own super-knowledge the freedom of mind and the freedom through wisdom that are cankerless, entering thereon, abide therein.[2]

Here Gotama rejects the popular notion (also widespread at the present day) that he is literally omniscient. He makes it clear that the essence of his enlightenment is his possession of the three knowledges. Furthermore, he states that the first and second knowledges are only intermittently present to his consciousness, though always accessible; he can call them up whenever he pleases.

Throughout the centuries this statement that Gotama was not literally omniscient has troubled devout Buddhists, no doubt because it suggests that the Blessed One was less than perfect. An early example of this concern is recorded in the *Questions of King Milinda* (second century B.C.), in which the king discusses the matter with the learned monk Nāgasena. Nāgasena at first affirms that Gotama *was* omniscient, but then qualifies this by saying: 'The insight of knowledge was not always and continuously (consciously) present with him. The omniscience of the Blessed One was dependent on reflection.'[3]

It appears, then, that Gotama's enlightenment consisted not in omniscience but in mastery of the three knowledges. Having attained the three knowledges under the Bodhi Tree at Gayā, he was subsequently able to call up the first and second of them whenever he wished, while the third became his permanent condition thenceforth.

With a view to clarifying Gotama's teaching on insight meditation, we now examine these three knowledges in turn.

The First Knowledge

As described in the texts, the first knowledge consists in pushing the memory back beyond the moment of birth to one's preceding existence in *saṃsāra*, and then, by an extension of the process, penetrating back through hundreds of thousands of previous lives, and even through many previous phases in the alternating evolution and dissolution of the universe. Gotama says this is like recollecting the villages one has passed through in the course of a journey, but he gives no advice on how to do it.[4] Some attempt to fill this gap in the Tipiṭaka account is made in two later manuals, the *Visuddhi-magga* and the *Abhidharma-kośa*. The *Visuddhi-magga* contains the following instructions:

> The monk who is a beginner, wishing to recall thus, should enter into the Four Jhanas in their due order after he, having finished his meal and returned from the alms-round, has gone into solitude and seclusion. And emerging from the Fourth Jhana, the basis of higher

> knowledge, he should contemplate his having sat himself down, the last of his acts. He should then contemplate in reverse order all that he had done during the night and day thus: The preparation of the seat, the entering into the dwelling, the putting by of the bowl and robe, the time of eating, the time of return from the village, the time of roaming the village for alms, the time of entering the village for alms, . . . all that he had done at the dawn, all that he had done in the last watch [of the night], all that he had done in the first watch . . . Thus in reverse order should he contemplate all his actions on the second day, the third, fourth, fifth day, the tenth day, . . . as far back as a year. Thus contemplating what he had done during ten years, twenty years, as far back as his birth in the present lifetime, he should contemplate name and form that arose at the moment of decease in the immediately preceding existence.[5]

The description then tells how the meditator penetrates back through many previous physical existences and many eons of evolution and dissolution, as in the Tipiṭaka account.

The *Abhidharma-kośa* of Vasubandhu, a Sarvāstivādin text of the fourth century A.D., gives instructions which emphasize recollection of previous thoughts rather than of previous physical activities:

> The ascetic who wants to remember his earlier lives begins by grasping the character of the thought that has just perished; from this thought he proceeds back, considering the immediately successive states of his present existence, to the thought of his conception. When he remembers a moment of thought in the intermediate existence . . . *abhijñā* [supernormal knowledge] is realized.[6]

Most present-day scholars have little or nothing to say on recollection of former existences. An exception is Eliade, who attaches some importance to it. He offers the following description-interpretation:

> The method is to cast off from a precise instant of Time, the nearest to the present moment, and to retrace the time backwards (*pratiloman* or 'against the stream') in order to arrive *ad originem*, the point where existence first 'burst' into the world and unleashed Time. Then one rejoins that paradoxical instant before which Time was not, because nothing had been manifested. We can grasp the meaning and the aim of this technique: to reascend the stream of Time would necessarily bring one back ultimately to the point of departure, which coincides with that of the cosmogony. To relive one's past lives would also be to understand them and, to a certain degree, 'burn up' one's 'sins'; that

is, the sum of the deeds done in the state of ignorance and capitalised from one life to the next by the law of *karma*.[7]

Eliade also suggests that to retrace the course of one's former lives would be to 'transcend the human condition and to regain the non-conditioned state, which preceded the fall into Time and the wheel of existence'.[8]

Recollection of former existences presupposes the doctrine of *saṃsāra*. According to that doctrine, one's present existence is but one in an enormously long series of such existences: after death each individual is reborn in another form, determined by his *karma*; and he will continue a prisoner in this weary cycle unless and until, by following the Path of the Buddhas, he attains enlightenment and thereby *nirvāṇa*, liberation from *saṃsāra*. For anyone who accepts this basic notion that his present existence is one in a long series of such existences, it is perhaps not difficult to accept the proposition that recollection of his earlier existences could contribute to bringing that process to an end.

Most believing Buddhists do accept the doctrine of *saṃsāra* quite literally, though they are usually more concerned with ensuring a better existence next time than with attaining complete liberation from the process. However, some Buddhists, including certain leading monks and scholars, consider that the doctrine has to be understood non-literally. Their interpretations, while differing in details, all agree on one crucial point: the birth and death referred to in the *saṃsāra* doctrine are not the birth and death of the physical body but the frequently repeated arising and ceasing of certain momentary phenomena in this present life. What those momentary phenomena actually are is usually left unclear.

For example, Dhiravamsa says: 'Rebirth is in this life . . . Rebirth is a process of dying and being reborn in life, from moment to moment.'[9] The Tibetan master Chögyam Trungpa, in his commentary on the *Tibetan Book of the Dead*, states: 'Birth and death apply to everybody constantly at this very moment . . . There is a continual experience of death and birth.'[10] And the Lama Govinda, also commenting on the *Tibetan Book of the Dead*, says: 'For all who are familiar with Buddhist philosophy, it is clear that birth and death are not phenomena that happen only once in human life, but something that happens uninterruptedly within us. At every moment something within us dies and something is reborn.'[11]

Sometimes the interpretation is formulated more precisely. In his *Psychological Attitude of Early Buddhist Philosophy* Govinda gives a hint about the identity of the 'something' that dies and is reborn: 'Strictly speaking, the duration of the life of a living being is exceedingly brief, lasting only while a thought lasts . . . As soon as that thought has ceased the being is said to have ceased.'[12] This appears to equate 'birth' and 'death' with the arising and ceasing of thoughts. Alan Watts reports that a similar interpretation is commonly accepted in Zen Buddhism:

> Many Buddhists understand the Round of birth-and-death quite literally as a process of reincarnation, wherein the *karma* which shapes the individual does so again and again in life after life until, through insight and awakening, it is laid to rest. But in Zen, and in other schools of the Mahayana, it is often taken in a more figurative way, as that the process of rebirth is from moment to moment, so that one is being reborn so long as one identifies himself with a continuing ego which reincarnates itself afresh at each moment of time.[13]

On this view, 'rebirth' refers to the ever-repeated birth of 'a continuing ego'.

Buddhadasa independently advocates the same interpretation. In *Another Kind of Birth* and other works, he argues that the doctrine of rebirth as taught by Gotama is a clear example of Dharma Language, and must be interpreted in mental rather than physical terms. He maintains, in particular, that the word 'birth' refers to the arising of 'the idea of "I" ':

> The main difficulty lies in the interpretation of the word 'birth'. Most of us don't understand what the word 'birth' refers to and are likely to take it in the everyday sense of physical birth from a mother's body . . . It does *not* refer to physical birth, as generally supposed. *The mistaken assumption that this word 'birth' refers to physical birth is a major obstacle to comprehending the Buddha's teaching* . . .
>
> Now we hear talk of rebirth, birth again and again, and of the suffering that inevitably goes with it. Just what is this rebirth? What is it that is reborn? The birth referred to is a mental event, something taking place in the mind, the non-physical side of our make-up . . . 'Birth' in Everyday Language is birth from a mother; 'birth in Dharma Language is birth from ignorance, craving, clinging, the arising of the false notion of 'I' and 'mine'.
>
> Clearly 'birth' refers to nothing other than the arising of the idea 'I'.[14]

So while the majority of Buddhists take the *saṃsāra* doctrine literally as referring to physical events, a significant minority interpret it in terms of mental events. On this non-literal interpretation, the words 'birth' and 'death' refer to the ever-repeated arising and ceasing of momentary mental states; and the endless cycle of *saṃsāra*, from which every Buddhist is supposed to be seeking liberation, is an endless sequence of these mental arisings and ceasings.

This mentalistic interpretation has important implications for the doctrine of the three knowledges.[15] If *saṃsāra* is to be understood as a series of arising and ceasing mental states, it would seem to follow that 'recollection of former existences' is a process of recollecting that series of mental states in reverse order. This leads us to draw a comparison with the practice of retracing image sequences described in Chapter IV. The arising and ceasing of an image might appropriately be referred to metaphorically as a 'birth' and 'death'. It is often the case that the Pali has for 'birth' and 'death' not the literal terms *jāti* and *maraṇa* but the more metaphorical *upapāta* and *cuti*, which are etymologically 'arising' and 'falling'. (The latter pair of terms occurs in the name of the second knowledge, *cut'-ūpapāta-ñāṇa*, literally 'falling-arising-knowledge'.) In the stream of thought, images follow one another endlessly. The 'death' of each image is followed by the 'birth' of the next one, and so the process goes endlessly on and on. Thought is therefore like a miniature *saṃsāra*; and retracing thought sequences is like recollecting one's former existences in that *saṃsāra*. The resemblance is the closer because retracing of image sequences is in fact a kind of recollection.

The existence of this parallelism lends support to the non-literal interpretations outlined earlier, according to which 'birth' and 'death' are the arising and ceasing of momentary mental states. The correspondence would become complete if those momentary mental states were identified as mental images. Such an interpretation would be entirely in keeping with Govinda's 'thoughts', Alan Watt's 'continuing ego', and Buddhadasa's 'idea of "I" ' — for, as we have seen, the sense of I-ness coexists with thought unaccompanied by awareness. This refinement of the interpretation would have the effect of equating *saṃsāra* with the totality of thought sequences,[16] and recollection of former existences with the practice of retracing. The first of the three knowledges would thereby be explained as a cryptic reference to a valuable technique in insight meditation.

The passage cited earlier from the *Abhidharma-kośa* states that the meditator who wishes to recollect his former existences should begin by 'grasping the character of the thought that has just perished', then go back to the thought preceding it, and so retrace his mental steps to the moment of his conception and beyond. Anyone who seriously attempted to follow these instructions for recollecting his former existences would in fact be retracing image sequences. Whether or not he managed to push the process back beyond the moment of his conception, he would be practising precisely the technique of retracing described in Chapter IV. This fact strengthens our suggestion that 'recollection of former existences' may be a veiled reference to retracing of image sequences.

Now it could be objected, as an argument against this suggestion, that Gotama clearly believed in, and was concerned about, *saṃsāra* in the literal, physical sense. His description of the first knowledge specifically mentions his physical condition, caste, and so on in previous existences, evidence that he was after all referring to actual physical birth and death. This problem will be taken up after the remaining two knowledges have been examined.

The Second Knowledge

The second of the three knowledges, knowledge of the death and rebirth of beings according to their *karmas*, is described by Gotama as like watching from some high vantage point as people enter and leave a house.[17] The *suttas* as before give no advice on how the meditator should go about developing this special ability, and the later manuals are equally uninformative.

The canonical description of the second knowledge stresses the importance of *karma* in determining rebirth. According to the *karma* doctrine, which all Indian religions accept, the kind of existence one is reborn into after death is determined by the unexpended energy generated by one's previous actions or *karmas*. Thus a person's condition, pleasant or unpleasant, in this life is largely a result of his own actions, good or evil, in previous lives; and he is, by his present actions, determining his condition in future lives. The 'law of *karma*' is not enforced by some divine being sitting in judgement; it operates by a natural cause-and-effect mechanism, like any other law of nature. As the doctrine is understood in non-Buddhist schools, and in popular Buddhism also, the *karmas* or actions in question are physical actions, just as the births they condition are physical births. However, Gotama, though he does cite many examples of good or bad *physical* actions producing pleasant or unpleasant *physical* effects, also makes it clear that what counts is not the action itself but the motive or volition underlying it. In his explanation of *karma* recorded in the *Aṅguttara-nikāya*, he states: 'It is *cetanā* that I call *karma*.'[18] The term *cetanā* is defined as 'active thought, intention, purpose, will',[19] which would embrace all affective mental factors such as greed, lust, conceit, anger, hatred, etc.

With this mentalistic foundation, the Buddhist version of the *karma* doctrine is rather less implausible than its Hindu and Jaina counterparts.[20] However, it still calls for a substantial act of faith, since it assumes some mechanism whereby each good or evil volition in one physical existence can produce its commensurate result in a subsequent existence, perhaps eons later.

The only satisfactory solution is to make the interpretation consistently mentalistic throughout, and this is in fact what a number of Buddhist monks and scholars do. Such a mentalistic interpretation is adopted by the monk Khantipalo. He explains it as follows:

> The karma is said to 'perfume' the mental continuum, to leave a trace or pattern in the mind whereby habitual reactions, patterns of doing things, and character tendencies are built up.[21]

On this view, the law of *karma* refers to the process whereby an individual constantly forms and modifies his own thought habits or character traits. Buddhadasa adopts a similar interpretation. He explains the role of *karma* in the formation of thought habits using various examples involving desire and hatred.[22] Having desired a certain object, one is likely to recall that object with pleasure, and therefore to desire it again; and conversely, if one has reacted with hatred to a certain object, one is likely to recall it with displeasure, and therefore to hate it again. An individual's present mental condition is therefore in large part a result of his previous mental actions (desire, hatred, etc.), and in the same way his future mental condition is constantly being shaped by his present mental actions.

This mentalistic interpretation of *karma* implicitly assumes the mentalistic interpretation of rebirth examined above, according to which 'death' and 'birth' refer to the ceasing and arising of momentary mental phenomena. We have already examined the effect of refining that interpretation by identifying the mental phenomena in question as images in the flow of thought; one important effect is to convert the first knowledge into a description of a valuable meditative technique, retracing of image sequences. We now examine the effect of a comparable refinement of the mentalistic interpretation of *karma*.

In Chapter IV we noted that the process of linking between successive images in thought sequences is determined by the emotive charge inhering in the content of each image, and further that that emotive charge is ultimately a consequence of emotional involvement, both in the sensory data of which the image is a representation and in previous occurrences of the image itself. This principle closely resembles the 'law of *karma*'. This suggests that the mentalistic interpretation of *karma* described above might be refined by identifying *karma* more precisely as emotional involvement in mental content, whether primary sensations or images. As understood at the popular level, the law of *karma* states that each of one's many rebirths in *saṃsāra* is determined by one's physical actions or *karmas* in previous lives. In the completely mentalistic interpretation being suggested here, the law of *karma* states that each linking process in the flow of thought is determined by one's previous emotional involvement in mental content (sensations and images). The parallelism is complete.

Support for this interpretation of *karma* is to be found in the *Abhidhammattha-saṅgaha*, a synopsis of the Abhidhamma dated somewhere between the eighth and twelfth centuries A.D. In that text the mechanism of death-and-rebirth is succinctly described as follows: 'To one who is about to die, three "objects" (*ārammaṇa*) present themselves at the "mind-door": a *karma* (*kamma*), a *karma* image (*kamma-nimitta*), and a destiny image (*gati-nimitta*).'[23] Commentators explain these three 'objects' as follows: The *karma* is some 'weighty' action performed during the existence that is about to cease; the *karma* image is an image depicting the scene of that action; and the destiny image is an image depicting the new existence into which one is about to be reborn.[24] This is identical with our account of the process of linking between images. The *karma* image and destiny image are any two successive images in a thought sequence, and the *karma* is the previous emotional involvement, which guides the linking process between them. Thus the *Abhidhammattha-saṅgaha* description of the process of death-and-rebirth is at the same time a description of the process of linking between images in thought sequences. The two processes are tacitly equated.

The mentalistic interpretation of *karma* and rebirth here under consideration is directly relevant to the second knowledge. 'Knowledge of the death and rebirth of beings according to their *karmas*' may now be reworded as 'insight into the process of linking between images as determined by previous emotional involvement'. Thus the second of the three knowledges, if reworded in terms of the mentalistic interpretation of *karma* and rebirth, becomes identical with the practice that we have called 'observation of linking' (pp. 66 – 9). The death of a being is the ceasing of one image; rebirth — more correctly 'birth' or 'arising', since the Pali has simply *upapāta* — is the arising of the next image; and the *karma* which determines that birth is the previous emotional involvement which determines the course of the linking process.

The Third Knowledge

The third of the three knowledges, knowledge of the destruction of the *āsavas* or cankers (*āsava-kkhaya-ñāṇa*), is likened by Gotama to seeing clearly the sand, crabs, fish, and other things at the bottom of a limpid pool.[25] This indicates that its essential characteristic is unobscured insight.

The principal task in interpreting the third knowledge is to discover what is meant by the key term *āsava*.[26] The translation 'canker' is only one of many suggested; other common renderings include 'corruption, intoxicant, flood, taint, defilement, influence'. The generally accepted etymology, deriving the word *āsava* from the root *sru* 'to flow', suggests that 'influence' may be a literally correct translation.[27]

Usually there are said to be three *āsavas*: *kāmāsava, bhavāsava*, and *avijjāsava* — the *āsavas* of lust, becoming, and ignorance.[28] The first, *kāmāsava*, though usually translated 'lust', has a far wider connotation. This becomes evident when one considers the three *lokas* or 'realms of existence' recognized in Buddhism: the *kāmaloka, rūpaloka*, and *arūpaloka*.[29] The second and third of these correspond to the *jhānas*, in which consciousness of sense objects is progressively eliminated; the first is the ordinary everyday realm of the senses. The term *kāmāsava* therefore covers not only lust but all affective involvement in sense objects.

The second *āsava, bhavāsava*, is generally taken as desire for continued becoming or existence, that is, desire for continued rebirth in *saṃsāra*. Our interpretation of *saṃāra* suggests that this should be understood as affective involvement in the content of the thought-stream. Such an interpretation yields coherence and consistency in the *āsava* group since the first two *āsavas* then refer to the two recognized objects of affective involvement: (i) involvement in sense objects (*kāmāsava*), and (ii) involvement in the thought-stream (*bhavāsava*). *Bhava*, literally 'becoming', would be an appropriate term for the thought-stream; and there is in the late Abhidhamma tradition a term *bhavaṅga* which clearly does denote the thought-stream.[30]

The third *āsava, avijjāsava*, is literally 'ignorance'; however, as always in the Buddhist context, *avijjā* is not mere worldly ignorance, but a very subtle failure to perceive the true nature of things. (Its opposite, *vijjā*, denotes the three knowledges collectively.) The traditional grouping of *avijjāsava* with *kāmāsava* and *bhavāsava* indicates that it denotes in particular the lack of insight which coexists with, and is the condition for, emotional involvement in sense objects and images.

The *āsavas* therefore reduce to two basic categories: (1) 'ignorance', that is, failure to perceive the true nature of images and the mechanism of linking, and (2) emotional involvement in sense objects and images.[31] It is these that are destroyed in the third knowledge. Clearly then, the third knowledge is to be equated with awareness. Awareness is incompatible with 'ignorance' regarding the nature of mental content, and with emotional involvement of any kind. To attain awareness is to destroy the *āsavas*.

Interpretation of the Three Knowledges

It has been shown that there is a close parallelism between the three knowledges listed in the texts and the three techniques in insight meditation described in Chapter IV. The correspondences

Table 2. Correspondences between the three knowledges and the three insight techniques.

Knowledges	Insight techniques
1. Recollection of former existences in *saṃsāra*	1. Retracing of image sequences
2. Knowledge of the death and rebirth of beings according to their *karmas*	2. Observation of the ceasing and arising of images according to previous emotional involvement
3. Destruction of the *āsavas*	3. Awareness

are brought out in Table 2. The parallelism extends to the order of occurrence: the sequence in which the three knowledges are said to be developed is identical with the sequence in which the three insight techniques are applied in practice. But the sequential correspondence extends even further than this; for according to the textual account, the three knowledges are developed after the *jhānas* have been mastered, and as seen in Chapter IV, the three insight techniques are taken up after some proficiency in concentration has been attained. This far-reaching correspondence is strong evidence in support of the non-literal interpretation that we are advocating.

Macrocosm-microcosm Parallelism

We shall now consider the arguments foreshadowed earlier *against* this non-literal interpretation. Gotama refers to his clan, caste, and other physical circumstances in previous existences, to the beautiful or ugly appearance and high or low social status which beings acquire as a result of their earlier good or evil actions, etc. This suggests that the terms 'birth', 'death', '*karma*', etc. do after all refer to physical events. Clearly, then, it cannot be claimed that Gotama's teaching on *saṃsāra* and the three knowledges refers *exclusively* to momentary mental phenomena. The Tipiṭaka references to birth and death cannot be *purely* symbolic. However, in this connection it has to be remembered that an object or event may have symbolic meaning in certain contexts while retaining its original literal meaning in other contexts; indeed it may well have both meanings simultaneously. (For this reason Buddhadasa warns that one must always consider 'both meanings'.)[32]

In India in the sixth century B.C. the intellectual climate was particularly conducive to the development of double meanings in religious terminology. There existed a widely-held belief in what may be called macrocosm-microcosm parallelism, the idea that the microcosm (usually man himself) and the macrocosm (usually the world or universe which man inhabits) are reflections or replicas of each other.[33] This idea found its most graphic expression in certain cosmological diagrams depicting the universe in the form of a gigantic human figure; the earth (a flat disc) was located at the cosmic man's waist, and the tiered heavens and hells were at different levels in the upper and lower halves of his body.[34] As this idea developed, parallels between microcosm and macrocosm were found everywhere: the out-breath and in-breath were day and night, or on a grander scale, the alternating evolution and dissolution of the universe; the two main nerves of the body (*nāḍis*) were the rivers Gangā and Yamunā, while the spinal column was the world-axis, Mount Meru; and every object and gesture employed in Brahmanical sacrificial rituals was equivalent to some cosmic principle.[35]

It was believed, further, that appropriate manipulation of microcosmic objects and events could produce corresponding macrocosmic effects. This was the basis of the power wielded by the brahmans: their manipulations of ritual objects were believed to have macrocosmic consequences. The *śramaṇas* did not accept the exaggerated claims made by the brahmans; however, they did accept the notion of macrocosm-microcosm parallelism, with the implied possibility of human intervention in macrocosmic processes.[36]

This belief in macrocosm-microcosm parallelism is relevant and important in the present context. Gotama, as an accomplished meditator, would certainly have been familiar with the nature of thought processes. His devotees credit him with omniscience; we must at least credit him with insight into the dynamic structure of image sequences and the determining role of emotional involvement. As we have seen, there exists a remarkably close similarity in dynamic structure between image sequences (microcosm) and *saṃsāra* (macrocosm). It is therefore likely that Gotama, familiar with both the nature of image sequences and the doctrine of *saṃsāra*, observed this similarity and, applying the then widely-held notion of macrocosm-microcosm parallelism, drew the logical conclusion: liberation from *saṃsāra* could be attained through liberation from thought.

The kind of liberation from thought being advocated by most *śramaṇas* at that time, including Gotama's early teachers, was prolonged mental onepointedness (*jhāna, samatha*). But Gotama, once he had mastered the *jhānas*, perceived that this was a limited, transient achievement, and went in search of something higher. What did Gotama identify as the microcosmic counterpart of *nirvāṇa*? The answer is already implicit in the above-noted pattern of parallelism between the three knowledges and the insight practice: *Nirvāṇa* is attained by perfecting the third knowledge, that is by perfecting awareness.

Buddhadasa, in presenting his interpretation of rebirth, arrives at a similar conclusion, though he words it rather differently. Having identified *saṃsāra* as the repeated arising of 'the idea of

"I" ', he then states that arising of the I-idea can be prevented through the practice of awareness; and he identifies the resulting 'state of coolness' as a temporary form of *nirvāṇa*:

> So the direct practice of Dharma, the kernel of the Buddha's teaching, consists in keeping close watch on the mind, so that it does not give rise to the condition called the cycle of saṃsāra, so that it is always in the state called nirvāṇa. One has to be watchful, guarding the mind at all times so that the state of coolness is constantly there, and leaving no opportunity for the arising of saṃsāra.[37]

In addition he states that if awareness is practised continuously, this temporary *nirvāṇa* can become permanent:

> Keep watch, be aware, develop full insight. Whatever you do, . . . do it with awareness. Don't become involved in 'I' and 'mine'. Then saṃsāra will not be able to arise; the mind will remain in nirvāṇa until it has become fully accustomed to it and unable to relapse — and that is full or complete nirvāṇa.[38]

Thus Buddhadasa's interpretation of *nirvāṇa*, a logical extension of his basic interpretation of rebirth, agrees substantially with the conclusion we arrived at above through analysis of the three knowledges. (Buddhadasa does not discuss the three knowledges.)

In Chapter IV it was suggested that awareness, though usually difficult to maintain for more than a minute or two at a time, could probably be prolonged with consistent practice.[39] Buddhadasa goes further, accepting that awareness could become a permanent condition. His interpretation of *nirvāṇa* carries with it the implication that Gotama's achievement under the Bodhi Tree was actually the attainment of this condition of permanent awareness. This is in agreement with Gotama's statement in the *Tevijjā-Vacchagotta-sutta* (quoted on p. 79), which indicates that while his attainment of the first and second knowledges was intermittent, his attainment of the third was permanent.[40] Interpretation at this level is necessarily very speculative; only a *buddha* (or *arahant*) could know the nature of enlightenment. Nevertheless the evidence indicates that Buddhadasa's interpretation is correct: enlightenment (*sammā-sambodhi*) is the attainment of permanent awareness.

In popular Buddhism it is widely accepted that Gotama in his enlightenment knew and saw literally everything, from the finest component of the atom to the most distant reaches of the universe. However, the above interpretation indicates that Gotama's enlightenment consisted rather in continuous, unobscured insight into the functioning of his own mind. This less exalted attainment is more in accord with the spirit of Gotama's teaching, with its emphasis on mental rather than physical things; and as the above discussion has shown, it also fits in perfectly with the doctrine of the three knowledges.

One fault that we would, however, find in Buddhadasa's interpretation is its failure to distinguish between microcosmic and macrocosmic terms.[41] Enlightenment, permanent awareness, was what Gotama actually attained at the microcosmic level; *nirvāṇa*, liberation from the cycle of *saṃsāra*, was what he believed he had thereby achieved at the macrocosmic level. It seems essential to maintain the distinction between these two levels, while recognizing how they correspond to each other. We have recognized the correspondences shown in Table 3.

It is likely, however, that Gotama and his immediate followers actually perceived these correspondences as identities. For them the flow of thought probably did not merely correspond to *saṃsāra*, but actually *was saṃsāra*. Consequently each of the terms

Table 3. Macrocosmic-microcosmic correspondences relating to the three knowledges.

Macrocosm	Microcosm
saṃsāra	the stream of thought
an existence, a being	an image
birth	arising of an image
death	ceasing of an image
karma	affective mental state, emotional involvement
recollection of former existences	retracing image sequences
knowledge of death and rebirth of beings	observation of linking
destruction of *āsavas*	awareness
nirvāṇa	enlightenment, permanent awareness

'birth', '*nirvāṇa*', and so on, in effect had a double reference; each denoted both a physical (macrocosmic) phenomenon *and* its mental (microcosmic) counterpart.

In this chapter the non-literal interpretation of *karma* and rebirth, to which a limited number of Buddhist monks and scholars subscribe, has been examined and found to conform well with the account of mental processes presented in Chapters III and IV. As well, this interpretation has been applied to the three knowledges and shown to yield a remarkable correspondence with the three stages in the course of insight meditation described in Chapter IV. It has been inferred, on this basis, that much of Gotama's teaching implicitly assumes a detailed macrocosm-microcosm parallelism, and consequently that interpretation of the language of the Tipiṭaka must entail distinguishing macrocosmic terms from microcosmic, and identifying the correspondences between them.

It should be noted that this is not a rejection of rebirth in the literal, physical sense. We do not wish to suggest that the picture of *saṃsāra* painted in the Tipiṭaka, as an enormously long succession of physical existences, is without real foundation. It may be that *saṃsāra is* a reality. (The doctrine could probably never actually be disproved.) Acceptance of a non-literal interpretation in certain contexts does not entail rejection of the literal interpretation in all contexts. A committed Buddhist could, without being inconsistent, accept that 'recollection of former existences' is, in practical terms, a reference to retracing of image sequences, while still believing that he will be reborn after his physical death. To accept the non-literal interpretation is merely to acknowledge an extra dimension of meaning that had formerly been overlooked.

1

2

3

4

5

6

CHAPTER VI

THE FIVE SYMBOLIC GROUPS

Between the ambivalent language of the Tipiṭaka and the explicit symbolism of the *tantras* there is a historical gap of at least a thousand years. There is also a great difference in content and style, suggesting little likelihood of continuity of tradition between the two systems. Nevertheless, as pointed out earlier, certain pieces of evidence, in particular certain cross-references to events associated with Gotama's enlightenment, suggest that the two systems may after all be related, and may even belong to a single continuous esoteric tradition.[1] To this possibility we shall return below.

The interpretation of Tantric symbolism poses special problems. Buddhist Tantricism developed over a period of centuries, amassing a rich literature, a variety of complex rituals, and a bewildering array of symbols. Tantric symbolism appears unsystematic and confused. Sets of symbols are rarely consistent from text to text, and may even vary within one text.

Many of the symbols described in the *tantras* were already ancient when those texts were composed. It therefore probably often happened that the meaning given to a symbol in Tantric texts and rituals was *additional to* meanings that that symbol already had in other contexts. Indian and Tibetan religious symbols are multivalent; one cannot speak of '*the* meaning of a symbol'.[2] New meanings assigned to symbols do not supersede previous meanings, especially when those new meanings are the secret property of an élite few. The very act of assigning new secret meanings to symbols encourages speculative interpretation by the uninitiated, yielding still further 'meanings', which may become widely accepted. Again, it is likely that there exist many pseudo-symbols invented by well-intentioned scholastics, which are essentially devoid of meaning. The interpretation of Buddhist Tantric symbolism can therefore be pursued on a number of levels. Our interest here is in the possibility that certain symbols were given specific meanings in one particular context — always bearing in mind that any conclusion regarding those specific meanings in no way precludes the possibility that those same symbols may have had other meanings in other contexts.

Table 4. Structure of the maṇḍala. *The colours shown are those of the dhyāni Buddhas; the colours of the* maṇḍala *cells differ from these in that blue and white are interchanged. Amoghasiddhi's emblem is alternatively a double* vajra. *The consorts,* skandhas, *and wisdoms are not shown, as they are not dealt with in the analysis.*

location	element	colour	dhyāni Buddha	*mudrā*	emblem	*bīja*	*vāhana*
centre	space	white	Vairocana	Dharma-wheel	wheel	*Oṃ*	lion
north	air	green	Amoghasiddhi	no-danger	sword	*Āḥ/Hā*	*garuḍa*
west	fire	red	Amitābha	meditation	lotus	*Hrīḥ/Āḥ*	peacock
south	earth	yellow	Ratnasambhava	gift-bestowing	jewel	*Traṃ/Svā*	horse
east	water	blue	Akṣobhya	earth-touching	*vajra*	*Hūṃ*	elephant

Table 5. Structure of the cakra *system. (Since descriptions of the* cakras *vary greatly, this is only one of many different tables that could be drawn up.)*

cakra	element	dhyāni Buddha	*bīja*
crown	air	Vairocana	*Oṃ*
throat	fire	Amitābha	*Āḥ*
heart	water	Akṣobhya	*Hūṃ*
navel	earth		

Our examination will be limited to the sets of symbols associated with the *maṇḍala* and the *cakra* system, these being the best known and most clearly defined examples of Buddhist Tantric symbolism. Our approach will be essentially similar to that used in examining the three knowledges; however, because of the complexity of Tantric symbolism we first devote a chapter to discussing the general principles that appear to underlie it, and setting up a procedure for investigating it.

To facilitate discussion, the structures of the *maṇḍala* and *cakras* are presented in tabular form — see Tables 4 and 5. As these two tables make clear, both the *maṇḍala* and the *cakra* system contain several superimposed sets of entities — a set of elements, a set of colours, a set of dhyāni Buddhas, etc. — laid out in conventionalized geometrical arrangements.[3] Our task is to discover what significance, if any, these entities and arrangements have. In preparation for this we first discuss further the notion of symbolic parallelism introduced in the previous chapter.[4]

Symbolic Parallelism and the Fivefold Classification

As we have seen, Indian thought early came to be dominated by the idea that macrocosmic structures or processes and superficially similar microcosmic structures or processes were reflections or counterparts of each other. With the passage of time this basic notion was progressively extended, elaborated, and codified, in the manner outlined below.

The conspicuous division into female and male, which characterized the human and animal realms, came to be seen as applying throughout the physical universe: the moon was seen as female, the sun as male; the water element was female, the fire element male; the left side of the body was female, the right male; and so on.[5] Each such pair was seen as exemplifying a universal passive/active polarity in nature; there were two basic categories to which things could be allocated: a passive or female category and an active or male category.

In time it was recognized that this fundamental polarity implied a mid-point or balance or union, so a third category was created. This yielded parallel triads: female/male/sexual union, moon/sun/eclipse, water/fire/air, left/right/centre, and so on. This threefold classification was sometimes imposed arbitrarily on systems to which it was not naturally applicable; for example, the letters of the Indian alphabet were allocated to the three categories thus: vowels/consonants/*anusvāra* (the last being the nasalization, transcribed 'ṃ').[6] Things could thenceforth be classified into three groups: a passive group (female, moon, water, etc.), an active group (male, sun, fire, etc.), and a balance group (union, eclipse, air, etc.).

Later this threefold classification was in its turn extended. Indian cosmologists had long considered that matter was analysable into four elements: earth, water, fire, and air. Of these, water, fire, and air could be fitted into the threefold classification, but earth remained unaccounted for. Since the elements were of fundamental importance in the philosophical view of nature, a fourth group was recognized.[7] The resulting fourfold classification was found to accommodate neatly certain existing natural and conventional four-membered sets. For example, there had long existed a recognized set of four colours: blue, yellow, red, white.[8] This set fitted well with the elements, provided the sequence of the first two colours in the traditional listing was reversed: yellow = earth, blue = water, red = fire, white = air. A recognized set of four fundamental geometrical shapes, the cube, sphere, cone, and hemisphere, also fitted well.[9] (See Plate 7.) The cube belonged naturally in the same group as the earth element because both were characterized by stability; the sphere belonged with water, sharing with it the property of instability (the passive group); the cone, whose shape suggested a flame and upward movement, belonged with fire (active group); and the hollow hemisphere, suggesting emptiness, fitted well with air (balance group).

Later again the classification was extended still further. A refinement of cosmological theory had led to the recognition of a fifth element, geometrical space (*ākāśa*),[10] that in which the other four elements were contained. A fifth group was therefore created. To validate this new scheme, some attempt was made to extend existing three- or four-membered sets to five members. This attempt was occasionally successful, but usually entailed some distortion and artificiality. The difficulties involved are well illustrated by the case of the colours. The first three colours, yellow, blue, and red, were left as they were, grouped with earth, water, and fire respectively. However, white, originally grouped with air, was seen to belong properly with space, so was transferred accordingly. A new colour was then added to pair with air, namely green (or, in some versions, black) — clearly an arbitrary choice. The final distribution of the colours among the five groups was thus the outcome of several *ad hoc* adjustments: interchange of the serial positions of blue and yellow, transfer of white from air to space, and arbitrary recognition of a new colour to pair with air.[11] In addition there appears to have been some hesitation about how best to classify blue and white; sometimes blue is equated with space and white with water, rather than the reverse. (This uncertainty is reflected in the *maṇḍala*, where, as noted in the captions to Fig. 3 and Table 4, the two colours are inconsistently placed.)

With five groups the process of classification reached its effective limit. (A few sets with more than five members were recognized but explicit parallels between them were seldom drawn.) Thus, in general, things were recognized as falling into sets having up to five members: a set of five elements, a set of five colours, a set of four geometrical shapes, and so on. And each member of each set was recognized as belonging to one or another of five groups: the element earth, the colour yellow, the cube, etc. formed the first group; water, blue, the sphere, etc. formed the second group; and so on. This is shown in Table 6, which covers the principal recognized sets.

The features defining each group can, with one exception, be readily identified; they are summarized in Table 7. The exception is the fourth group, which is difficult to characterize because its members — air, green, eclipse, etc. — represent a miscellany of ill-defined and disparate properties. This is what might have been expected, given the patchwork historical development of this group as illustrated by the case of the colours; as regards its membership this fourth group is largely arbitrary and makeshift.

Though derived originally from the female/male polarity, the fivefold classification in its fully developed form is dominated by

Table 6. The principal sets arranged according to the five groups. This table is so laid out that the sets read upwards from the bottom, thus putting the elements in their natural relative positions (earth below, air above, etc.) and the shapes in the configuration depicted in the stūpa. *Since this arrangement has several other advantages, it is adhered to in most subsequent tables.*

5. space	white		union	light	centre	steady	syllable	Vairocana
4. air	green	hemisphere		eclipse			*anusvāra*	
3. fire	red	cone	male	sun	right	up	consonant	Akṣobhya
2. water	blue	sphere	female	moon	left	down	vowel	Amitābha
1. earth	yellow	cube						
element	colour	shape	sex	luminary	position	movement	sound	dhyāni Buddha

Table 7. Defining characteristics of the five groups.

group	defining characteristics
space	all-inclusiveness, supremacy, unification
air	?
fire	activity
water	passivity, instability
earth	immobility, stability

the elements. It appears to have been the elements more than any other set that determined the nature of the system. It was largely because there were five elements according to Indian cosmological speculation that five groups were recognized.[12] Also, in many cases affinity with the elements seems to have been the principal criterion for classification. For example, the basis for classifying the colour yellow in the first group was clearly not some fancied connection between yellow and the property of immobility, but rather the fact that yellow was, of the five colours, the one that most closely resembled the colour of earth.

Because the elements dominate the classification in this way, the five groups may appropriately be named after them. We shall therefore refer henceforth to 'the earth group', 'the water group', and so on.

The concept of parallelism is closely bound up with the process of symbolization, because it is the recognized parallels that determine the choice of objects which may serve as symbols. For example, when, as is done in certain contexts, the elements are symbolized by colours or shapes, it is naturally the case that earth is represented by yellow or the cube, water by blue or the sphere, and so on.[13] Symbolic correspondences are sometimes indirect, but are nevertheless usually found to be consistent throughout. For example, in Hindu astrology the two eclipses (lunar and solar) are symbolized by a bowl and a flag.[14] This symbolism is clearly based on the position of the referents in the fivefold classification (Table 6): the eclipses are in the air group; the bowl has the form of a hollow hemisphere, which is also in the air group; and the flag, which suggests wind and is the emblem of Vāyu, the Vedic god of wind, belongs naturally to the air group as well.[15] Thus any item may be symbolized by any other item from the same group in the fivefold classification.

The Buddhist *tantras* contain much symbolic parallelism, most of it based on the earlier threefold classification, passive/active/balance. Numerous parallel triads are listed, among them the old set of three dhyāni Buddhas. Amitābha, Akṣobhya, and Vairocana are identified with the qualities of passivity, activity, and balance respectively. The same classification applies to their emblems, the lotus, *vajra*, and wheel, and their *bījas, Āḥ, Hūṃ,* and *Oṃ*.[16] The rationale behind this classification is evident, at least in the case of the passive/active contrast. The lotus, being a flower, suggests femininity and passivity, and its aquatic habitat links it naturally with the water element; and the *vajra*, being a kind of weapon, suggests masculinity and activity. The *bījas Āḥ* and *Hūṃ* begin with a vowel and a consonant respectively, so in this respect follow the principle that vowels are female, and consonants male.

The structure of the Twilight Language is not, however, as simple as the above account may suggest. The objects in the *maṇḍala* and *cakras* are distributed in a way that appears to conflict in many respects with their symbolic correspondences according to the fivefold classification. For example, Amitābha, recognized as belonging to the passive or water group (Table 6), occupies the same *maṇḍala* cell as the fire element (Table 4). Again, the status of symbols according to the fivefold classification is sometimes not made explicit in the texts or elsewhere. For example, whereas Amitābha, Akṣobhya, and Vairocana clearly belong to the water, fire, and space groups respectively, the two remaining dhyāni Buddhas, Ratnasambhava and Amoghasiddhi, are of uncertain affinity. They must belong to the two remaining groups, namely earth and air, but which belongs to which is not immediately apparent. Thus the symbolism of the *maṇḍala* and *cakras*, though based on the essentially simple fivefold classification, is nevertheless of considerable complexity.

The fivefold classification presented in the *tantras* is remarkably comprehensive, embracing objects of every conceivable type; it includes the infamous set of 'five Ms' (fish, meat, wine, *mudrā*, sexual intercourse) and even a set of five 'body-fluids' (faeces, urine, blood, semen, flesh).[17] In addition it includes sets of doctrinal principles, such as the five *skandhas* (factors of existence), the four *kāyas* (Buddha-bodies) and the triad *prajñā, upāya, bodhicitta* (wisdom, means, enlightenment-mind). For example, *prajñā, upāya,* and *bodhicitta* are identified with the triads female/male/union, Amitābha/Akṣobhya/Vairocana, and so on, and are thus implicitly assigned to the water, fire, and space groups respectively.[18]

Though almost every other conceivable class of object is included in the Tantric classification, sets of meditative stages or attainments are lacking, or at least not readily identifiable. The 'five wisdoms', with which the five dhyāni Buddhas are explicitly association in the *maṇḍala*, may perhaps be such a set, since their names, 'mirror-like wisdom', 'discriminating wisdom', etc. do suggest meditative attainments.[19] However, the actual nature of these 'five wisdoms' is no less obscure than that of the three knowledges. We shall therefore approach the problem as we did that of the three knowledges, by seeking possible parallels with meditative practices.

Interpretative Methodology

Tantric symbolism is dominated by the notion of parallelism, in particular by the all-embracing classification into five groups. It will therefore be assumed as a working hypothesis that the *siddhas* (the adept masters in the élite meditative tradition who are said to have created the Twilight Language) followed the above-noted general principle of symbolization: a given entity could be symbolized by any object belonging to the same group as that entity in the fivefold classification. It follows that if the *siddhas* had wished to symbolize the stages in a course of meditative practice, they would probably have begun by classifying those stages according to the already existing fivefold scheme. By so doing they would have provided themselves with a ready-made fund of symbols, while at the same time endowing their teaching with cosmic significance. Our search for possible correlations between meditative stages and symbols will therefore entail, in the first instance, identifying which of the five groups each stage would belong to.

In doing this we shall naturally follow the traditional criteria for classifying objects according to the fivefold scheme. The position of any given object in this scheme is determined not only by that object's individual properties but also by its status relative to the other members of its set. For example, the moon belongs to the water group not only because it is naturally associated with water (through its connection, real or mythological, with the tides, dew, etc.), but also because of the way in which it contrasts with the sun: the moon is to the sun as water is to fire, as female is to male, and so on. So in classifying the meditative stages in terms of the five groups we shall have to consider not only the properties of each stage, but also the features in respect of which each stage contrasts with other stages in the course of meditative practice, or with other mental states. Given the group characteristics as summarized in Table 7, we may expect to have relatively little difficulty identifying affinities with the earth, water, fire, and space groups, but considerable difficulty discerning affinities with the unclearly defined air group.

Symbolic Classification of the Meditative Stages

We begin with the most basic meditative practice, concentration. The condition in which the mind is concentrated or onepointed contrasts with the normal condition, in which thought runs uncontrolled; we therefore first identify the characterizing features of these two contrasting conditions. This we may best do by considering, to begin with, how they have been described by Buddhist meditation masters since the time of Gotama.

In Buddhist literature the mental condition in which sequences of imagery and verbalizing run on endlessly is often compared to a flowing stream. We find in the oldest section of the Tipiṭaka the term 'stream of consciousness' (*viññāṇa-sotaṃ*).[20] The same metaphor is often found in the Tibetan literature. The guru Padma Karpo spoke of 'thoughts . . . following one after the other as if in a continuous stream';[21] Mipham Nampar Gyalba observed that the 'stream of images flows unbroken';[22] and in the *Vow of Mahāmudrā*, there is reference to 'the mind river'.[23] This manner of speaking is also common at the present day. Tarthang Tülku refers to 'the stream of mental images',[24] and 'the flow of thoughts and images';[25] and David-Neel, in a discussion of the meditation practices she observed in Tibet, speaks of 'the continual, swift, flowing stream of thoughts and mental images . . .'[26]

The stream metaphor has also been found appropriate by western psychologists. William James wrote: 'It flows. A "river" or a "stream" are the metaphors by which it is most naturally described. *In talking of it hereafter, let us call it the stream of thought, of consciousness, or of subjective life.*'[27] James's term

What focuses. Keeping focus!
Creation of objects — form. *Focus!*

No.

'stream of consciousness' has since become widely adopted in a variety of contexts.

If the normal unconcentrated condition of the mind resembles a flowing stream, the practice of concentration, which consists in bringing thought to a stop, is like building a dam across that stream. Mircea Eliade adopts this analogy in his *Yoga: Immortality and Freedom*. He describes how the practice of concentration 'dams the mental stream and thus constitutes a "psychic mass", a solid and unified continuum'.[28] One could put it another way by comparing the meditator who succeeds in attaining mental onepointedness to a person who saves himself from a flooded river by reaching the bank and pulling himself out on to dry land.

Such figures of speech focus attention on the distinguishing characteristics of these two mental states: the concentrated condition, in which the mind remains fixed on a single object, is characterized by immobility and stability; the normal unconcentrated condition, in which mental imagery and verbalizing run on unhindered, is characterized by movement and instability. These characteristics may therefore be identified as the criteria for classifying the two states according to the fivefold scheme: the concentrated state partakes of the properties of the earth group, while the normal unconcentrated state partakes of the properties of the water group. We conclude, therefore, that if the *siddhas* had been familiar with the course of meditative practice we have described, and had wished to classify its component stages according to the fivefold scheme, they would have assigned the concentrated or onepointed condition to the earth group, and the normal unconcentrated condition to the water group.

We now apply the same procedure to the next stage in the course of meditative practice, namely retracing of thought sequences. The normal movement of thought, which goes on incessantly and effortlessly, is essentially a passive process, resembling, as we have seen, the downhill movement of a stream of water; retracing, which consists in *reversing* this normal movement, working one's way back upstream to the starting point of each train of thought, requires conscious effort. This is the essence of the contrast: the normal flow of thought is a passive, 'downhill' process; retracing is an active, 'uphill' process.[29]

The contrast between the normally flowing thought-stream and the practice of retracing is therefore an instance of the supposedly universal passive/active dichotomy. In the fivefold classification this is the distinction that holds between the water group and the fire group. It follows that in the fivefold classification, while the thought-stream would belong to the passive or water group (along with moon, female, downward movement, etc.), retracing would belong to the active or fire group (sun, male, upward movement, etc.).

From retracing we now proceed, as we did in our original description of meditative practices (Chapter IV), directly to the final stage, awareness. Awareness can be practised in all situations. It is possible, in principle at least, to be aware throughout one's entire waking day, regardless of what activity, physical or mental, one is engaged in. Thus awareness is universal, all-inclusive. In terms of practical technique, awareness is a delicate state of balance between a passive component and an active component; it consists in the coexistence of the thought-stream (passive) with a form of insightful scrutiny (active). Awareness is therefore a union of opposites. A further characteristic of awareness was mentioned earlier in our description of meditative practices. In the evaluation of the relative merits of the different techniques as means to insight, awareness was recognized as occupying the highest place. Thus as regards its value as a means to insight, awareness is superlative.

The practice of awareness can therefore be characterized as all-inclusive, superlative, and a union of opposites. All of these are also characteristics of the fifth or space group. It is therefore to the space group that awareness would belong, in a classification of the meditative practices according to the fivefold scheme.

One meditative stage remains, namely observation of linking. This practice possesses no genuinely individual characteristics. It is a transitional stage, bridging the gap between retracing and awareness, and having some characteristics in common with both. Now the only group with which no meditative stage has yet been brought into symbolic correspondence is the air group. We noted earlier that the air group is difficult to define in terms of distinguishing features. Its members — air, hemisphere, green, eclipse, *anusvāra* (ṃ), etc. — have virtually no properties in common, their combination into a single group being based on a variety of other considerations, including symmetry, traditional sequence of listing, even mere historical accident. For example, green was grouped with air not because it was seen as in any way resembling air, but because it was the only major colour that had not yet been included in the fivefold classification; and the eclipses were grouped with air simply because the moon and sun belonged in the water and fire groups respectively, and the air group was next in the series.

In the case of observation of linking, the only satisfactory criterion for classification is sequential position. In the course of meditative practice, observation of linking comes between retracing and awareness, as in the conventional listing of the five groups air comes between fire and space. This sequential parallelism indicates that observation of linking belongs to the air group. The complete set of correspondences is therefore as shown in Table 8.

Table 8. Group classification of the five meditative stages.

awareness	space
observation of linking	air
retracing	fire
thought-stream	water
concentration	earth
meditative stage	group

One feature of this set of correspondences calls for comment. In our earlier account of the course of meditative practice, the throught-stream was not spoken of as a meditative stage. As the normal everyday condition of the mind, the condition in which sequences of imagery and verbalizing run unhindered, the thought-stream may appear to lie outside the course of practice. In fact, however, the thought-stream has an essential place *within* the course of practice. A meditator who has established concentration and wishes to go on to practise retracing can do so only if he first allows the flow of thought to resume. The transition from concentration to retracing, that is from tranquillity meditation to insight meditation, is possible only by way of an intervening stage, however brief, in which the thought-stream flows again as usual. Failure to recognize this important fact prevents many meditators from progressing beyond concentration.[30] The condition in which the thought-stream flows normally has therefore to be recognized as a meditative stage in its own right, coming between concentration and retracing. The full course of meditative practice described in Chapters III and IV is therefore a sequence of five stages: 1. concentration, 2. thought-stream, 3. retracing, 4. observation of linking, 5. awareness.

The above comparison has shown that these five stages fit into the fivefold classification remarkably well. Not only is it clearly apparent to which group each stage belongs; in addition the sequence of the five stages in the practice — concentration, thought-stream, retracing, observation of linking, awareness — is identical with the traditional order of listing the corresponding groups — earth, water, fire, air, space.[31]

Twilight Language and Meditative Practice

The notion of symbolic parallelism long pervaded all aspects of Indian thought and was particularly prominent in Tantric Buddhism. The five groups were all-embracing, covering even the most outlandish objects and the most abstract concepts. If the five-stage course of meditative practice described here was known and applied in the Tantric tradition, it would almost certainly have been seen to fit into the fivefold scheme in the manner demonstrated above. But the numerous lists of parallel sets given in the *tantras* never include concentration, retracing, etc. Two conclusions are therefore possible: *Either* the authors of the *tantras* did not know of this five-stage course of meditative practice, *or* they did know of it but intentionally refrained from mentioning it.

The latter alternative would accord well with the notion of a Twilight Language. If there did exist masters of meditation in an élite tradition who were familiar with the five-stage course of practice and concerned, for whatever reasons, to keep it a secret, they would have had at their disposal an excellent means for representing that course in cryptic symbolic form. They needed only to recognize the remarkable correspondence between the five meditative stages and the five groups, while intentionally refraining from stating it explicitly. It would then have been possible for them to symbolize each of the five stages by any entity from the same group. For example, the practice of concentration could be symbolized by earth, the cube, the colour yellow, etc.; the normal flow of thought could be symbolized by water, the sphere, blue, . . . and so on. This would have provided a means for ensuring the secrecy of the élite tradition: as long as the symbolic correspondences were not spelled out in the texts, only initiates could know what the symbols stood for. This suggestion, though necessarily speculative, accords with widely-held views regarding the purpose and message of the Twilight Language. It provides a working basis for the interpretative analysis of the *maṇḍala* and *cakras* as associated in some specific way with meditation.

CHAPTER VII

THE MAṆḌALA AND CAKRAS

It has been shown that the five meditative stages described in Chapters III and IV fit neatly into the system of five symbolic groups. It follows that the table of parallel sets (Table 6) can be extended by adding a column for the meditative stages, as shown in Table 9. This amounts to an explicit recognition that the five meditative stages constitute a set, of a type with the elements, colours, and so on. It brings each of the stages into symbolic correspondence with all of the other items in its group: concentration with earth, yellow, the cube, . . .; the thought-stream with water, blue, the sphere, . . .; and so on. In the previous chapter it was suggested that these symbolic correspondences may provide a basis for interpreting the *maṇḍala* and *cakras*. That suggestion will now be pursued. Attention will be limited initially to the more complete and consistent of the two devices, the *maṇḍala*, and the sets of symbols will be grouped for convenience of presentation.

Table 9. Correspondences between principal sets, with meditative stages included.

awareness	space	white		union	light	. . .
observation of linking	air	green	hemisphere		eclipse	. . .
retracing	fire	red	cone	male	sun	. . .
thought-stream	water	blue	sphere	female	moon	. . .
concentration	earth	yellow	cube			. . .
meditative stage	element	colour	shape	sex	luminary	. . .

The Elements and Colours

The positions of the elements and colours in the *maṇḍala* are as shown in Fig. 5. Of the elements, all but air would be remarkably well suited as symbols for the meditative stages. For example, a meditation master could very aptly refer to the transition from concentration to the thought-stream as a movement from earth to water, and so on. The likelihood that such symbolic language was actually used will be discussed shortly.

Each colour occupies the same *maṇḍala* cell as the element to which it corresponds symbolically. Indeed, the colours in the *maṇḍala* are often thought of as *standing in for* the elements, which themselves would be difficult to depict.[1] By virtue of the correspondence shown in Table 9, the five colours could, like the elements, serve as symbols for the five meditative stages; however, unlike the element symbolism suggested above, such a colour symbolism would be only partially based on direct natural resemblances. Red does suggest the active nature of retracing, and white the all-inclusiveness and supremacy of awareness; but for the three remaining colours such shared properties are lacking. A symbolic connection between the colours and the meditative stages would therefore be largely indirect, a consequence of common group membership in the fivefold classification. For example, yellow could appropriately serve as a symbol for concentration not because of any shared properties — yellow and concentration have in themselves nothing in common — but because yellow and concentration both belong to the earth group.

Both the elements and the colours are associated with meditation in the *kasiṇa* practice described in Chapter III. In that practice the meditator gazes at a series of discs or *kasiṇas*, usually ten in number. The first four are composed of the elements earth, water, fire, and air, and the next four are coloured blue, yellow, red, and white. Of the remaining two (evidently later additions to an earlier list of eight), one is composed of space and the other of either light or 'consciousness' (*viññāṇa*).[2] The meditator first gazes at the earth disc until he attains onepointedness, acquires a *nimitta*, and so passes to the deeper levels of concentration; and having mastered this practice with the earth disc, he does the same with the water disc, and so on through the series.[3] We noted in Chapter III that the composition of the object used in concentration practice is irrelevant once onepointedness has been attained. The use of a definite series of different discs as meditation objects is therefore pointless — which is no doubt why, at the present

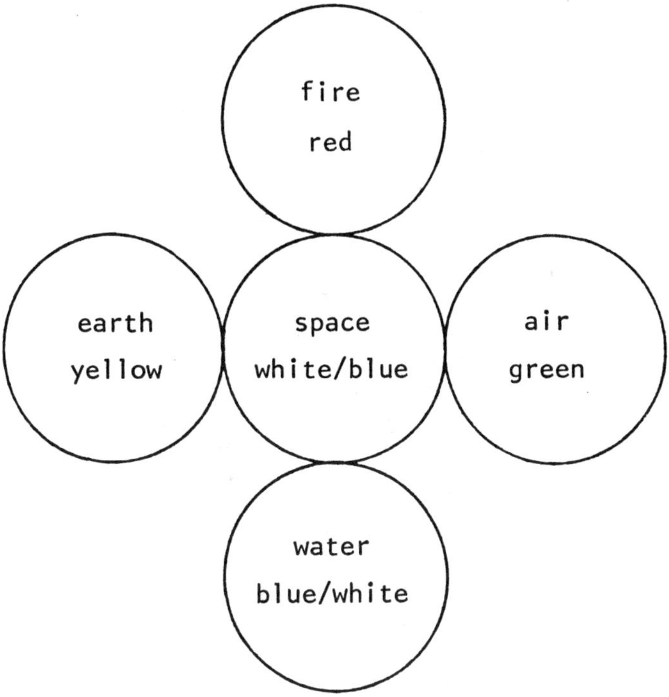

Fig. 5. Positions of the elements and colours in the *maṇḍala*.

day, the *kasiṇa* meditation is more a textual curiosity than a living practice. This being the case, what is the true significance of the *kasiṇas*?

The quaint account given in the *Visuddhi-magga* of how the meditator should prepare 'discs' of fire, air, and space suggests that the entire '*kasiṇa* meditation' is a product of scholastic elaboration. Here it is appropriate to draw a comparison with the practice mentioned in Chapter I, in which the meditator gazes at the five cells of the *maṇḍala* in turn, beginning with the eastern cell, going clockwise, and finishing at the centre. As we have seen, authorities in a position to judge consider that this practice betrays a fundamental misunderstanding of the *maṇḍala*. The *maṇḍala* was intended not as a meditation object but as a symbolic map of the course of practice to be followed; gazing at it is therefore — to borrow a well-known Zen simile — like looking at the finger instead of at the moon to which it is pointing. Since each *maṇḍala* cell is basically a coloured disc, this practice of gazing at the cells in turn closely resembles the *kasiṇa* meditation. This suggests that the *maṇḍala* and the *kasiṇas* may have a common origin. In view of the remarkable appropriateness of the elements as a symbolic representation of the course of meditative practice, it may be that both *maṇḍala* cells and *kasiṇas* were derived, by divergent lines of development, from an earlier set of coloured discs understood as corresponding to the elements and used as an aid in teaching meditation.

This is not to suggest that every reference to meditation on the elements is to be interpreted symbolically. The Tipiṭaka contains descriptions of a meditation practice in which the physical body is mentally analysed into the four elements earth, water, fire, and air.[4] (Space was a later addition.) The meditator recognizes the bones and other solid parts as belonging to the earth element, and so on. There is no reason for supposing that this was anything other than it appears to be: a means for developing an appropriate attitude of detachment toward the body. However, the fact that there existed such a practice, in which references to the elements were intended literally, does not diminish the likelihood that in the centuries following Gotama's death, and especially following the development of the fivefold classification, meditation masters might have adopted the elements as symbols for the stages of a different kind of meditative practice. And once the symbolic correspondences, earth = concentration; water = thought-stream; etc., had been established, it would have been a short step to the adopting of a set of coloured discs to stand for stages of meditation. How this set of coloured discs might have become part of the *maṇḍala* will be discussed later after the other symbol sets have been analysed.

The Dhyāni Buddhas, Mudrās, and Emblems

The positions of the five dhyāni Buddhas with their *mudrās* (hand-poses) and emblems are shown in Fig. 6. (The colours are included for comparison.)

The *tantras* equate the pair Amitābha/Akṣobhya with the pairs female/male, passive/active, *prajñā/upāya*, etc., as shown in Table 6. But, as can be seen by comparing Table 6 and Fig. 6, these traditionally recognized parallels entail a conflict with the dhyāni Buddhas, colours and elements. Amitābha (passive) is red and occupies the same *maṇḍala* cell as fire (active), while Akṣobhya (active) is blue and occupies the same cell as water (passive). The objects sharing any particular *maṇḍala* cell are therefore not necessarily members of the same symbolic group. This fact will have to be taken into account when interpreting the dhyāni Buddhas; for example, if Amitābha belongs to a different symbolic group from his colour, perhaps he also belongs to a different group from his *mudrā* and/or emblem.

However, on further examination the situation proves not so complicated. Logic indicates that each *mudrā* does, after all, belong to the same group as the dhyāni Buddha it identifies. A dhyāni Buddha and his *mudrā* are inseparable; whereas the dhyāni Buddhas can be, and often are, depicted without their characteristic colours, emblems, *bījas* (seed syllables), and/or *vāhanas* (animal mounts), they cannot be depicted without their *mudrās*.

It can also be demonstrated that each of the five emblems belongs to the same group as the dhyāni Buddha who holds it. We noted earlier that there is a natural basis for the association of the lotus with Amitābha (passive), and of the *vajra* with Akṣobhya (active). That the jewel belongs with Ratnasambhava, the dhyāni Buddha who holds it, is demonstrated not by any shared characteristics (little information is given on this dhyāni Buddha's distinguishing features), but by the fact that the name 'Ratnasambhava' means 'Jewel-birth'. Similar reasoning shows that the wheel is genuinely associated with Vairocana, since this dhyāni Buddha's *mudrā* is the Dharma-wheel *mudrā*. For Amoghasiddhi and the sword or double *vajra* he holds, no direct links of this sort

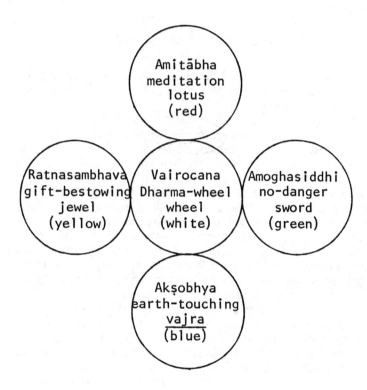

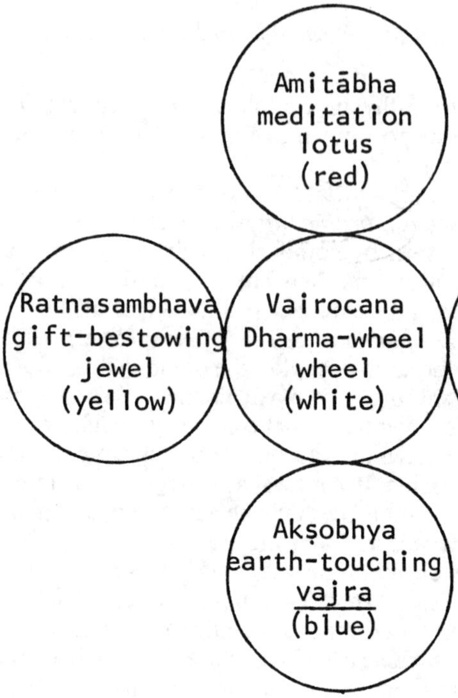

Fig. 6. Positions of the dhyāni Buddhas, *mudrās,* and emblems in the *maṇḍala*. The colours of the dhyāni Buddhas are included for comparison.

exist, but the conclusion follows nevertheless: since each of the other four emblems has been shown to belong to the same group as the dhyāni Buddha who holds it, the one remaining emblem can only belong with the one remaining dhyāni Buddha. So whereas a dhyāni Buddha does not necessarily belong to the same group as his colour, he does belong to the same group as his *mudrā* and his emblem. (The *bījas* and *vāhanas* are less straightforward and will be considered later.)[5]

Table 10. Group classification of dhyāni Buddhas, mudrās, *and emblems.*

Vairocana	Dharma-wheel	wheel	space
Ratnasambhava	gift-bestowing	jewel	?
Akṣobhya	earth-touching	*vajra*	fire
Amitābha	meditation	lotus	water
Amoghasiddhi	no-danger	sword or double *vajra*	?
dhyāni Buddha	*mudrā*	emblem	group

Table 10 sets out the correspondences between dhyāni Buddhas, *mudrās*, and emblems, together with the positions of Amitābha, Akṣobhya, and Vairocana in the fivefold classification. The status of Amoghasiddhi and Ratnasambhava in the fivefold classification has yet to be established. These two dhyāni Buddhas must belong to the two remaining groups, earth and air, but which belongs to which is not clear from the texts. On this question the *mudrās* give no immediate guidance, indeed they can be positively misleading, as the case of Akṣobhya demonstrates. Akṣobhya is identified by the earth-touching *mudrā*, though he himself belongs to the fire group. There is no real contradiction here, however, because the primary reference of the earth-touching *mudrā* is not, as the name may suggest, to an element, but to an event in Gotama's life-story. By virtue of a long-standing iconographic convention, the earth-touching *mudrā* is associated with the occasion on which Gotama repulsed Māra the tempter by calling on the earth to bear witness to his merit in former existences. It is clearly this association, rather than the

Table 11. Biographical references of the mudrās.

Dharma-wheel (Vairocana)	first discourse on Dharma
gift-bestowing (Ratnasambhava)	magnanimity
earth-touching (Akṣobhya)	repulsing Māra
meditation (Amitābha)	Māra's attack
no-danger (Amoghasiddhi)	subduing wild elephant
mudrā	biographical reference

mudrā's name or outward appearance, that is relevant symbolically. Similar associations exist for the other *mudrās*. The full set is as shown in Table 11. We now examine these associations with a view to clarifying the symbolic status of the dhyāni Buddhas themselves.[6]

The meditation *mudrā* (Amitābha) is associated in the iconography with the attack by Māra on the meditating Gotama. As noted in Chapter I, this incident is widely recognized as a metaphorical reference to the arising of distracting thoughts in the mind of the meditator. Whatever their specific content, the thoughts that may distract a meditator from his practice are all part of the thought-stream. It follows that the meditation *mudrā* is linked symbolically with the thought-stream. Now Amitābha, whom this *mudrā* identifies, is regarded as belonging to the passive or water group, and it is also to that group that the thought-stream has been shown to belong. There is therefore agreement among the various symbols involved: Amitābha's *mudrā* refers to the attack by Māra, which symbolizes the thought-stream; and the thought-stream belongs to the water group, to which Amitābha himself and his lotus emblem also belong.

The earth-touching *mudrā* (Akṣobhya) is associated with Gotama's calling on the earth to bear witness to his merit in former existences, in order to repulse Māra's attack. This event has to be viewed in the light of our earlier interpretation of 'recollection of former existences'. How one might go about bearing witness to a person's merit in former existences is not clear from the texts; however, we may assume it would entail, minimally, *recollecting* those former existences. This, together with the already established significance of Māra's attack, leads us to infer that the action of bearing witness to merit in former existences, whereby the attack was repulsed, is a cryptic reference to the practice of retracing thought sequences. Retracing very effectively deprives images of their power to dominate; it is therefore, in metaphorical terms, a powerful means for repulsing Māra. Now Akṣobhya, whom the earth-touching *mudrā* identifies, is traditionally considered to belong to the active or fire group, and it is also to this group that the practice of retracing belongs. So here again there is agreement among the various symbols involved.

The Dharma-wheel *mudrā* (Vairocana) is associated with the 'setting in motion of the Dharma-wheel', the occasion when Gotama first taught his Dharma to others. There is here no recognized connection with meditative practice; however, such a connection is worth considering in view of the already noted close link in the case of the meditation and earth-touching *mudrās*. Whereas those two *mudrās* refer to events leading up to the enlightenment (Māra's attack and defeat), the Dharma-wheel *mudrā* refers to the first major event *after* the enlightenment. Gotama depicted in the meditation or earth-touching *mudrā* is still engaged in striving for enlightenment; depicted in the Dharma-wheel *mudrā* he is fully enlightened. Consequently the Dharma-wheel *mudrā* is associated indirectly with awareness. This is not to suggest that the icon in Dharma-wheel *mudrā* was created as a symbolic representation of awareness; rather it is to suggest that that icon, created originally as a representation of the first teaching of the Dharma, could well have been seen by masters in the élite meditative tradition as suitable for symbolizing awareness, and therefore adopted for that purpose.

The no-danger *mudrā* (Amoghasiddhi) refers to an occasion when Gotama subdued a savage wild elephant which had been turned loose in his vicinity by a jealous rival named Devadatta. As the vicious creature charged towards him, Gotama spoke a few words, whereupon it stopped in its tracks and tamely knelt down to pay him homage.

Here again there is no explicit link with meditative practice; however, an indirect connection becomes apparently when one considers textual references to the taming of elephants. In one of his best-known similes Gotama likens the practice of mindfulness to the process of taming a wild forest elephant: the elephant is the mind in its normal unruly condition, and the technique of taming it by tying it to a strong stake is the practice of mindfulness.[7] The same simile is found in the writings of the seventh-century Buddhist master Śāntideva. In his *Compendium of Training* Śāntideva says: 'But if that unruly elephant, the mind, has been completely bound by the rope of mindfulness, then all danger has ended and everything good has come.'[8] As noted in Chapter IV, mindfulness is basically a preliminary form of concentration practice. We may infer therefore that the reference in the elephant simile is to concentration, the practice which consists in 'tying' the mind to the meditation object.

Support for this conclusion comes from the status of the elephant in Indian symbolism in general.[9] Although a terrestrial creature, the elephant is widely recognized as belonging to the water group. In the iconography of all Indian sects, the elephant is frequently depicted standing in water, spraying water over himself, or pouring water from a pot over the head of some deity, most commonly the goddess Śrī (Lakṣmī); and the connection with the water element is reinforced by mythological associations with rainclouds and with Indra, the Vedic god of storms. In addition, the elephant is closely connected with various other water-associated symbols, for example the lotus (he is often depicted holding a lotus in his trunk) and birth (Gotama's birth was foretold by his mother's dream of an elephant).

The tale of Gotama's stopping the charging elephant depicts a contrast of movement versus rest, of instability and danger versus stability and safety ('no-danger').[10] If the elephant himself belongs to the water group, the action of stopping him in his tracks belongs to the earth group. This reinforces our conclusion that the no-danger *mudrā* is symbolically connected with the practice of concentration.

The qualification made above applies here also. We are not suggesting that the story of Gotama's taming the charging elephant was intended as a symbolic account of concentration practice, but rather that it may have been intentionally re-interpreted as such on the basis of the Tipiṭaka link between elephant-taming and concentration.

The one remaining *mudrā*, the gift-bestowing *mudrā* (Ratnasambhava), differs from the others in referring not to an event in Gotama's life-story, but to one of his distinguishing qualities, his magnanimity. This quality does not suggest any of the five meditative stages, but as Table 12 shows, there remains only one stage with which it might be paired, namely observation of linking. The significance of the pattern of correspondences shown in Table 12 will be assessed after the emblems have been examined.

Table 12. Correspondences between mudrās *and meditative stages, as inferred from biographical references.*

Dharma-wheel	first discourse	awareness
gift-bestowing	magnanimity	?
earth-touching	repulsing Māra	retracing
meditation	Māra's attack	thought-stream
no-danger	subduing elephant	concentration
mudrā	biographical reference	meditative stage

Two of the emblems have already been considered briefly. We noted in Chapter VI that the lotus and the *vajra* both partake of the qualities traditionally ascribed to the dhyāni Buddhas who hold them: the lotus (Amitābha) suggests passivity and femininity, and by virtue of its aquatic habitat is closely associated with the water element; and the *vajra* (Akṣobhya), being a powerful weapon, suggests activity and masculinity. These two emblems would therefore be appropriate as symbols for the thought-stream and the practice of retracing respectively. Three emblems remain to be considered.

The wheel (Vairocana) is, like its corresponding *mudrā*, associated with the first teaching of the Dharma, and would, for the same reasons, be appropriate as a symbol for enlightenment or awareness. In addition, the wheel has come to symbolize the Dharma itself, the totality of Gotama's teaching, and thus has become the most highly esteemed of all Buddhist symbols, comparable in status to the cross in Christianity. The wheel's supreme status augments its suitability as a symbol for the highest meditative stage and as a member of the space group.

Amoghasiddhi is identified by either a sword or a double *vajra*. The sword suggests a sudden 'cutting off'. In Chapter IV we cited the following instruction given by Padmo Karpo: 'Let these thoughts now do whatever they want, not *cutting them off* at all . . . Thus you feel your thoughts occur, but you yourself neither *cut them off* nor react to them . . . Now you know how to leave every thought and passion entirely alone, not *cutting it off* at all . . .'[11] We noted that 'cutting off thoughts' would be an apt way

Table 13. Interpretation of dhyāni Buddhas and attributes in terms of meditative stages.

Vairocana	Dharma-wheel	first discourse	wheel	space	awareness
Ratnasambhava	gift-bestowing	magnanimity	jewel	air	observation of linking
Akṣobhya	earth-touching	repulsing Māra	*vajra*	fire	retracing
Amitābha	meditation	Māra's attack	lotus	water	thought-stream
Amoghasiddhi	no-danger	subduing elephant	sword	earth	concen-tration
dhyāni Buddha	*mudrā*	biographical reference	emblem	group	meditative stage

of describing concentration practice. For the same reasons the sword would be an appropriate symbol for concentration.

Amoghasiddhi's alternative emblem, the double *vajra*, does not in itself suggest any particular meditative stage. Geshe Nyawang interprets it as 'symbolizing steadiness and firmness'.[12] This interpretation — for which, unfortunately, Nyawang gives neither textual references nor a reasoned argument — would make the double *vajra* a suitable symbol for concentration. It would thus be in agreement with our interpretation of Amoghasiddhi's other emblem (the sword) and of his no-danger *mudrā*.

Ratnasambhava's jewel emblem, like his gift-bestowing *mudrā*, does not suggest any one of the five meditative stages, but here again there remains only one stage, observation of linking, with which it might be paired.

The demonstrated correspondences between emblems and meditative stages are in all cases in agreement with those of the associated *mudrās*. If, applying the 'process of elimination', we pair Ratnasambhava's *mudrā* and emblem with observation of linking, the result is the set of correspondences shown in Table 13.

The dhyāni Buddhas are widely regarded as symbolic representations of meditative stages on the path to enlightenment. The above analysis lends support to that view by pointing out how the biographical associations of the *mudrās* link them, more or less directly, with particular meditative techniques. More specifically, it indicates that the techniques symbolized are the five stages of the course of meditative practice described in Chapters III and IV.

How this symbolic set developed historically is not altogether clear.[13] The development of the icons themselves is relatively straightforward, but the process whereby those icons acquired their esoteric associations is, not surprisingly, obscure. The earliest Buddha icons appear about the first century A.D.[14] Conventionalized associations linking certain *mudrās* with specific events in Gotama's life-story quickly became established. Icons in the meditation, earth-touching, and Dharma-wheel *mudrās* were the most popular, particularly the first, which, in the developing Mahāyāna, became identified with Amitābha, the cosmic Buddha of the Western Paradise. At some time between the first and fifth centuries these three icons, as Amitābha, Akṣobhya, and Vairocana, came to be recognized as a discrete set of *tathāgatas* or *jinas* (now improperly called dhyāni Buddhas), and were assigned to the passive, active, and balance categories respectively in the already well-established three-way classification. As the Tantric tradition recognizes, these same three were also at some time brought into symbolic association with meditative stages. Our analysis indicates that the stages in question were the thought-stream, retracing, and awareness. When this association with meditative stages came about is difficult to say. It may have come into existence as a consequence of the symbolic associations evident in the Māra legend: the same associations would have automatically applied to the icons representing that legend; or it may have been introduced centuries later, perhaps as a development from the three-way classification. The former possibility seems to us the more likely, for reasons that will be set out fully in the next chapter.

The extension from three dhyāni Buddhas to five would have followed naturally to meet the requirements of the full system of five symbolic groups based on the elements. The two new members, Amoghasiddhi and Ratnasambhava, were again already popular forms of the Buddha icon. The choice of the no-danger *mudrā* for concentration and the earth group was based on the appropriate associations of the *mudrā*; the choice of the gift-bestowing *mudrā* for observation of linking and the air group was probably arbitrary, there being no other more appropriate *mudrā* available. (Cf. the similarly arbitrary choice of the colour green for the air group.) The five icons were provided with emblems, probably in imitation of Hindu deities, but with due regard for symbolic appropriateness. The subsequent arranging in a cross pattern, and the acquiring of inappropriate colours etc. will be discussed after the remaining components of the *maṇḍala* have been examined.

The set of five seated Buddha figures is remarkably appropriate as a medium for symbolizing the course of meditative practice; however, it is hard to see how it could have had practical value as a teaching aid. Perhaps its inclusion in the esoteric tradition was motivated by a desire to give the popular Buddha icons a place in the fivefold symbolism. In any case, it has provided a durable graphic representation of the course of meditative practice, which later generations have preserved out of reverence, even if unaware of its hidden meaning.

The Bījas

As regards the *bījas* or 'seed syllables', the *maṇḍala* is variable. The most common version, which we shall call Version 1, is that shown without parentheses in Fig. 7.[15] At least four other versions, relatively much rarer, are recognized in different branches of the Vajrayāna. Most of them can readily be explained as derived from Version 1 through minor errors in transmission, for example misreading *Traṃ* as *Traḥ*, and *Oṃ* as *Vaṃ* or *Vuṃ*.[16] However, one of these less common alternatives does have to be recognized as significantly different, namely that shown in parentheses in Fig. 7. We shall call it Version 2.[17] Version 2 cannot be derived in any immediately obvious way from Version 1, and must therefore be taken account of in any attempt to interpret the *bīja* symbolism.

Āḥ, Hūṃ, and *Oṃ* are common to both versions. These three together make up the 'root *mantra*', *Oṃ Āḥ Hūṃ*, which is said to underlie all *mantras.*[18] In the *tantras Āḥ, Hūṃ*, and *Oṃ* are consistently assigned to the water, fire, and space groups, and associated with Amitābha, Akṣobhya, and Vairocana respectively. As regards this Tantric classification, Version 2 conforms to the tradition; Version 1 conflicts with it, placing *Āḥ* in the northern *maṇḍala* cell with Amoghasiddhi, while giving Amitābha a different *bīja, Hrīḥ*. Such conflicts within the *maṇḍala* have already been observed (e.g. the red colour of Amitābha). While they will have to be accounted for in due course, they pose no immediate problem for the process of interpretation. It remains to

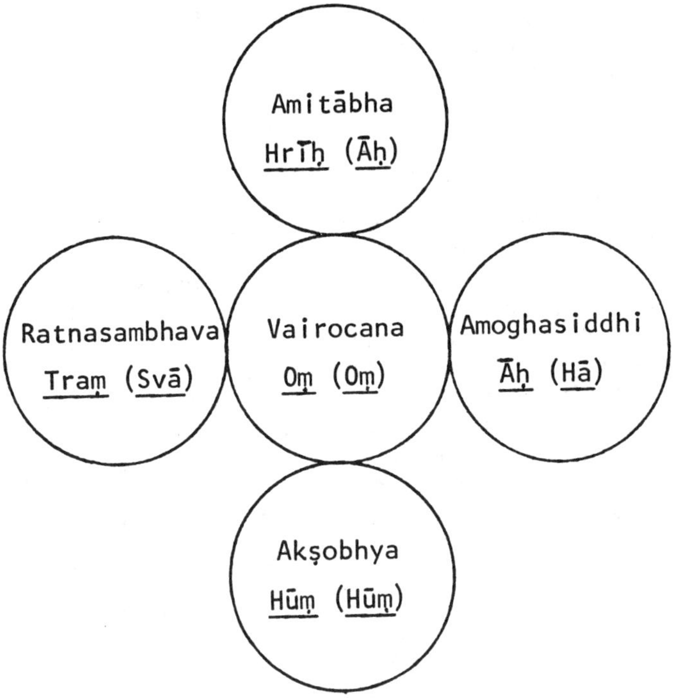

Fig. 7. Positions of the *bījas* in the *maṇḍala*. The most common version (Version 1) is shown without parentheses; the only significant variant (Version 2) is shown in parentheses.

discover the symbolic affinities of *Traṃ* and *Hrīḥ* in Version 1, and of *Svā* and *Hā* in Version 2.

For *Traṃ* and *Hrīḥ* there exists no information comparable to that provided for *Āḥ, Hūm*, and *Oṃ*, so a different approach to the problem has to be sought. We find it in that most popular and potent of all Buddhist *mantras, Oṃ Maṇi Padme Hūṃ Hrīḥ* (often abbreviated to *Oṃ Maṇi Padme Hūṃ*). Of the five components of this *mantra*, only *Hrīḥ* remains unidentified. The symbolic status of *Oṃ* and *Hūṃ* is already known, and the two remaining components are also already familiar, since *maṇi* means 'jewel' and *padme* is an inflexional form of *padma*, 'lotus'.

Because of the conspicuous place it occupies in Tibetan Buddhism, the *mantra Oṃ Maṇi Padme Hūṃ Hrīḥ* has often attracted the attention of would-be interpreters of the Twilight Language.[19] The problem of interpretation is compounded by a high degree of grammatical ambiguity in the inflexional form *padme*.[20] Westerners have usually taken this form to be the locative singular, and therefore translated *Maṇi padme* as 'The jewel [is] in the lotus'; however, this is grammatically impossible since *maṇi* is not in the nominative case. A plausible alternative, favoured by Bharati and others, is that we are dealing here with a compound word *Maṇipadme*, and that this is the vocative form of a feminine personal name *Maṇipadmā*. (Sanskrit in the traditional written form had neither capitals nor spacing between words; hence the transliterations *maṇi padme, maṇipadme*, and *Maṇipadme* are all equally valid.) According to this interpretation, the *mantra* is an invocation to a female deity: '*Oṃ!* O Maṇipadmā! *Hūṃ! Hrīḥ!*'.[21] However, no deity named Maṇipadmā is to be found anywhere in the extensive Mahāyāna pantheon. This is therefore hardly an adequate explanation for the most popular of all Buddhist *mantras*.

From the point of view of grammar, there is another, equally valid interpretation, namely that we have here a *dvandva* or coordinative compound, *maṇi-padme*, meaning 'jewel and lotus'.[22] On this interpretation, the *mantra* is simply a list of five items: *Oṃ, jewel, lotus, Hūṃ, Hrīḥ*. This list contains two of the five dhyāni Buddha emblems (jewel and lotus) and three of the five *bījas* (*Oṃ, Hūṃ, Hrīḥ*). Of the five, all but *Hrīḥ* have already been assigned places in the fivefold classification, as shown in Table 14.

Now the root mantra, *Oṃ Āḥ Hūṃ*, represents the three groups that predominated in the earlier Tantric classification, namely balance, passive, and active. One might therefore expect to find,

Table 14. Group classification of components of the mantra Oṃ Maṇi Padme Hūṃ Hrīḥ

Oṃ	space
jewel	air
Hūṃ	fire
lotus	water
Hrīh	?
mantra component	group

in the later Tantric tradition, a *mantra* with five components representing the later set of five groups. Table 14 indicates that this is in fact the role of *Oṃ Maṇi-padme Hūṃ Hrīḥ*. If *Hrīḥ* is taken as belonging to the earth group, the *mantra* covers the full set of five groups, and its remarkably high status in the Vajrayāna is thereby accounted for. Many investigators have advocated interpretations such as '*Oṃ! Nirvāṇa* is in *saṃsāra. Hūṃ! Hrīḥ!*' and '*Oṃ!* The Buddha is in the world. *Hūṃ! Hrīḥ!*'; but these, quite apart from their dependence on the inaccurate translation of *maṇi-padme*, leave unexplained a large part of the *mantra*, namely the three *bījas*. By contrast, the above interpretation in terms of the five groups accounts for every one of the *mantra's* components.[23]

For our present purpose, the important point is the identification of *Hrīḥ* as belonging to the earth group. The one remaining

Table 15. Group classsification of the bījas.

Oṃ	space
Traṃ	air
Hūṃ	fire
Āḥ	water
Hrīḥ	earth
bīja	group

bīja in the *maṇḍala, Traṃ*, is thereby automatically identified with the one remaining group, air. The basic interpretation of Version 1 in terms of groups is now complete — see Table 15.

In Version 2 the unidentified *bījas* are *Svā* and *Hā*. Here it is relevant to note two general points regarding the structure of *mantras* and *bījas*. The first is that many *mantras* end with the word *Svāhā*, which is an exclamation used in making offerings. A typical example is the following invocation to the goddess Pāṇḍaravāsinī: *Oṃ Āḥ Paṃ Hūṃ Svāhā*.[24] This combines the root *mantra Oṃ Āḥ Hūṃ* with the syllable *Paṃ*, standing for the goddess's name, and the final *Svāhā*. The second point is that there has often occurred a process of coining pseudo-*bījas* by splitting ordinary words into their component syllables. For example, *maṇi-padme* is sometimes split to yield the pseudo-*bījas, Ma, Ṇi, Pa, Dme*.[25] It is now clear that the *Svā* and *Hā* of Version 2 derive from an expanded version of the root *mantra, Oṃ Āh Hūṃ Svāhā*.[26] The syllables of *Svāhā* were probably assigned to Ratnasambhava and Amoghasiddhi about the time when the set of dhyāni Buddhas was extended from three members to five. This being the case, and since *Svā* and *Hā* occur nowhere else in the system of *bīja* symbolism, these two syllables are of little real symbolic importance and will not be considered further.[27]

Version 2 is nevertheless of symbolic interest in that, unlike Version 1, is places *Āḥ* where it seems to belong, with Amitābha in the western *maādala* cell rather than with Amoghasiddhi in the northern. A probable explanation for this discrepancy between the two versions emerges when one examines actual written specimens of the *bījas*. In the archaic and very ornate *lan-tsha* script, the one normally used in Tibet in graphic representations of the *bījas*, the syllables *Āḥ* and *Hrīḥ* are often almost identical in appearance. This, together with the fact that the *lan-tsha* script was little used for other purposes and was therefore unfamiliar to all but specialists, could have caused the *bījas Āḥ* and *Hrīḥ* to become confused, and thereby accidentally interchanged in the *maṇḍala*.[28] It would follow that the original and 'correct' arrangement of the *bījas* in the *maṇḍala* is as shown in Fig. 8.

Unlike the *mudrās*, the *bījas* show no direct evidence of a symbolic connection with the meditative stages. If such a connection existed, if could only have been derivative, a secondary consequence of the *bījas*' membership of the five groups.

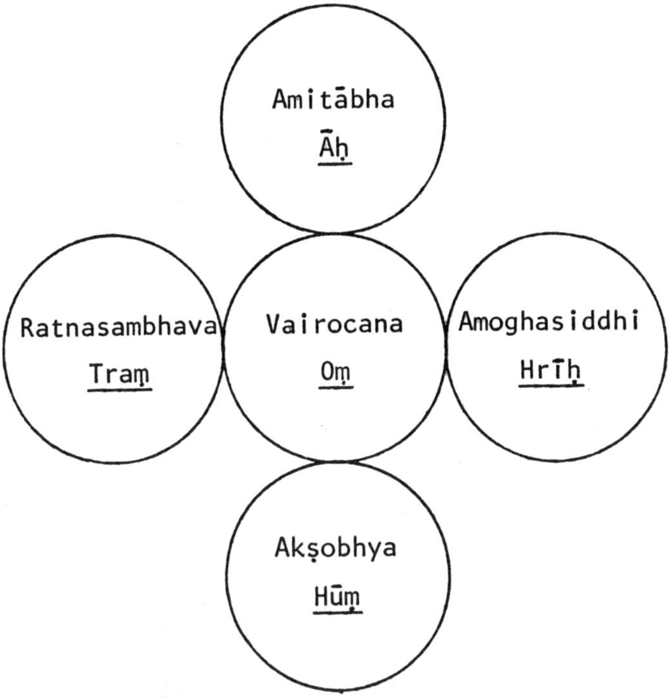

Fig. 8. Inferred original positions of the *bījas* in the *maṇḍala*.

The Vāhanas

The five *vāhanas* or animal mounts are located in the *maṇḍala* as shown in Fig. 9. The elephant has already been shown to belong to the water group, and to be linked in the Tipiṭaka with the thought-stream. We therefore pass on to the remaining four animals, beginning with the lion.

In the Tipiṭaka, metaphorical references to lions are frequent. Gotama explains such references as follows: 'As for the word "lion", monks, this is a term for the wayfarer who is arahant, a fully-awakened one.'[29] The lion is thus equated symbolically with enlightenment, and so with awareness. This symbolic connection is in keeping with the fact that in India, as elsewhere, the lion enjoys supreme status among the beasts, and therefore would belong to the space group.

The *garuḍa*, a mythological creature that is half man half bird, is less well known in the Buddhist context than in the Hindu, where he serves as the *vāhana* of Viṣṇu. The principal characteristic of the *garuḍa* is his enmity towards serpents; he destroys serpents in large numbers and is often depicted in the act of killing or devouring them. It is in this role that the *garuḍa* figures in the following incident, recounted in one of the later biographies of Gotama. Once a heretic named Agnidatta assumed the form of a many-headed serpent (*nāga*) and attacked Gotama; but Gotama's principal disciple, Sāriputta, assumed the form of a *garuḍa* and killed it.[30] This tale resembles in certain important respects that of the attack by the savage wild elephant. The Sanskrit/Pali word for 'many-headed serpent', *nāga*, is ambiguous: it also means 'elephant'. In addition, the names of the evil-doers are closely similar to the two tales: Agnidatta in the one case, Devadatta in the other. It is likely, then, that the two tales, that of the attacking serpent and that of the attacking elephant, are divergent variants of a single original. In any case it is clear that the two closely parallel each other symbolically. The serpent, a creature traditionally linked with water, birth, etc., belongs, like the elephant, to the water group;[31] and the serpent-devouring *garuḍa* belongs, like the no-danger *mudrā*, to the earth group.

The peacock (or goose, in some versions) is the easiest of the five *vāhanas* to place. As a bird it naturally belongs to the air group.

The horse has no evident connection with any of the five groups, whether it is compared with the elements or with the

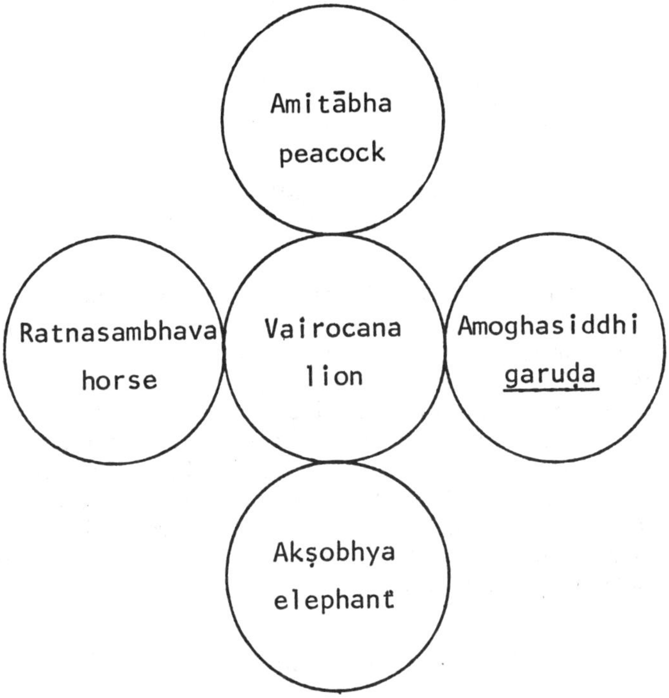

Fig. 9. Positions of the *vāhanas* in the *maṇḍala*.

Table 16. Group classification of the vāhanas

lion	space
peacock	air
horse	fire
elephant	water
garuḍa	earth
vāhana	group

meditative stages. However, there now remains only one group to which no *vāhana* has been assigned, namely the fire group, whence we infer that the horse belongs with fire.

The full interpretation of the *vāhanas* in terms of symbolic groups is therefore as shown in Table 16. Of the five, the elephant is explicitly connected with the thought-stream, and the lion is linked indirectly with awareness by way of the association with enlightenment. Apart from these two cases there is no indication that the set of *vāhanas* was intended as a representation of the course of meditative practice. The reasons for its inclusion in the *maṇḍala* are discussed below.

Interpretation of the Maṇḍala

The principal symbols comprising the *maṇḍala* have been examined set by set and assigned places in the fivefold classification. The result is the set of correspondences shown in Table 17.

Having clarified the status of the individual symbols, we now attempt to account for their characteristic spatial arrangement. Why the symbols should have been arranged in a cross is not difficult to see, when one considers the importance of cruciform arrangements in Indian cosmography, iconography, and temple architecture. The Indian world-map is basically cruciform, with four continents located to the north, east, south, and west of the world-axis, Mount Meru. Different versions of the map further emphasize this basic pattern in various ways: Mount Meru is shown as square in section; its four sides are coloured blue (or

Table 17. Group correspondences among maṇḍala *components.*

space	white	Vairocana	Dharma-wheel	wheel	*Oṃ*	lion
air	green	Ratnasambhava	gift-bestowing	jewel	*Traṃ*	peacock
fire	red	Akṣobhya	earth-touching	*vajra*	*Hūṃ*	horse
water	blue	Amitābha	meditation	lotus	*Āḥ*	elephant
earth	yellow	Amoghasiddhi	no-danger	sword	*Hrīḥ*	*garuḍa*
element	colour	dhyāni Buddha	*mudrā*	emblem	*bīja*	*vāhana*

white), yellow, red, and green; it is surrounded by four subsidiary mountains; it has four world-guardians posted around it, one on each side; and so on.[32] A good example of cruciform arrangement in iconography is the god Brahmā; he has four heads facing the four directions, and four arms each holding a different emblem. Another is the set of four Tīrthaṅkaras (enlightened masters in the Jaina tradition), often depicted in front of Jaina temples; this group resembles that of the dhyāni Buddhas so closely as to indicate direct mutual influence.[33] The tendency to see things in terms of four axes about a central point or origin has strongly influenced the outward form of Indian symbolism from Harappan times to the present day. The *siddhas*, in setting out the five coloured discs, the five dhyāni Buddhas, and so on in a cruciform pattern, were therefore merely conforming to a long-standing convention, which happened to fit in well with the concept of five symbolic groups.

The cruciform arrangement defines five positions: the four cardinal points and the centre. On what principle were the five groups distributed among those five positions? As noted several times in the course of the analysis, the symbols in any particular cell of the *maṇḍala* often belong to different symbolic groups; for example, the western cell contains Amitābha (belonging to the water group), the colour red (fire group), and the peacock (air group). Such seeming contradictions have long challenged the ingenuity of scholars attempting to make sense of Tantric symbolism. Several more or less plausible theories have been advanced to account for them. Perhaps the simplest is Eliade's suggestion that the Twilight Language was designed 'to project the yogin into the "paradoxical situation" indispensable to his training';

the contradictions are then readily accounted for as part of a deliberate attempt to confront the meditator with *kōan*-like paradoxes.[34] The theory favoured by Govinda is that the symbolic contradictions reflect conflicting forces in the meditator's mental makeup; in each pair of conflicting symbols one member represents a mental state that must be given up through meditation practice, the other an opposing state that must be cultivated.[35] According to Wayman, the explanation lies in the existence of more than one system of correspondences among symbol sets. He maintains that in addition to the generally recognized 'basic-time correspondences' there exists a system of 'fruitional-time correspondences', in which many of the familiar equivalences no longer apply. The basic-time correspondences represent the condition of the ordinary worldling, while the fruitional-time correspondences represent that of the meditator who has successfully completed the practice. Seeming contradictions can thus be explained as due to the discrepancies between these two sets of correspondences.[36]

The problem is usually expressed, as above, by stating that the symbols in any given *maṇḍala* cell often belong to different groups. But it can be more readily explicated if stated the other way about: the symbols belonging to any particular group are often located in different *maṇḍala* cells. For example, the symbols that belong to the fire group are distributed as follows: fire itself and the colour red are in the western cell; Akṣobhya, the *vajra*, and *Hūṃ* are in the eastern cell; and the horse is in the southern cell. The total situation is made clear in Table 18.

Table 18. Positions of maṇḍala *components. N, S, E, W, = north, etc.; C = centre. The* mudrās, *being inseparable from the dhyāni Buddhas they identify, are not included.* Āḥ *and* Hrīḥ *are shown in their inferred original positions.*

space	C	white	C	Vairocana	C	wheel	C	*Oṃ*	C	lion	C
air	N	green	N	Ratnasambhava	S	jewel	S	*Traṃ*	S	peacock	W
fire	W	red	W	Akṣobhya	E	*vajra*	E	*Hūṃ*	E	horse	S
water	E	blue	E	Amitābha	W	lotus	W	*Āḥ*	W	elephant	E
earth	S	yellow	S	Amoghasiddhi	N	sword	N	*Hrīḥ*	N	*garuḍa*	N
element		colour		dhyāni Buddha		emblem		*bīja*		*vāhana*	
(a)		(a)		(b)		(b)		(b)		(c)	

Only the space group is totally consistent; all symbols in this group are in the central cell. The other four groups are consistently distributed among the four peripheral cells. However, beneath this inconsistency a certain order is discernible. The elements and the colours are identically distributed and so also are the dhyāni Buddhas, emblems, and *bījas*. Only the *vāhanas* are unique in their distribution. These distributional properties are indicated in Table 18 by labelled brackets. The symbols in the *maṇḍala* therefore fall into three distributional classes: (a) the elements and colours; (b) the dhyāni Buddhas, emblems, and *bījas*; and (c) the *vāhanas*. The problem now is to account for the existence of these three classes.

In considering why the symbol sets in the *maṇḍala* are arranged as they are, one has to bear in mind that the *maṇḍala* does not always contain the same total number of symbol sets. One or more of the sets usually depicted may be omitted. For example, a *maṇḍala* engraved on a brass plaque naturally lacks the set of colours; and in the extreme case, as in a representation of the dhyāni Buddhas' emblems around a *stūpa*, only one set is depicted. On the other hand, some versions of the *maṇḍala* contain more than the usual number of sets. For example, there exist relatively rare representations of the *maṇḍala* which include the two-dimensional counterparts of the four geometrical shapes.[37] In such *maṇḍalas* the square, circle, triangle, and semicircle are located in the north, east, south, and west respectively. We noted earlier that the four shapes belong to the first four symbolic groups as shown in Table 19. Considered on this basis, the shapes agree with the *vāhanas* as regards their distribution in the *maṇḍala*, while conflicting with all the other symbol sets. This is clear

Table 19. Group classification of the four shapes.

	space
hemisphere/semicircle	air
cone/triangle	fire
sphere/circle	water
cube/square	earth
shape	group

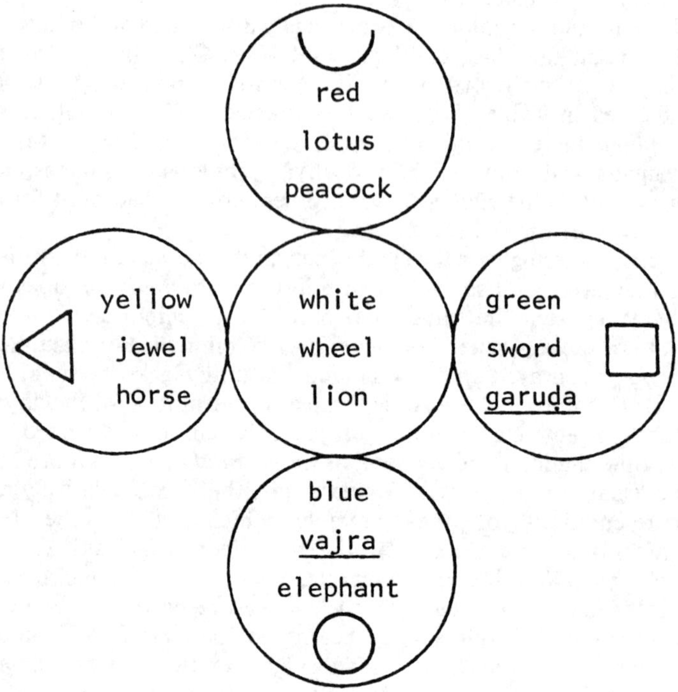

Fig. 10. Positions of the shapes relative to the three distributional classes, namely: (a) the colours, (b) the emblems, and (c) the *vāhanas*.

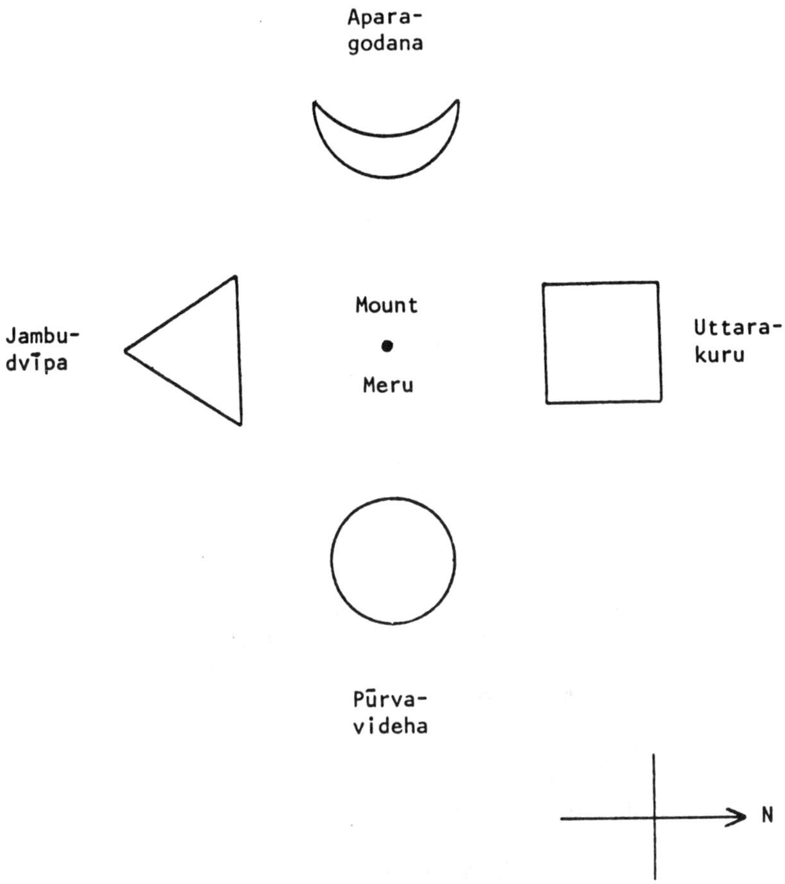

Fig. 11. Mount Meru and the four continents.

from Fig. 10, which shows the shapes together with a representative from each of the three distributional classes (a) the colours, (b) the emblems, and (c) the *vāhanas*. For example, in the western cell, the semicircle (air) agrees with the peacock (air) while conflicting with the colour red (fire) and the lotus (water).

To discover why the shapes are arranged in this particular way in the *maṇḍala*, we turn to the Indian cosmography, in which the four shapes figure prominently. The four continents that surround the central Mount Meru are as shown in Fig. 11.[38] The triangular continent in the south, Jambu-dvīpa, is identified with India — appropriately since India is roughly triangular in shape and is located south of the Eurasian landmass. The three other continents are vaguely identified with various 'barbarian' regions.

It is now self-evident why the shapes in the *maṇḍala* are arranged as they are: the adding of the shapes to the *maṇḍala* consisted in mechanically superimposing the world-map on the *maṇḍala* arrangement without regard for symbolic correspondences.

The world-map in its turn represents an attempt at assimilating the traditional set of four shapes to known geographical facts — a special case of macrocosm-microcosm parallelism. The factors determining the arrangement of the four shapes relative to the compass points were clearly as follows. The shapes were naturally always listed in the sequence square, circle, triangle, semicircle, since they corresponded to the elements earth, water, fire, air. Now in India anticlockwise movement is inauspicious to the point of being virtually taboo, while clockwise movement is auspicious; when circumambulating a temple or *stūpa* one always proceeds clockwise, never anticlockwise. Unless prevented in some way, for example by an unusual temple layout, one begins this clockwise movement in the east. This is the so-called *pradakṣiṇa* movement: clockwise, preferably beginning in the east. The spatial arrangement of the four shapes therefore had to be such that clockwise movement around the 'map' would yield the correct sequence. This was easily achieved. However, the second, less stringent requirement, that the sequence should begin in the east, could not be met because of another overriding consideration: the triangle had to be in the south in order to conform with the actual position of India, with which it was identified. The result was a compromise: the shapes were so arranged that the correct sequence — square, circle, triangle, semicircle — resulted from clockwise movement beginning in the *north*.

When the conventionalized arrangement of the shapes was superimposed on the *maṇḍala*, contradictions naturally resulted.

As the above analysis demonstrates, these contradictions are devoid of symbolic significance. For example, if in the southern cell, the triangle (fire) was brought together with yellow (earth), this was not intended as a *kōan*-like paradox that would shock the meditator into a new mode of consciousness; nor was it meant to represent some inner conflict which the meditator must resolve. It was simply a consequence of mechanically combining the two originally independent cruciform designs. The triangle was placed in the southern cell of the *maṇḍala* simply because it already occupied the southern position in the world-map.

The principles illustrated by the case of the four shapes adequately account for the existence of the three distributional classes in the *maṇḍala* arrangement. The *maṇḍala*'s present form can be explained as due to a mechanical superimposing of three formerly distinct and independent proto-*maṇḍalas* (Fig. 12) corresponding to the three distributional classes (Table 18). Each of the three was consistent within itself but different from the others. It remains to account for the arrangement of the symbols within each of these three patterns.

The case of the elements and colours (distributional class (a)) is the simplest. Earlier we advanced the suggestion that the coloured *maṇḍala* cells probably arose from the same original source as the *kasiṇas*, namely a set of coloured discs used by *siddhas* to represent the course of meditative practice. To this we would now add that the *siddhas* adopted the convention of arranging those discs in a cross, in such a way that the traditional *pradakṣiṇa* movement (clockwise from the east) yielded the traditional sequence blue, yellow, red, (green), white. The resulting pattern conflicted with the traditional listing of the elements, since water now preceded earth rather than following it. However, because it was the colours rather than the elements that were actually depicted, the traditional listing of the colours prevailed.

In the case of the dhyāni Buddhas it is clear that the principal factor determining the arrangement was the symbolic relationship existing among the three oldest members: Amitābha, Akṣobhya, and Vairocana belonged to the passive, active, and balance groups respectively. In recognition of this relationship, Vairocana (balance) was placed in the centre with the contrasting Amitābha and Akṣobhya (passive and active) on either side of him. Because Amitābha was traditionally associated with the Western Paradise, he was placed to the west of Vairocana, which left Akṣobhya in the east. The subsequent addition of Ratnasambhava and Amoghasiddhi to this original pattern probably entailed an

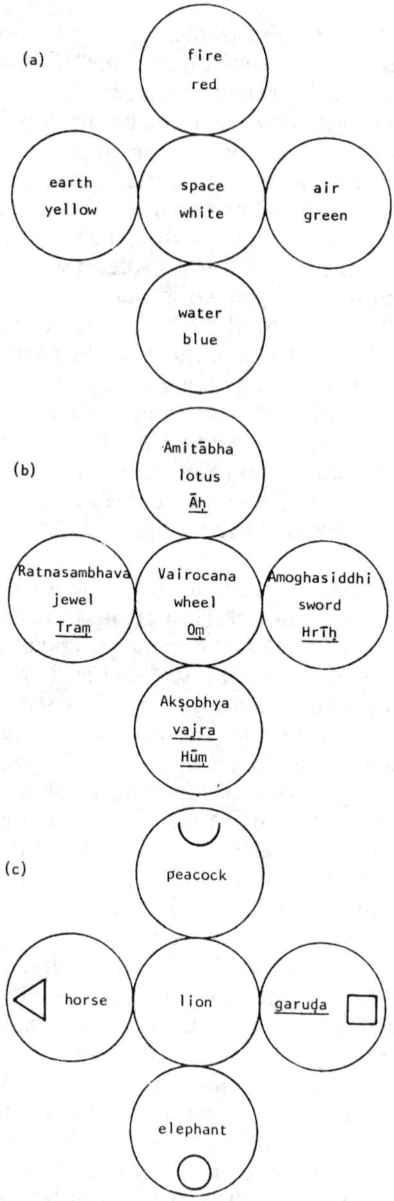

Fig. 12. The three proto-*maṇḍalas*, corresponding to the three distributional classes (a), (b), and (c).

arbitrary choice between the two possible positions — whence the present arrangement.

The emblems were almost certainly assigned to the dhyāni Buddhas directly, without being first set out as an independent proto-*maṇḍala*; if there now exist *maṇḍalas* depicting the emblems alone, these have been secondarily derived by abstracting from the full *maṇḍala*. The same, we may infer, is true of the *bījas*: they were assigned to the dhyāni Buddhas directly. Cases where the *bījas* exist as an independent cruciform pattern are secondary derivatives.

The arrangement of the colours differed from that of the dhyāni Buddhas because the two sets had different historical origins. The colours had long existed as a recognized list of four (later five); their spatial arrangement had to preserve the order of that ancient list. The dhyāni Buddhas developed from an earlier set of three, in which the emphasis was on the passive/active/balance relationship; their spatial arrangement had to reflect that relationship.

It appears that at some relatively late stage the cruciform arrangement of dhyāni Buddhas (Fig. 12b) and the cruciform arrangement of coloured discs (Fig. 12a) were superimposed. This was done mechanically, without regard for symbolic correspondences, which explains why all the dhyāni Buddhas except Vairocana in the centre have inappropriate colours.[39]

The *vāhanas* are arranged in a manner identical with that of the four shapes. Now the *vāhanas* occur not only in the *maṇḍala* but also in the Tibetan version of the world-map, which makes it likely that the identity of arrangement between *vāhanas* and shapes stems from an earlier close association of the two sets: the shapes were arranged according to the principles discussed earlier, and the *vāhanas* simply followed suit (just as the arrangement of the elements followed that of the colours).[40] The *vāhanas* and shapes therefore probably existed as a third proto-*maṇḍala* (Fig. 12c), which was later mechanically superimposed on the colours and the dhyāni Buddhas, again without regard for symbolic correspondences.

This completes our analysis of the *maṇḍala*.[41] Each of the component symbols has been classified according to the fivefold scheme. The combinations of symbols in the different cells have been explained as resulting from superimposition of three formerly separate, differently arranged proto-*maṇḍalas*: (a) the elements and colours; (b) the dhyāni Buddhas, emblems, and *bījas*; (c) the *vāhanas* (and the four shapes). Finally, the arrangement of the symbols within each of these proto-*maṇḍalas* has been accounted for.

Occasional reference has been made to symbolic correspondences with stages in the meditative practice; however, the analysis has been only minimally dependent on those correspondences. This being the case, it would be possible to propose a self-consistent interpretation of the *maṇḍala* which would make no reference to meditation. For example, one could explain the *maṇḍala* as nothing more than a combination of several different parallel sets from the fivefold classification, having no referent outside itself. However, such an interpretation would be unacceptable. It is implied in the notion of a Twilight Language, and widely believed both by practising Vajrayanists and by Western scholars, that the *maṇḍala* does have symbolic meaning, and, more explicitly, that it symbolizes the meditative path to enlightenment. An interpretation of the *maṇḍala* can therefore be judged adequate and acceptable only if it demonstrates a clear symbolic connection between the components of the *maṇḍala* and a course of meditative practice that is demonstrably in line with Buddhist teachings.

This requirement has been met. It has been shown that there exists a far-reaching symbolic correspondence between the components of the *maṇḍala* and the course of meditative practice described in Chapters III and IV. To begin with it was shown that the set of five meditative stages — concentration, thought-stream, retracing, observation of linking, and awareness — fits perfectly into the fivefold scheme of classification: each stage partakes of the properties that characterize one or other of the five symbolic groups, and may therefore be said to belong to that group; and the sequence of the stages in practice is identical with the traditional order of listing the groups. It follows that the full course of practice could appropriately be symbolized by any of the recognized five-membered sets: the elements, the colours, the dhyāni Buddhas, and so on. (See Table 20 for the complete pattern of correspondences.) The assumption that the elements and colours were used in this way not only explains the role of those two sets in the *maṇḍala* but also goes some way towards accounting for the puzzling *kasiṇa* meditation. In the case of the dhyāni Buddhas, evidence of a link with the meditative practice is provided by the biographical references of the *mudrās*. For two of the five (Amitābha and Akṣobhya) the link with meditative stages is direct and explicit, for another two (Vairocana and Amoghasiddhi) it is indirect. Evidence of a symbolic connection with meditative

Table 20. Interpretation of maṇḍala *and* cakras *in terms of meditative stages.*

space	white	Vairocana	Dharma-wheel	wheel	*Oṃ*	lion		awareness
air	green	Ratnasambhava	gift-bestowing	jewel	*Traṃ*	peacock	hemi-sphere	observation of linking
fire	red	Akṣobhya	earth-touching	*vajra*	*Hūṃ*	horse	cone	retracing
water	blue	Amitābha	meditation	lotus	*Āḥ*	elephant	sphere	thought-stream
earth	yellow	Amoghasiddhi	no-danger	sword	*Hrīḥ*	*garuḍa*	cube	concentration
element	colour	dhyāni Buddha	*mudrā*	emblem	*bīja*	*vāhana*	shape	meditative stage

stages has also been noted in two of the *vāhanas*, the elephant and the lion.

For the elements/colours and the dhyāni Buddhas we have suggested ways in which the symbol sets might have been created by *siddhas* and employed to represent the course of meditative practice. We do not wish to imply that the remaining symbol sets were created and used in the same way. On the contrary, it seems likely that some of the sets, for example the *bījas*, never served any useful function, their incorporation into the *maṇḍala* having been simply a consequence of their prior membership of the symbolic groups. We therefore interpret the *maṇḍala* as being in part a conscious creation, and in part a product of a mechanical process of growth and accretion. An extreme example of the latter process is the mechanical superimposing of the proto-*maṇḍalas*. This indicates a degenerate phase in the history of the *maṇḍala*, in which symbolic correspondences were disregarded, either out of ignorance or out of an exaggerated reverence for long-established arrangements.

A still more degenerate phase is represented in the 'visions' described in the *Tibetan Book of the Dead*. As mentioned in Chapter I, the first five of the visions allegedly seen by a dying person are based on the five *maṇḍala* cells. The series begins at the centre, then goes clockwise from the east (a common variant of the *pradakṣiṇa* movement). We quoted the description of the first vision (corresponding to the western cell), in which the dying person sees, among other things, 'a red light, the purified element of fire' (fire group) and 'Blessed Amitābha' who 'holds a lotus in his hand' (water group) and 'sits on a peacock throne' (air group). Not only are these associations of symbols self-contradictory; in addition the clockwise listing has yielded an inappropriate sequence of symbols within each set. For example, the dhyāni Buddhas appear in the sequence Vairocana, Akṣobhya, Ratnasambhava, Amitābha, Amoghasiddhi, which is symbolically meaningless. Thus mechanical conversion of the cruciform pattern into a list has obscured even further the underlying significance of the symbols.

The Cakra System

Compared with the *maṇḍala*, the *cakra* system is simple and straightforward, at least in its earliest, most basic form, as described in Chapter I. Being a linear series, rather than a two-

Table 21. The fivefold cakra *system according to Govinda.*

cakra	element	colour	shape	dhyāni Buddha	*bīja*
crown	space	blue		Vairocana	*Oṃ*
throat	air	green	hemi-sphere	Amitābha	*Hrīḥ*
heart	fire	red	cone	Akṣobhya	*Hūṃ*
navel	water	white	sphere	Ratnasambhava	*Traṃ*
basal	earth	yellow	cube	Amoghasiddhi	*Āḥ*

dimensional layout, the *cakra* system escaped most of the problems associated with superimposition. However, it did not escape them entirely, as is evident from Table 5 (page 105).[42] Here the dhyāni Buddhas and *bījas* agree with each other but together conflict with the elements. The arrangement of the elements is based on the traditional listing and an upward movement from navel to crown; that of the dhyāni Buddhas and *bījas* is based on the sequence in the root-*mantra, Oṃ Āḥ Hūṃ*, and a downward movement from crown to heart.

The contradictions persist in more complex versions of the *cakra* system such as the one summarized in Table 21.[43] Here a fifth *cakra* has been added, necessitating some rearrangement of the symbols. Each of the first four elements has been moved down one place, and the fifth element, space, has been added at the crown. Also *Āḥ* has been interchanged with *Hrīḥ*, as in the *maṇḍala*. The colours, elements and shapes agree with one another, as do also the dhyāni Buddhas and *bījas* (except for the confusion of *Āḥ* and *Hrīḥ*); however, between these two distributional categories there is disagreement in two of the *cakras*, navel and throat. This pattern of partial agreement is a largely fortuitous result of the haphazard process of development. It appears that when the fifth element, space, was added, the positions of the other four elements were adjusted to preserve the correct order of listing; but that when the fourth and fifth dhyāni Buddhas, Ratnasambhava and Amoghasiddhi, were added, they were simply assigned indiscriminately to the two vacant places.

This variability constitutes strong evidence that the *cakra* system is a purely man-made device. Yet in spite of such evidence the notion persists that the *cakras* are real 'psychic centres', which can be 'opened' if one applies the right meditative techniques. It is widely believed that the meditator should inwardly contemplate each *cakra* in turn, beginning at the basal *cakra* and proceeding upwards step by step to the crown.[44] The popularity of this belief seems to derive in large part from the superficial plausibility of the notion that 'spiritual progress' might come about through some kind of opening or activation of psychic nodes (plexuses?) along the spinal cord. The upward movement, away from body-parts concerned with sex and excretion, and towards the brain, suggests a progression away from worldliness and ignorance, and towards purity and enlightenment. It was perhaps such considerations that originally inspired the *siddhas* to adopt the human body as a frame in which to locate their symbols. There were partial precedents for such a system in various anthropomorphic diagrams of the universe, which equated different levels in the body with various hells and heavens (cf. page 90). To substitute meditative stages for the heavens in the upper half of the body would have been a small step. The whole development is yet another example of macrocosm-microcosm parallelism.

The *cakra* system and the *maṇḍala* represent two different attempts at providing an appropriately shaped frame or matrix to accommodate the various symbol sets. The existence of these two different frames — with their different and in many respects mutually contradictory collocations of symbols — indicates two partially independent lines of development. It may reflect a major geographical separation of monastic communities, or perhaps a sectarian split within the élite tradition. It may be that *siddhas* in one geographical region or school retained the linear arrangement of the symbols, and assimilated this to the human body, while *siddhas* in another adopted the cruciform arrangement. Again, it may be that one school traditionally used the colours and/or elements as the medium for symbolizing the practice while another traditionally used the dhyāni Buddhas. A subsequent mechanical combining of these different sub-traditions, by scribes or artists unaware of their significance, would then have produced the existing composite arrangments with all their inner contradictions. The details of these developments, as also of the early stages in the creation of the *maṇḍala* and *cakras* will perhaps be revealed by future historical research. Such details are, however, only marginally relevant to our present purpose, which is to discover the meaning of the symbolism.

The *maṇḍala* and the *cakra* system have been analysed using the methodology established in Chapter VI. On the basis of this analysis, and in the light of their traditional association with meditation, they have been interpreted as symbolic diagrams of the five-stage course of meditative practice — rather distorted diagrams, however, in which earlier simple layouts have been obscured through mechanical combining and rearrangement, by people who probably had little idea what the symbols were meant to represent.

Here let us reiterate a qualification made earlier. In assigning specific meanings to the symbols of the *maṇḍala* and *cakras* we do not exclude the possibility of other meanings in other contexts. For example, in concluding that the lotus which Amitābha holds, and which figures in the *mantra Oṃ Maṇi-padme Hūṃ Hrīḥ*, denotes the thought-stream, we do not wish to imply that this is *the* meaning of the lotus. The lotus clearly means different things in different Indian contexts. In the Tipiṭaka and other ancient texts it symbolizes purity; as a common motif on early Buddhist *stūpas*, it is said to denote Gotama's birth; and as an emblem of various Hindu deities, for example Sūrya and Viṣṇu, it appears to mean something else again. Even in the Tantric context the lotus has meanings other than the one we have assigned to it; for example, it often denotes the female organ (the *vajra* being the male). Our interpretation in terms of meditation applies only in a very specific context, and should be understood as qualified accordingly: 'As one of the set of five dhyāni Buddha emblems, the lotus was, for initiates in the secretive meditative tradition, a symbol for the thought-stream.' This special intentional meaning was additional to the many other meanings which the lotus had — and would later acquire — in other contexts. Similar qualifications apply for all the other symbols, and for the entire *maṇḍala*. Some of the ritual purposes to which *maṇḍalas* are put, in Balinese religion and elsewhere, indicate no connection with insight meditation; our interpretation applies only to the *maṇḍala* as it was understood by *siddhas* in the élite meditative tradition.

CHAPTER VIII

DOCTRINAL AND HISTORICAL IMPLICATIONS

In Chapter I we noted that Gotama's overt doctrine, as we find it in the Tipiṭaka, is incomplete and unclear at the very places where full, clear explanation seems most needed. The path of practice is adequately explained as far as the *jhānas* (right concentration); however, the insight practice that should follow mastery of the *jhānas* is rarely discussed, and such descriptions as *are* given are expressed in cryptic, seemingly symbolic language. Our analysis of the three knowledges and of the *maṇḍala* and *cakras* has, as anticipated, helped fill this gap. It has indicated that mastery of the *jhānas* should be followed by a course of introspective practice in three stages, which brings a progressively deepening insight into the nature of thought processes.

In Chapter II we sought to explain the silence of the Tipiṭaka on insight meditation, arguing that Gotama would have taught higher meditation only in private, refraining from dealing with it in any detail in his public discourses. In spite of this, one would expect that the course of insight meditation we have reconstructed, if it was indeed taught by Gotama in his private meetings with advanced students, would be somewhere echoed in his public teaching. Even if the course of insight meditation was never directly and overtly described, one would expect that knowledge of that course would facilitate understanding of the overt teaching. Our reconstruction of Gotama's course of insight practice could therefore be evaluated by testing its explanatory power when applied to the overt teaching, observing to what extent it illuminates obscure aspects of the Dharma as we find it in the Tipiṭaka. This we do in the first half of this chapter by applying our interpretation to some well-known Buddhist doctrines.

We also noted in Chapter II that while there are indirect indications of an esoteric tradition in early Buddhism, solid historical evidence is totally lacking. Our interpretation of symbolism both in the Tipiṭaka and in the *tantras* clearly has far-reaching implications in this connection. They will be discussed in the second half of this chapter.

Doctrinal Implications

Under this heading we shall examine the following important doctrines: the three grades of 'trainee' (*sekha*) that precede the attainment of arahantship, the three 'universal characteristics' (*tilakkhaṇa*), the four Noble Truths, and the Noble Path. Since all of these impinge also on other less central doctrines, examination of them in the light of our conclusions in earlier chapters will serve as a good test of the explanatory power of our interpretations.

The Three Trainees

In our analysis of the three knowledges, we examined the suggestion, advanced initially by Buddhadasa, that enlightenment is to be equated with the attainment of permanent awareness. Now a person who has attained enlightenment is said to have become an *arahant*, this being the highest grade in the Tipiṭaka classification according to spiritual status.[1] That classification may be represented schematically as in Table 22.

The first division is into two groups, *ariyas* and 'worldlings' (*puthujjana*). *Ariyas* differ from worldlings in having passed a certain critical transition point on the path, an attainment which guarantees them *nirvāṇa* within at most eight lifetimes. *Ariyas* are divided into trainees (*sekhas*) and non-trainees (*asekhas*). The latter are *arahants*, beings who, having replicated Gotama's experience, have attained full enlightenment and liberation; they will not be reborn in any realm after their physical death. Trainees, on the other hand, still have some way to go on the

Table 22. Classification of human beings according to spiritual status.

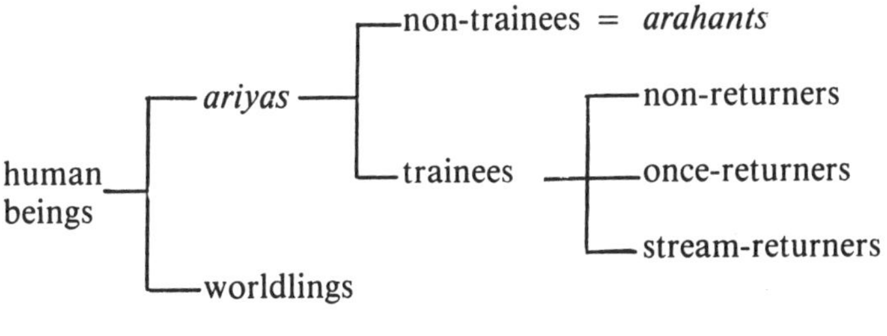

path. Three grades of trainee are recognized: the stream-enterer (*sotāpanna*), who will be reborn in the world of men no more than seven times before attaining *nirvāṇa*; the once-returner (*sakadāgāmi*), who will be reborn here only once more before attaining *nirvāṇa*; and the non-returner (*anāgāmi*), who will not be reborn here, but will go after death to one of the highest heavens and from there attain arahantship. The differences in the number of rebirths required by the three trainees are related to differences in the extent to which they have succeeded in throwing off the 'fetters' (*saṃyojana*), a set of 'unskilful states' broadly equivalent to the *āsavas*.[2]

Arahantship, as enlightenment, can be equated with the attainment of permanent awareness; the three trainees will now be examined in the light of that interpretation. We begin by reviewing certain features of the insight practice.

In the three-stage insight practice there is a progressive reduction in the number of images employed. In the first stage, retracing or 'recollection of former existences', an entire sequence of images is retraced to its source; the number of images is variable but would normally be of the order of half a dozen. In the second stage, observation of linking, the meditator goes back only one step to the preceding image, before allowing linking to take place again and repeating the process. In the third stage, awareness, retracing is dispensed with; the meditator observes thought as it arises, without interfering with it.

Table 23. Correlation between trainee grades and insight techniques.

non-returner	none	awareness	none
once-returner	one	observation of linking	one
stream-enterer	seven or fewer	retracing	indefinite
trainee grade	number of rebirths in this world	insight technique	number of images retraced
doctrine		practice	

There is a close parallelism between this series (number of images retraced) and that of the trainees (number of rebirths in this world) — see Table 23. Given our interpretation of 'birth' as referring to the arising of images, this close parallelism suggests that the three trainee grades correspond to the three stages in the insight practice; the number of times each trainee will be reborn in this world denotes the number of images retraced in each stage. The correspondence becomes complete if we postulate that the maximum number for the first stage was arbitrarily set at seven — a 'mystical' number in ancient India, as it was also in west Asia and Europe. Support for this postulate can be found in a statement made in the *Vimutti-magga* (*Path of Freedom*), a treatise on meditation similar to, but earlier than, the *Visuddhi-magga*. The *Vimutti-magga* says, in its discussion of recollection of former existences: 'The recollection of seven past lives is the best.'[3] This otherwise unintelligible statement makes good sense as soon as it is allowed that the reference is to retracing image sequences whose length is arbitrarily set at seven images. This interpretation of the trainees also accounts for the term 'stream-enterer' applied to the first of the three grades: the term is appropriate since the corresponding stage in the insight practice consists in tracing the thought-stream back to its source.

But in the texts the terms 'stream-enterer', 'once-returner' etc. are applied to *people*, often specific monks in the Sangha. We therefore infer that these terms denoted not the insight practices themselves but the meditators engaged in those practices. To say that this or that monk had become a stream-enterer was to say that he had advanced in his practice to the stage of retracing. More generally, an *ariya* was any disciple who was practising, or had already mastered, one or more of the three techniques in insight meditation.

That the three trainees can be interpreted in this way further strengthens the case for the non-literal interpretation of rebirth, as well as lending support to our overall interpretation of Buddhist symbolism, centring on the three insight techniques.

The Three Characteristics

One of the best-known Buddhist doctrines is that of the three 'universal characteristics' (*tilakkhaṇa*), the statement of which is as follows.

1. *Sabbe saṅkhārā aniccā.*
2. *Sabbe saṅkhārā dukkhā.*
3. *Sabbe dhammā anattā.*[4]

This formula can be translated provisionally as,

1. All compounded things are transient.
2. All compounded things are suffering.
3. All things are devoid of selfhood.

The three characteristics, transience, suffering, and non-selfhood, are normally overlooked by ordinary beings, but become apparent to the monk in his progress towards enlightenment, indeed recognition of them is essential to the attainment of enlightenment. The gaining of insight into the three characteristics is, nominally at least, the goal of some widely-practised meditation techniques, including Burmese *vipassanā*. The traditional order of listing the three — *anicca, dukkha, anattā* — is invariable, and although it is nowhere clearly stated that this represents the order in which they will be perceived in practice, most meditators take for granted that it does. For the purposes of this discussion it is convenient to examine the three in the reverse of the traditional order.

The third characteristic, *anattā* (non-selfhood) is attributed to 'all *dhammas*'. Now the Pali term *dhamma* has many meanings; depending on context it may signify 'thing', 'phenomenon', 'mental state', 'mental object', 'law', or — the most familiar meaning — 'the Buddha's teaching' (Sanskrit *Dharma*).[5] However, it is to be expected that the relevant meaning of *dhamma* in the present context is the one that the word has as a specialized term in Buddhist psychology. The significance of *dhamma* in that context becomes clear when one examines textual accounts of the sense-organs and their objects. Six sense-organs are recognized, the usual five — eye, ear, nose, tongue, and body — and as sixth

Table 24. The six sense-organs and their objects.

Organ	Object
eye	forms
ear	sounds
nose	odours
tongue	tastes
body	contacts
mind	*dhammas*

mano, 'mind'. The objects sensed with these organs are stated to be as in Table 24.[6] In this usage *dhamma* is usually translated 'mental object'[7] — a safe rendering since it yields a tautology: 'The objects sensed with the mind are mental objects.' But since it is stated that *dhammas* are to the mind as forms are to the eye or sounds to the ear, one can conclude that the term *dhamma* in this particular context has the meaning 'mental image'. (We use 'image' here in the broad sense preferred in modern western psychology, to denote not only visual images but also their counterparts in the other modalities — auditory, olfactory, etc. The term thus includes mental verbalizing.)

This is an important conclusion. Our account of insight meditation contained frequent references to images — naturally, since thought, whose true nature the practice is designed to reveal, is composed of images. The central importance of images in the insight practice is reflected in the frequency of symbolic references to images in the Tipiṭaka; as we have interpreted them, the terms, 'being', 'lifetime', 'birth', and 'death' all refer indirectly to images or related mental phenomena. It would therefore be surprising if images were never mentioned explicitly in the overt doctrine.

In our earlier discussion we did mention, on two occasions, a Pali term with the meaning 'image', namely *nimitta*. But the first occurrence of this term was rather specialized, the reference being to the peculiar (usually visual) images that may develop in the advanced stages of concentration practice; and the second was from the historically late *Abhidhammattha-saṅgaha* account of the mechanism of rebirth (pp. 44, 87). In the Sutta-piṭaka *nimitta* appears not to occur with the simple meaning 'image'. It is now apparent that the standard Pali term for 'image' is *dhamma*. As noted above, *dhamma* also has other meanings; however, 'image' does often prove to be the appropriate translation.

To illustrate we may consider briefly an early reference to *dhammas* in Gotama's description of events on the day preceding his enlightenment (quoted in Chapter I). There Gotama states that, having reflected on the futility of the ascetic practices he had been engaged in, he suddenly realized what he *ought* to be practising: just as a cowherd may suddenly recall that he ought to be keeping watch over his cows, so Gotama realized that he ought to be keeping watch over his *dhammas*.[8] Equating *dhammas* with mental images renders this statement intelligible in itself and consistent with the remainder of the account of the enlightenment, which — as we have interpreted it — describes a course of practice based on systematic examination of the nature of images.

Applying this meaning of *dhamma* to the statement of the third characteristic, *Sabbe dhammā anattā*, yields: 'All images are devoid of self.' This is precisely the central insight of awareness: 'There are only the images; there is no "I", no "thinker" behind them.' We therefore conclude that the third characteristic is perceived in the third and final stage of the insight practice — or, in the language of the Tipiṭaka, in the third knowledge.

This identification of *anattā* with the central insight of awareness does not rule out the possibility that Gotama may have meant, as many Buddhists assume he did, to attribute non-selfhood to all things in the universe. For Gotama that all-inclusive characterization would have followed automatically, either through application of the principle of macrocosm-microcosm parallelism or by simple extrapolation. What we suggest, however, is that the basis for such a generalization would have been the realization of non-selfhood in the most difficult case of all, that of 'the meditator' and 'his own mind'.

The second characteristic is *dukkha* (suffering). It is attributed to *sabbe saṅkhārā*, 'all compounded things', and is unique among the three characteristics in that it not only is perceived in the course of insight practice but also is totally eliminated in the final attainment, as discussed below under the four Noble Truths.

The term *dukkha* is usually translated 'suffering', less often 'anguish', 'unsatisfactoriness', or 'ill'.[9] Gotama explains it as referring to birth, ageing, death, grief, lamentation, bodily pain, mental suffering, despair, and 'not getting what is wished for'.[10] *Dukkha* therefore covers both physical and mental suffering. However, it is clear that in attaining liberation from *dukkha* Gotama had *not* attained liberation from physical pain in his current life, for the texts often mention that in his old age he experienced pains of various kinds, including backaches severe enough to interfere with his teaching activities.[11] It appears, then, that in speaking of the suffering of birth, ageing, and death, Gotama was referring to *future* existences: he would never again experience those sufferings because, unlike all unenlightened beings, he would not be reborn after his present life was ended. On the other hand, in speaking of his liberation from *mental* suffering, Gotama clearly *was* referring to his present existence; he *had* freed himself from grief, lamentation, and so on.

But although the term *dukkha* as used in the texts covers both physical pain and mental distress, these two clearly do not exhaust its range of meaning. Even prolonged happiness is said to be permeated with *dukkha*, a fact which seems to justify 'unsatisfactoriness' as the best translation. Thus *dukkha* at the most subtle level appears to refer to a normally unperceived unsatisfactory quality present even in blissful states of consciousness, a quality that becomes clearly apparent only through insight meditation.

We shall approach the problem of identifying this subtle microcosmic *dukkha* by applying our non-literal interpretations to its macrocosmic counterpart, that is to *dukkha* as an attribute of the ever-repeated process of death and rebirth in *saṃsāra*. We have identified *saṃsāra* with the thought-stream, and the process of death and rebirth determined by *karma* with the process of linking between images determined by previous affective involvement. The meditative practice that reveals the mechanism of that process is the technique we have called observation of linking — in macrocosmic terms 'knowledge of the death and rebirth of beings according to their *karmas*' (the second knowledge). The parallelism indicates that the microcosmic *dukkha* is a characteristic of the process whereby linking between images is determined by previous affective involvement. It is the 'unsatisfactory' nature of this process, as perceived by the meditator practising observation of linking, that is to be identified as the subtle, hidden form of *dukkha*, the kind of *dukkha* that is said to pervade even happy mental states.

The characteristic *dukkha* is attributed to 'all *saṅkhāras*'. The Pali word *saṅkhāra* (plural *saṅkhārā*) is most literally translated 'compounded thing' or 'compound'. However, as used in the Tipiṭaka it has a wide range of derived meanings.[12] As in the case of *dhamma*, the meaning of *saṅkhāra* most likely to be applicable in the present context is the one that the term has in Buddhist psychology, where it denotes the fourth of the five *khandhas*. The *khandhas* (Sanskrit *skandha*) are the 'aggregates' or components into which the being or person is analysed; the fourth of them, *saṅkhārā*, is fairly consistently interpreted by scholars as referring either to the totality of affective states or to the resulting habitual tendencies.[13] In either case the dictum 'All *saṅkhāras* are *dukkha*' amounts to a statement of the insight attained in the practice of observation of linking: 'Mental processes involving affective states and their subsequent determining effects have an inherently unsatisfactory quality.'

Now the term *saṅkhāra* is clearly to be equated with *āsava* (p. 88), and recognition of this reveals the following striking correlation. Whereas the first and second characteristics are attributed to all *saṅkhāras*, the third, *anattā*, is attributed to all *dhammas*; and this transition from *saṅkhāras* to *dhammas* correlates with the destruction of the *āsavas* in the third knowledge — in our terminology, with the elimination of affective states in the third stage of the insight practice. The second and third characteristics thus correlate closely with the insights attained in the second and third stages of the insight practice, observation of linking and awareness.

The one remaining characteristic, *anicca*, transience and insubstantiality, is commonly understood by Buddhists as referring to the rather obvious impermanence of physical things, in particular the human body, and the textual accounts of it tend to support that view. At the same time, given the predominantly mentalistic bias in Gotama's teaching, it seems likely that *anicca* was meant to refer more specifically to the transience of mental phenomena.[14] Now the meditative practice which above all others reveals the transience of mental phenomena is retracing. Through retracing the meditator realizes, to his astonishment, how rapidly image sequences move, and how insubstantial the component images are. He comes to see thought as resembling an ever-flowing stream. Thus in so far as *anicca* refers to the normally hidden processes of thought, the first of the three characteristics is perceived in the first of the three knowledges, 'recollection of former existences'. It should be noted, however, that the same conclusion follows if *anicca* is taken as having a wider reference, including the visible physical world, one's immensely long journey through *saṃsāra*, and even the beginningless evolution of the universe, because the first knowledge, as described by Gotama, takes in 'a hundred, . . . a thousand, . . . a hundred thousand births, and many an eon of integration and many an eon of disintegration [of the universe] . . .' The microcosmic interpretation does not rule out the macrocosmic interpretation.

The above analysis has demonstrated that the three characteristics correspond to the insights attained in the last three stages of the meditative practice as shown in Table 25. We conclude that the three characteristics are in fact the insights attained in the last three stages of the course of meditative practice.

It has now been shown that two important doctrinal sets, the three characteristics and the three trainees, yield to interpretation in terms of the three-stage course of introspective practice in much the same way as do more explicitly symbolic sets such as the three knowledges. In all of these sets the distinction between macrocosm and microcosm is blurred, terms from the two realms

Table 25. Correlation between characteristics and insight techniques.

dhammas	*anattā*	awareness	images	There is no 'thinker', no 'I'.
saṅkhāras	*dukkha*	observation of linking	images plus involvement	Linking is determined by earlier involvement.
saṅkhāras	*anicca*	retracing	images plus involvement	Thought is streamlike; images are transient.
object	characteristic	technique	object	insight
doctrine		practice		

being freely mixed or used with double reference. This is in keeping with the suggestion made in Chapter V that Gotama did not regard his references to rebirth, *saṃsāra*, etc. as symbolic; he perceived the relationship between macrocosm and microcosm not as mere symbolic correspondence but as identity. This blurring of the distinction between macrocosm and microcosm results in a corresponding blurring of the distinction between the two categories that we have called 'symbolic language' and 'overt doctrine'. We have discussed the three knowledges under the former heading, and the three characteristics under the latter. But in retrospect it can be seen that the difference is only one of degree; in the knowledges the terminology is predominantly macrocosmic, in the characteristics it is predominantly microcosmic. For Gotama there was no distinction.

It may appear superficially that the teaching is needlessly repetitious, stating the same three stages several times over. Closer examination reveals, however, that the various triads are not quite identical. The knowledges are the actual meditative techniques, the characteristics are the insights thereby attained, and the trainees are the people practising those techniques and attaining those insights.

On the other hand it *would* be accurate to describe the presentation as unduly cryptic. Why were several quite dissimilar terminologies used for sets of entities so closely related? And why were the relationships among those sets — here clarified only after lengthy analysis — not spelled out in simple language? The answer, we suggest, is that such details were explained only in private, to those advanced meditators who were actually practising the techniques in question. In the overt teaching only the lists of terms were given, with minimal supporting information provided in stereotyped formulae. Explanation in terms of actual meditative practices and mental processes was reserved for members of the meditative élite.

The Four Noble Truths

The totality of Gotama's teaching is summed up in his four Noble Truths concerning the arising and the cessation of *dukkha*:

1. the truth of *dukkha*,
2. the truth of the arising of *dukkha* — through *taṇhā* (desire),
3. the truth of the cessation of *dukkha* — through the cessation of *taṇhā*,
4. the truth of the way to the cessation of *dukkha* — that is, the Noble Eightfold Path.[15]

In the texts the first and second Truths, dealing with *dukkha* and its arising, are expounded in terms of the chain of conditioned arising (*paṭicca-samuppāda*), the five aggregates (*khandhas*), and other related doctrines. This aspect of Gotama's teaching has received relatively little attention in this book; it was discussed briefly in the section on *karma* and the second of the three knowledges. The third and fourth Truths, dealing with the attaining of liberation from *dukkha*, are expounded in the texts in terms of the Noble Path and many other essentially similar lists of stages such as the Footprints of a Buddha. It is on this aspect of Gotama's teaching, and in particular on the advanced stages of the Path, that we have concentrated in this book, our objective being to discover what, in practical terms, the aspirant should actually do to attain the promised goal. Now, however, we shall seek to place the Path in its broader traditional context by examining the complete set of four Noble Truths.

The significance of the central notion of *dukkha* at the microcosmic level has already been discussed. *Dukkha* is an inherently unsatisfactory quality characterizing all thought-processes in which affective states (*saṅkhāras*) are operative. If one reacts to a sense-object with some emotion such as desire or anger, the subsequent arising of images depicting that object is more frequent than if one had not so reacted; and those images carry an emotive charge reflecting the quality of the original emotional reaction. This emotive charge has the following two principal effects. (1) It leads to a repetition of the emotional reaction: one reacts with desire, hatred, etc. to the content of the image just as one did to the original sense-object, thus reinforcing the emotive charge and ensuring that the image will arise even more frequently in the future, with similar results. (2) It determines the direction of the linking process, ensuring that the next image in the sequence is one that focuses even more directly on the desired or hated object, or on other similar or related objects. As a result of these two effects, the content of the thought-stream is very largely determined by prior emotional involvement in primary sensations and images. Rarely does it seem to be guided by choice on the part of 'the thinker'.

The inherent unsatisfactoriness of this situation (*dukkha*) is not normally noticed. However, through insight meditation the mechanism of the process becomes apparent. In the practice of observation of linking the role of affective involvement in determining linking is clearly seen; and in the practice of awareness affective involvement of every kind is eliminated for as long as the awareness is maintained.

This understanding of *dukkha* will now be applied to the four Noble Truths. In his explanation of the Truths Gotama declares that the underlying cause of *dukkha* is *taṇhā*,[16] and that it is through eradicating *taṇhā* that liberation from *dukkha* can be achieved.[17] *Taṇhā*, literally 'thirst', is usually translated 'desire' or 'craving'. The texts explain it as being of three kinds: *kāma-taṇhā, bhava-taṇhā*, and *vibhava-taṇhā*.[18] The terms *kāma* and *bhava* were encountered earlier in the first and second of the three *āsavas*; we identified them as denoting respectively sense objects and the thought-stream. Pursuing that interpretation, and taking it that *taṇhā*, like *āsava*, covers *all* affective states, we conclude that the first and second types of *taṇhā* are affective involvement in sense objects (*kāma-taṇhā*) and in the thought-stream (*bhava-taṇhā*). It follows that *vibhava-taṇhā*, literally 'thirst for non-becoming', is affective involvment having as its object image-free states, such as those attained in *jhāna* practice. (Many meditators are strongly attached to the *jhānas*, to the detriment of their further meditative progress.)

The three forms of *taṇhā* constitute one of many sets of 'unskilful states' enumerated in the texts. Others are the *āsavas*: *kāma, bhava, avijjā* (sensuality, 'becoming', ignorance); the three *akusala-mūlas* (unskilful roots): *lobha* (or *rāga*), *dosa, moha* (desire, aversion, delusion); the five *nīvaraṇas* (hindrances): *kāmacchanda, vyāpāda, . . . vicikicchā* (sensuality, ill-will, . . . doubt); and the seven (or ten) *saṃyojanas* (fetters): *kāmacchanda, vyāpāda, . . . avijjā* (sensuality, ill-will, . . . ignorance).[19] In discussing the *āsavas* in Chapter V we recognized two categories: (1) 'ignorance' (*avijjā*) and (2) affective states (*kāma, bhava*). These same two categories are clearly recognizable in the sets listed above; for example, in the *akusala-mūlas* or unskilful roots, *moha* represents (1) ignorance, while *lobha* and *dosa* represent (2) affective states. In some cases a representative of the 'ignorance' category is not actually named; however, its presence is implied since, as noted in Chapter IV, affective involvement is conditional on lack of insight.[20]

Where the above sets of terms differ is in their manner of subdividing the second category, affective states. In the *āsavas* and *taṇhā* the classification is according to the object of the affective states: sense objects, the thought-stream, (and, in the case of *taṇhā*, the image-free condition of the *jhānas*). In the unskilful roots, the hindrances, and the fetters, the classification is according to the nature of the affective state itself: there are two basic sub-categories, a 'positive' (desire, sensuality) and a 'negative' (aversion, ill-will). Some further, less fundamental divisions are also inconsistently recognized, indicating that the lists have in some cases grown with the passage of time. For example, there is sometimes a fourth *āsava, diṭṭhi* (false view),[21] and the list of fetters is particularly variable. Such differences do not, however, invalidate the conclusion that all the above sets are essentially identical.

For our present purpose the important point is that *taṇhā* may be equated with the *āsavas*. It follows that Gotama's explanation of the third Noble Truth parallels closely his description of the third knowledge:

Third Truth: Liberation from *dukkha* is attained through eradiction of *taṇhā*.

Third Knowledge: Liberation from *saṃsāra* is attained through destruction of the *āsavas*.

This parallelism is made explicit in Gotama's account of how he himself attained the third knowledge and perceived the Noble Truths:

> Then . . . I directed my mind to the knowledge of the destruction of the *āsavas*. I understood as it really is: This is *dukkha*, . . . this is the arising of *dukkha*, . . . this is the cessation of *dukkha*, . . . this is the

> course leading to the cessation of *dukkha*. I understood as it really is: These are the *āsavas*, . . . this is the arising of the *āsavas*, . . . this is the cessation of the *āsavas*, . . . this is the course leading to the cessation of the *āsavas*.[22]

Here Gotama states the four-membered formula twice: first in terms of *dukkha*, and then in terms of the *āsavas*, that is, *taṇhā*.

We have interpreted the *āsavas*, and thereby also *taṇhā*, as covering all affective states, that is, emotional involvement both in primary sensations and in the contents of the thought-stream. Thus liberation from *dukkha* is attained through the elimination of all emotional involvement, that is, through the attainment of permanent awareness, or enlightenment.[23] The quality *dukkha*, perceived in the second insight practice (observation of linking), is eliminated in the third (awareness), along with the *taṇhā/āsavas/saṅkhāras* that immediately condition it.

In summary, then, the four Noble Truths are interpreted as follows.

1st Truth: The mechanism of thought processes is such that, once seen, it is bound to be recognized as inherently unsatisfactory in nature. Despite appearances to the contrary, the direction taken by thought sequences is for the most part determined not by 'the thinker' but by a blindly operating causal mechanism.

2nd Truth: The source of this unsatisfactory situation is affective states, that is emotional involvement, however slight, in sense objects and, more particularly, in the images that subsequently represent them. And this occurs because of a deep-seated delusion regarding the nature of the process, in particular a failure to see images *as images*.

3rd Truth: This situation can be changed; the unsatisfactory quality can be eliminated by eliminating the emotional involvement. And this can only really be achieved by eliminating the underlying delusion, in particular by coming to see images in their true nature.

4th Truth: The way to attain this is by following the 'Noble Tenfold Path', the course of practice summarized under the headings of morality, concentration, and insight, and culminating in permanent awareness into the nature of thought processes.

The Noble Path

We noted in Chapter I that the Noble Eightfold Path, stopping short at right concentration (*sammā samādhi*), appears to be incomplete, while the less well-known Tenfold Path, with its two extra stages right insight and right liberation (*sammā ñāṇa, sammā vimutti*), appears to cover the full course of Buddhist practice. We also cited evidence indicating that right insight is identical with the three knowledges. The case has now been presented for identifying the three knowledges with the three-stage practice described in Chapter IV. This, then, is our answer to the principal question raised in Chapter I: The insight meditation practice (*vipassanā*) that should follow the perfecting of the *jhānas* (*samatha*) is in fact the series of three introspective techniques: (1) retracing, (2) observation of linking, (3) awareness. The gap between right concentration and right liberation has thus been bridged, and we are now in a position to set out the Noble Tenfold Path in full. In preparation for this, however, we first look again at the *Eight*fold Path and at the problems it has posed for interpreters of Buddhist doctrine.[24]

Most Buddhists take for granted that the Eightfold Path is a complete summary of Gotama's course of practice leading to enlightenment and liberation. They are thus faced with the problem of finding in this eightfold path a stage or stages corresponding to the insight practice (*vipassanā*) that should follow concentration. This problem has been recognized since earliest times. The first recorded reference to it is in a *sutta* called the *Cūḷa-Vedalla*, the Lesser Miscellany.[25] There the problem is expressed in terms of a teaching, often mentioned in the texts, that the course of training has three major divisions called Dharma-groups or trainings (*dhammakkhandha, sikkhā*), namely *sīla, samādhi*, and *paññā* — morality, concentration, and insight or wisdom. In the *sutta* a nun named Dhammadinnā is asked by a layman how the three Dharma-groups are related to the Noble Eightfold Path. She replies that the two sets correspond as in Table 26. Thus Dhammadinnā equates *paññā* with the first two stages of the path, right view and right aspiration.

This explanation has been widely accepted by Buddhists ever since. It is not entirely implausible since right view is defined as 'knowledge about the four Noble Truths';[26] however, it does necessitate a serious distortion of the Path sequence: the first two stages have to be transferred to the end of the series. This problem is usually explained away with the statement that the traditional

Table 26. Correspondences between Dharma-group and Eightfold Path according to Dhammadinnā.

Dharma-groups	Eightfold Path
1. *sīla*	3. right speech 4. right action 5. right livelihood
2. *samādhi*	6. right effort 7. right mindfulness 8. right concentration
3. *paññā*	1. right view 2. right aspiration

order of listing the stages of the Path has no particular significance, being not necessarily the order in which those stages will be developed in practice. But from the Tipiṭaka it is clear that the order of listing the stages *is* significant, and *does* represent the practical sequence. The most direct statement of this is a paragraph in the *Mahācattārīsaka-sutta*, which says:

> As to this, monks, right view comes first. And how, monks, does right view come first? From right view proceeds right aspiration, from right aspiration proceeds right speech, . . . from right concentration proceeds right insight, from right insight proceeds right liberation.[27]

This is not to say that earlier stages would be abandoned as later ones are taken up; on the contrary, the same *sutta* makes clear that as far as right concentration (but not beyond) the Path series is cumulative:

> And what, monks, is noble right concentration with its causal associations and accompaniments? It is this: right view, right aspiration, right speech, . . . right mindfulness. Whatever mental one-pointedness, monks, is accompanied by these seven, this is called noble right concentration with its causal associations and accompaniments.[28]

Clearly, then, the Path is both sequential and cumulative, and Dhammadinnā's explanation, entailing as it does modification of the traditional Path sequence, is unsatisfactory.

From our interpretation of Buddhist practice it is evident that the root of the problem lies in the incompleteness of the eightfold path. When one considers the tenfold path rather than the eightfold, it becomes clear that the *paññā* group ought to be equated instead with the ninth stage, right insight (*sammā ñāṇa*). Support for this explanation is provided by the existence of a less common alternative set of *four* Dharma-groups, in which *sīla, samādhi,* and *paññā* are followed by *vimutti* (liberation).[29] This set of four clearly corresponds with the Tenfold Path as shown in Table 27.[30]

Right view (which Dhammadinnā equates with *paññā*) and right insight (which we suggest *ought* to be equated with *paññā*) are both said to entail knowledge of the four Noble Truths. However, the kind of knowing involved is very different in the two cases. The knowledge which constitutes right view is

Table 27. Proposed correspondences between Dharma-groups and Tenfold Path.

Dharma-groups	Tenfold Path
	1. right view
	2. right aspiration
1. *sīla*	3. right speech 4. right action 5. right livelihood
2. *samādhi*	6. right effort 7. right mindfulness 8. right concentration
3. *paññā*	9. right insight
4. *vimutti*	10. right liberation

described simply as 'knowledge about *dukkha*, knowledge about the arising of *dukkha*, . . .'; the knowledge which constitutes right insight, that is which comes with the destruction of the *āsavas*, is described thus: 'He knows as it really is: "This is *dukkha*"; he knows as it really is: "This is the arising of *dukkha*"; . . .'[31] This second description indicates a penetrating and direct realization, very different from the mere 'knowing about' represented by right view. This suggests that right view is merely an intellectual understanding of the Truths sufficient to motivate a beginner to set out on the Path, while right insight (as perfected in the third of the three knowledges) is the direct inner realization of the Truths which brings liberation.

That this is in fact the nature of the distinction between right view and right insight becomes clear when the Path is compared with some other extant lists of the stages to be passed through by the Buddhist aspirant. An example is the list of 'footprints' discussed in Chapter I.[32] That list begins with the layman hearing a Buddha teach the Dharma, coming to have faith in it, and resolving to embark on the course of practice; it then continues with a series of stages perfectly paralleling those of the Path, as shown in Table 28.[33] This indicates that in the footprint series the counterpart of right view is hearing a Buddha teach the Dharma, that is, acquiring a preliminary intellectual understanding of the teaching; while the counterpart of right aspiration is the developing of faith in the teaching and resolving to put it into practice.

Having thus clarified the first two stages of the Path, we now go on to discuss the remaining eight stages. Stages 3, 4, and 5, right speech, action, and livelihood, together constitute the *sīla* section of the Path. They are elaborated in the texts in various lists of precepts, ranging from the basic five abstentions (*pañcasīla*) adopted by all Buddhists, to the 227 or more very detailed rules binding on monks. Most lay people do not progress beyond this point on the Path. For them the basic precepts of right speech, action, and livelihood provide an adequate moral code for daily living, founded on the doctrine of *karma*, and promising that good behaviour in the present life will be rewarded in the next or some subsequent life, as well as making for happiness here and now.[34]

For more committed followers, especially those who take ordination in the Sangha, practice of this section of the Path provides the basis in moral discipline (*sīla*) that is essential for the successful practice of mental discipline (*samādhi*). Within the meditative context, and quite apart from more general moral

Table 28. Correspondences between Tenfold Path and Footprints of a Buddha.

Tenfold Path	Footprints of a Buddha
1. right view 2. right aspiration	1. hearing Dharma, gaining faith, and resolving to practise
3. right speech 4. right action 5. right livelihood	2. adopting the moral precepts
6. right effort	3. guarding the 'sense-doors'
7. right mindfulness	4. mindfulness
8. right concentration	5. *jhāna* 1 6. *jhāna* 2 7. *jhāna* 3 8. *jhāna* 4
9. right insight	9. recollection of former existences 10. seeing death and rebirth of beings 11. destruction of the *āsavas*
10. right liberation	12. liberation

considerations, the rationale for adopting the precepts is that this is conducive to good meditation. For example, any violent action or word, being a manifestation of a violent emotional state, inevitably has mental repercussions that make meditation the more difficult. On the other hand, abstaining from violence, though it may require a temporary suppression of emotions, is an example of right effort (Stage 6, to follow), and facilitates progress in meditation.[35] And even such minor disciplines as personal cleanliness and neatness conduce to good meditation by perceptibly reducing mental distraction. As Krishnamurṭi puts it, 'How can you keep your mind tidy if you can't even keep your room tidy?'[36]

Stage 6, right effort (*sammā vāyāma*) is defined as the practice of the four exertions (*padhāna*): (i) preventing the arising of unarisen unskilful mental states, (ii) eliminating already arisen unskilful states, (iii) encouraging the arising of unarisen skilful states, and (iv) consolidating already arisen skilful states.[37] The same practice is present in the footprint series under the more colourful title 'guarding the sense-doors'. The sense-doors are the five physical senses and the mind (*mano*), it being recognized that the arising of affective states occurs in response to sense stimuli and mental images.[38] The eliminating of affective states that takes place in the practice of right effort is achieved through simple suppression; no insight is involved. This practice is therefore very different from destruction of the *āsavas*, which entails the cessation of all affective states through eliminating the ignorance (*avijjā*) which is their root cause. Thus of the two subdivisions within the *āsava* category, (1) ignorance and (2) affective states, only the second is eliminated by right effort. The first, ignorance, remains.

On the positive side, right effort consists in the practice of the *brahma-vihāras*, which consists in cultivating attitudes of loving-kindness, compassion, sympathetic joy, and equanimity (*mettā, karuṇā, muditā, upekkhā*).[39] Of these four the highest is *upekkhā*, a condition of detachment in which all affective states have ceased. (This condition becomes progressively better established in Stages 7, 8, and 9.) Thus the overall aim of right effort is temporary elimination of affective states.

Stage 7, right mindfulness (*sammā sati*), is seen by many Buddhists as the most important stage of the entire Path. Many consider that the textual account of right mindfulness contains all that the meditator needs to know for the practice of insight meditation — implying that the lack of a stage right insight in the Eightfold Plan is no defect.[40] The nature of right mindfulness will now be examined in the light of this claim. Four categories of mindfulness are recognized: mindfulness of the body, of feelings, of *citta* (mind?), and of *dhammas*. As noted in Chapter IV, the first two of these would be applicable in developing the *jhānas*: the basic practice for attaining the *jhānas* is mindfulness of the breathing, a form of mindfulness of the body; and the development of the higher *rūpa-jhānas* entails the arising and subsequent cessation of *sukha*, pleasant bodily feeling. (See Stage 8, below.) Mindfulness of the body would also be effective in overcoming the unskilful state of lust; it includes contemplation of the body as composed of revolting substances, as analysable into four elements, and as subject to decay — all of which are conducive to an attitude of detachment (*upekkhā*).

The remaining two categories, mindfulness of *citta* and of *dhammas*, sound superficially as if they could yield insight into the nature of the mind, especially in view of our demonstration that *dhamma* frequently means 'image'; however, closer examination indicates otherwise. Mindfulness of *citta* entails (1) observing the presence or absence of the three 'unskilful roots', desire, aversion, and delusion (*rāga, dosa, moha*), noted earlier as one of the many sets of 'unskilful states' equivalent to the *āsavas*; and (2) observing whether or not the mind is attentive, 'grown great', 'supreme', concentrated, and — finally — liberated.[41] The practice of simply observing the presence or absence of these unskilful and skilful states amounts to a monitoring of one's meditative progress. This facilitates the practice of Stage 6, right effort, by alerting the meditator to the presence of states that have to be developed or eliminated. It would also clearly be a valuable adjunct to insight practice; however, it would not constitute an insight practice in its own right. For example, noting whether or not delusion is present would be useful as a measure of progress in the application of any practice aimed at overcoming delusion; but it would be only an *adjunct* to such a practice.

Mindfulness of *dhammas* is divided into five sections. Two of these consist again in observing the presence or absence of unskilful states, namely (i) the 'hindrances' (*nīvaraṇa*) and (ii) the 'fetters' (*saṃyojana*) as they arise in association with the six 'sense-doors'.[42] Both of these sets are, as noted earlier, equivalent to the 'unskilful roots' and the *āsavas*, and therefore duplicate the practice (1) under mindfulness of *citta*. A third practice consists in observing the presence or absence of the 'factors of enlightenment'. These are seven factors broadly equivalent to the skilful qualities listed under (2) in mindfulness of *citta*;[43] the practice of observing their presence or absence thus duplicates the practice (2), being again a monitoring of meditative progress.

A further practice covered by mindfulness of *dhammas* entails observing the arising and ceasing of the five *khandhas*, that is, the body, feelings, *saññā* (perceptions?), *saṅkhāras* (affective states), and *viññāṇa* (consciousness?).[44] Here again there is much duplication: body and feelings are included under the first two categories of mindfulness, and, as just noted, affective states (skilful and unskilful) are already represented several times over. The remaining two *khandhas, saññā* and *viññāṇa*, are difficult to distinguish and considerable doubt exists regarding their actual psychological identities. This being the case, it could be that mindfulness of their arising and ceasing constitutes a form of insight practice.

The fifth and last practice included under mindfulness of *dhammas* is mindfulness of the four Noble Truths. This is described as follows:

> And again, monks, a monk remains contemplating *dhammas* in *dhammas* from the point of view of the four Noble Truths. And how, monks, does a monk remain contemplating *dhammas* in *dhammas* from the point of view of the four Noble Truths? Herein, monks, a monk knows as it really is: 'This is *dukkha*'; he knows as it really is: 'This is the arising of *dukkha*'; he knows as it really is: 'This is the cessation of *dukkha*'; he knows as it really is: 'This is the Path leading to the cessation of *dukkha*'.[45]

This description is identical with that contained in the account of the third knowledge. The latter begins with a brief statement that the monk directs his mind to the destruction of the *āsavas*, then gives the above description of how the monk perceives the four Noble Truths, and concludes with an exactly parallel description in which the word *dukkha* is replaced by *āsavas*.[46] We have noted that this parallelism in the account of the third knowledge reaffirms the intimate connection between the cessation of *dukkha* and the cessation of the *āsavas*: the two occur together; each implies the other. It follows that the description of how the monk practises mindfulness of the four Noble Truths is in fact a description of destruction of the *āsavas*, that is, the third knowledge. This being the case, mindfulness of the four Noble Truths is to be recognized as an insight practice, indeed as the most advanced of insight practices.

This appears to justify the view often expressed by interpreters of the Path that right mindfulness represents *vipassanā* (insight meditation), which it is recognized should follow the perfecting of *samatha* (tranquillity meditation, concentration). For adherents of this view the fact that right mindfulness comes before right concentration rather than after it in the traditional listing of the Path stages poses no problem; because, as we have seen, it has long been held — even since Dhammadinnā's attempt to reconcile the Path with the three Dharma-groups — that the traditional Path sequence is without significance and does not represent the practical sequence.

Our examination of the practices covered by mindfulness of *citta* and mindfulness of *dhammas* has shown that mindfulness of the *khandhas* could, in part, be construed as an insight practice, and that mindfulness of the four Noble Truths definitely *is* an insight practice. But closer examination of the texts introduces another important factor into the discussion. Comparison of the Pali account of mindfulness with its counterpart in the Chinese Tripiṭaka (a useful means of checking the authenticity of doubtful sections of text) reveals close agreement throughout, except in one respect: in the Chinese version, counterparts for the sections on the *khandhas* and the four Noble Truths are lacking.[47] This indicates that those two sections probably did not form part of Gotama's exposition of mindfulness, but were later additions made within the Pali (Theravāda) tradition. In other words, precisely those sections of the account of mindfulness which appear to describe insight practices are late interpolations; hence right mindfulness can *not* be interpreted as representing *vipassanā*.

The fact that sections describing insight practices were added to the earlier account of mindfulness suggests an attempt by the custodians of the Pali texts to compensate for the incompleteness of the Eightfold Path. Whereas Dhammadinnā attempted to compensate for the lack of a ninth stage, right insight, by reinterpreting the first stage, right view, other unknown members of the Sangha sought to achieve the same effect by upgrading the seventh stage, right mindfulness.

We have seen that mindfulness is essentially a monitoring of meditative progress. As such it plays an important role throughout the second half of the Tenfold Path. Through the practice of mindfulness the meditator alerts himself to the presence of affective states (developed or suppressed through right effort), of feelings (developed in the first three *jhānas* and then eliminated in the fourth), and of delusion (progressively eliminated in right insight). In addition, mindfulness of the body is instrumental in the initial attaining of the *rūpa jhānas*, and indeed even in the practice of the *sīlas*. The recognition of two distinct categories, mindfulness of *citta* and mindfulness of *dhammas*, is puzzling in view of their observed broad overlap. But in any case it is apparent that mindfulness of *dhammas*, at least as described in the texts, does not refer to some kind of insight practice based on mental images.

Stage 8, right concentration (*sammā samādhi*), is a very well-defined stage of the Path; it consists in mastery of a basic set of four *rūpa jhānas* (material *jhānas*), followed optionally by a further set of four *arūpa jhānas* (non-material *jhānas*). However, the subject of *jhāna* itself is rendered confusing by the existence of two rather different textual accounts, the Sutta version and the

Abhidhamma version.[48] Analysis of these two versions reveals that the Abhidhamma version, in which *ekaggatā* (one-pointedness) is said to be present in the first *rūpa jhāna*, is self-contradictory and in conflict with meditative experience, while the Sutta version is self-consistent and in good agreement with meditative experience.[49] The Sutta version ought therefore to be accepted as authentic; the Abhidhamma version is probably a product of scholastic systematization. Unfortunately most commentators, including the author of the *Visuddhi-magga*, have chosen to regard the Abhidhamma version as the authentic one, with the result that some very confusing interpretations of the *jhānas* have appeared.[50]

The following summary of the stages passed through in concentration meditation shows how these correlate with the *jhāna* series as described in the Sutta-piṭaka.[51] The concentration object used is usually the sensation experienced at the nostril rim in breathing, less often a coloured disc or a chanted *mantra*.

Rūpa jhāna 1: Through an effortful, but at this stage still unsuccessful, attempt to keep attention focused on the designated object, the meditator attains temporary freedom (*viveka*) from the 'hindrances'. (This stage therefore overlaps with right effort.) The thought-stream (*vitakka-vicāra*) continues to flow as usual.

Rūpa jhāna 2: The attempt to keep attention focused on the designated object is finally successful; thought stops and the state of mental onepointedness (*cetaso ekodibhāva, samādhi, avitakka avicāra*) is attained. At this stage the effort employed in focusing is often excessive and 'overflows' into involuntary physical movements such as twitching and gooseflesh (*pīti*), accompanied by pleasurable bodily feelings (*sukha*).

Rūpa jhāna 3: The involuntary movements cease and the pleasurable feelings become intense, suffusing the meditator's entire body.

Rūpa jhāna 4: These feelings cease and a neutral state of pure mental onepointedness is attained. The meditation object is now perceived with remarkable clarity.

Arūpa jhāna 1 = 'endless space':[52] (This stage occurs only in the case of a visual object (such as a coloured disc) or a chanted *mantra*.) The meditator finds that on closing his eyes or ceasing to chant his *mantra*, he experiences a vivid mental (*arūpa*) replica of it. This replica (*uggaha-nimitta*) then becomes his meditation object. (This stage is also called *upacāra-samādhi*.)

Arūpa jhāna 2 = 'endless *viññāṇa*': The mental replica of the original meditation object gives way to a more 'abstract' image (*paṭibhāga-nimitta*). The latter, while still resembling the former in general shape and orientation, is usually more radiant and colourful, and is usually a visual image, regardless of the original sense modality. (In the case of an original tactile object such as the breathing, the clear sensation experienced in the fourth *rūpa jhāna* is replaced directly by the 'abstract' image of the second *arūpa jhāna*.)[53] (This stage is also called *anuloma*.)

Arūpa jhāna 3 = 'nothingness': The abstract image suddenly vanishes, leaving the meditator with a feeling of having been cast into an endless black vacuum. (This stage is also called *gotrabū*.)

Arūpa jhāna 4 = 'neither perception nor non-perception': The meditator completely loses consciousness. But he realizes this only in retrospect, after returning to normal consciousness; and it is only by consulting a clock or other reliable indicator of the passage of time that he can judge how long the condition lasted. (This stage is also called *appanā* or *nirodha*.)

For a meditator wishing to proceed to insight meditation, the onepointedness of the second *rūpa jhāna* is a sufficiently secure foundation. The deep concentration of the *arūpa jhānas* is unnecessary, and may even seriously hinder progress if it becomes an object of attachment (*vibhava-taṇhā*).

Stage 9 of the Path, right insight (*sammā ñāṇa*), has been shown on textual grounds to be identical with the three knowledges described in the footprint series, in Gotama's account of his own enlightenment, and elsewhere. The three knowledges have been shown, in their turn, to be identical with the three introspective techniques, retracing of image sequences, observation of linking, and awareness. We infer that the perfection of this stage would be attained when awareness has become permanent, and that it is to be identified with enlightenment (*sammā sambodhi*).

Stage 10, right liberation (*sammā vimutti*). We have inferred that Gotama interpreted his attainment of permanent awareness or enlightenment in macrocosmic terms as the attainment of *nirvāṇa*, liberation from *saṃsāra*. So much is indicated in his accounts of the third knowledge, where, having described how he freed himself from the *āsavas*, he then says: '. . . and I comprehended: Destroyed is birth, brought to a close is the Brahma-faring, done is what was to be done, there is no more of being such or such [i.e. no more of being reborn in *saṃsāra*]'.[54] This states Gotama's macrocosmic interpretation (attainment of *nirvāṇa*) of his microcosmic experience (perfecting of awareness). It corresponds to the tenth stage of the Tenfold Path. It appears, then, that of the ten stages the first nine, ending at right insight, are the actual course of practice, while the tenth is the interpretation of what has thereby been achieved. This would explain the frequent omission of liberation (*vimutti*) from summaries of the Path, for example, the usual recognition of three Dharma-groups (*sīla, samādhi, pañña*) rather than four (the same plus *vimutti*). The usual omission of right insight as well as right liberation is in keeping with our contention that Gotama would not have dealt with the techniques of insight meditation in his public discourses but would have imparted them to individual students in private. The Eightfold Path was familiar to all disciples; the secrets of the Tenfold Path were known only to the *ariyas*.

One further characteristic of the Path will be noted before we conclude this section on doctrinal implications. Gotama referred to his path of practice as the 'Middle Way' (*majjhimā paṭipadā*), explaining that the reference was to the need for the aspirant to avoid two extremes in his practice: on the one hand severe asceticism, and on the other luxurious comfort.[55] Our description of the practice leading to awareness indicates, however, that Gotama's injunction to keep to the middle way between the extremes is applicable not only to the *sīla* section of the Path (asceticism/luxury) but also to the *samādhi* and *paññā* sections. In assessing the value of concentration we noted that deep concentration (as in the *arūpa jhānas*) is no less a hindrance to insight than total lack of concentration. What the meditator needs is concentration sufficiently shallow that it intermittently breaks down, giving him the opportunity to retrace (See pp. 53 – 4). This is 'right concentration', the Middle Way between the extremes of deep *jhāna* and a totally undisciplined thought-stream.

A similar principle applies in insight practice: the meditator has to develop the critical state of balance in which his insightful scrutiny of images can coexist with the forward linking process. (See pp. 69 – 70). This is the Middle Way as applied to insight practice.

The above discussion of doctrinal implications has demonstrated that the methodology employed in interpreting Buddhist symbolism can be applied equally effectively to some important Buddhist doctrines. It thereby provides further evidence for the validity of our interpretation. In addition it suggests that the overt teaching as a whole, perhaps even including Abhidhamma and Mahāyāna developments, might profitably be studied from this new perspective.

Historical Implications

In Chapters I and II we examined the evidence for and against an esoteric transmission in early Buddhism, and concluded that Gotama probably did initiate such a transmission. We noted that textual and historical references, the sources of evidence normally appealed to in approaching this kind of question, are naturally very meagre. We therefore relied mainly on other, less direct data, in particular (1) our knowledge of how gurus in ancient India traditionally communicated spiritual instruction to their disciples, and (2) the 'argument from silence', the surprising lack, in the Tipiṭaka, of explicit information on the technique of insight meditation.

Our subsequent examination of meditation and symbolism has revealed some far-reaching correspondences which clearly have important implications for the question of an esoteric transmission, and indeed for the history of Buddhism as a whole. Some of these implications will now be considered — not with a view to resolving the historical problems raised, but rather in order to suggest the kinds of questions that historians of Buddhism might begin asking.

We may begin by noting that our conclusions about the relationship between meditation and symbolism in the Tipiṭaka have subtly modified the argument from silence. As presented in Chapters I and II the argument from silence consisted in pointing out a serious gap in the Tipiṭaka account of meditation practice. We noted that various sources, such as the Tenfold Path and the division of Buddhist practice into *samatha* and *vipassanā*, indicate that mastery of concentration has to be followed by some form of insight practice, and we pointed out that no description of such a practice is to be found in the Tipiṭaka. This we saw as evidence that Gotama did withhold important information from all but a select few of his disciples. The subsequent discussion (Chapters III to VII), by revealing systematic relationships between meditative stages and symbolic language, has provided evidence that important information was indeed secretly imparted. However, by coming to specific conclusions regarding the content of this information (the techniques of insight meditation), we have also revealed that the texts do after all contain a number of references to that content. The silence is therefore not a total silence; the information is there, but expressed very cryptically or inadequately. The three knowledges, the three characteristics, and the three trainees are all frequently mentioned in the texts.

However, they are never adequately explained in terms of mental states or meditative techniques: no information is given on how in practice the meditator should recollect his former existences, perceive transience, or attain the path of stream-entry. All we have is the terms, together with, at best, very brief descriptions that tend to obscure rather than clarify. We conclude that if Gotama ever explained these terms in straightforward language, he must have done so in secret. Our analysis of Buddhist symbolic language has therefore in effect both modified and strengthened the argument from silence by identifying more precisely what it is that Gotama was silent about. In so doing it has thrown new light not only on the life and thought of Gotama himself, but also on an important strand in the development of Buddhism (the élite meditative tradition), which — because of that same silence — has usually been overlooked.

The Life and Thought of Gotama, the Buddha

Very little is really known about Gotama as an historical figure. Most of the 'biographical information' found in the texts must be discounted as pious hagiographic accretion. Only the frequently mentioned principal events of his life — his religious quest, asceticism, enlightenment, teaching, and death — can be accepted with any confidence. Attempts to flesh out this meagre outline have naturally concentrated on discussion of his teaching. But here too there are difficulties. The Tipiṭaka is evidently the product of an established monastic order. Much of what passes for Gotama's teaching bears the marks of later systematization. It is difficult to know how much of the recorded Dharma can be ascribed to Gotama himself.

In this connection our interpretation of the three knowledges and associated doctrines is of value in throwing light on some of the basic presuppositions of Gotama's thought. It has demonstrated the dominant role of macrocosm-microcosm parallelism in Gotama's world-view, and thereby situated him squarely in the intellectual-spiritual environment of his times. This make possible a better estimate of Gotama's achievement, and of his stature and originality as a religious reformer and thinker. Our interpretation has shown how the supposed effectiveness of Gotama's path of insight practice in bringing liberation from *saṃsāra* depended on a particular understanding of the world and of man's circumstances in it. In so doing it incidentally lends support to the Theravāda conception of Gotama as a human, historical figure — albeit a very remarkable one. Thus our interpretation has important implications both for the study of Gotama's role as teacher of Dharma and founder of the Sangha, and also for research into the development of early Buddhism.

Early Buddhism and the Élite Tradition

The conclusion arrived at in Chapter II that Gotama probably did initiate an esoteric transmission carries with it the implication that there existed an élite group of disciples who received this special secret teaching and put it into practice. This élite group would, we suggested, have been composed of dedicated meditators who had qualified for initiation by demonstrating high moral calibre (*sīla*) and proficiency in the basic practice of concentration (*samādhi*). But is there in the Tipiṭaka any reference to such a group?

In the previous section evidence was presented which indicates that the term *ariya* referred to monks practising stages in insight meditation. It was shown that the stream-enterer, once-returner, and non-returner correspond to the practices of retracing, observation of linking, and awareness respectively, while the *arahant* (as suggested already by Buddhadasa) corresponds to the attainment of permanent awareness. The transition from worldling to *ariya* status therefore corresponds to the transition from concentration practice (*samatha*) to insight practice (*vipassanā*). Now it is precisely at this transition point in the meditative practice that the Tipiṭaka becomes silent; concentration is fully described, but retracing is not even mentioned. This indicates that the attainment of *ariya* status coincided with entry into the élite meditative tradition. The term *ariya* referred simultaneously to practitioners of insight meditation and to members of the élite tradition, for the two were one and the same. So the Tipiṭaka does mention an élite group of meditators. What is more it tells us something about them by mentioning a primary division into adepts (*asekhas*, i.e. *arahants*) and trainees (*sekhas*), and enumerating the grades in the latter group. Here again the symbolic analysis-interpretation has strengthened one of the arguments advanced in Chapters I and II. By putting a precise meaning to an important set of terms in the Tipiṭaka, it has provided textual support for the claim that there existed an élite meditative tradition in early Buddhism.

This in turn throws light on the debate, all too briefly hinted at in the Tipiṭaka, between the *jhāyins* (meditators) and the remaining monks who devoted their energies to memorizing and discussing texts. Regarding this division within the Sangha, it should be remembered that the Tipiṭaka was compiled by the memorizers and would therefore not be expected to portray the *jhāyins* very favourably. Advanced meditation could hardly be ignored altogether in the Tipiṭaka; however, it does seem to have been deliberately played down, with reference to practitioners of the higher meditative stages limited to stereotyped descriptions of the grades of *ariyas*.

The evidence that we have put forward concerning the existence of an élite meditative tradition in early Buddhism also has implications for the role of meditation in the early Sangha, and thus for the development of the Sangha itself. As de Jong has observed, Gotama's teaching was 'an aristocratic doctrine of deliverance, making high ethical and intellectual demands'.[56] It is likely that only a minority of monks met those demands, especially during the period of Aśoka's generous imperial patronage, when unprecedented numbers flocked to join the order. With the rise of popular Buddhism, monks would have spent an ever-increasing proportion of their time ministering to the needs of the lay community. How did these changes affect the position of the *jhāyins*? Did the élite meditative tradition manage to keep alive the original ideal of meditation? Or did the changing nature of the Sangha reduce the *jhāyins* to an idiosyncratic minority, perhaps destroying some lines of transmission altogether? These are questions which any study of the evolution of the early Sangha will have to address.

Continuity of the Esoteric Tradition

In Chapter I we suggested the possibility of a historical connection between the Twilight Language and the seemingly symbolic language of the Tipiṭaka. We pointed out that the *mudrās* of the dhyāni Buddhas Amitābha and Akṣobhya are widely recognized as referring to the legendary encounter between Māra the tempter and Gotama on the evening of his enlightenment; and we suggested that this reference ought to be taken into account in interpreting the *mudrās*. Our symbolic analysis of the *mudrās* (Chapter VII) has revealed that the role of these two dhyāni Buddhas as representing events associated with the enlightenment, is closely and consistently connected with their status as members of the passive and active groups in the early threefold classification. This fact has implications for the question of continuity of tradition, which will now be considered. We begin by summarizing the relevant historical events.

Māra, the Evil One, figures prominently in the Tipiṭaka as lord of the realm of desire (*kāma-loka*), and thus as tempter of all who would overcome desire in the search for release from *saṃsāra.*[57] However, except for a brief reference in the Vinaya, Māra does not figure in any of the accounts of Gotama's enlightement found in the Pali Tipiṭaka. A full account of the attempt by Māra and his three daughters to distract the meditating Gotama does not appear until the *Mahāvastu*, a 'biography' of the Buddha, of which part dates from the second century B.C. but much is later. We may take it, then, that the story of Māra's attack and subsequent defeat was a later accretion, and was probably not widely known until perhaps the third century B.C. The legend was first given iconographic form, as a Buddha icon in the earth-touching *mudrā*, about the first century A.D., that is (if the above-mentioned dating of the *Mahāvastu* is reliable) about four centuries after the legend itself became current. The earth-touching *mudrā* came to symbolize Gotama's overcoming of Māra, just as the Dharma-wheel *mudrā* symbolized his first teaching of the Dharma.

At some later time, in the developing Mahāyāna tradition, another form of the Buddha icon, that in the meditation *mudrā*, was brought into association with the icons in earth-touching and Dharma-wheel *mudrās* to form a recognized triad, the dhyāni Buddhas Amitābha, Akṣobhya, and Vairocana, associated with the passive, active, and balance groups respectively in the threefold classification. Later again, about the fourth or fifth century A.D., this set of three was extended to yield the full five-membered set found in the dhyāni Buddha *maṇḍala*.

In addition to the above two widely acknowledged associations with the Māra legend and with the threefold classification — it is considered in the Tantric tradition that a secret symbolic correspondence with meditative techniques was also recognized. Our symbolic analysis of the dhyāni Buddhas has led us to identify the techniques in question as the five stages of the course of meditative practice described in Chapter IV. This raises a question which has a direct bearing on the problem of continuity of tradition: How and when did this association with meditative stages come about?

The importance of this question arises out of the following facts, noted in Chapter VII:

(i) *The meditation mudrā*: Māra's attack on Gotama is widely recognized as a metaphorical reference to the arising of distracting thoughts in the mind of the meditator. The meditation *mudrā* which denotes that incident, is therefore associated symbolically with the thought-stream. The thought-stream belongs to the passive or water group in the fivefold classification. Amitābha, whom the meditation *mudrā* identifies, is regarded in Tantric symbolism as also belonging to the passive or water group.

(ii) *The earth-touching mudrā*: Gotama's repulsing of Māra is interpreted (in Chapter VII) as referring to the practice of retracing, firstly because of the direct contrast with the attack (which represents the thought-stream), and secondly because of the reference to former existences. The earth-touching *mudrā* is thereby associated with retracing. Retracing belongs to the active or fire group. Akṣobhya, whom the earth-touching *mudrā* identifies, is regarded in Tantric Buddhism as also belonging to the active or fire group.

In each case the *mudrā*'s role in the Māra legend, when interpreted in terms of the five-stage course of practice, is found to belong to the same symbolic group as the dhyāni Buddha who has that *mudrā*. How did this symbolic agreement come about? There would seem to be two possible explanations, depending on whether the association with meditative stages is considered to have come *before* or *after* the association with the passive and active groups, namely the following: (a) The meditation and earth-touching *mudrās* were brought into symbolic association with the thought-stream and retracing respectively, because Māra's attack and defeat, with which they were already identified, were seen as suggesting those stages. On the basis of this association, the same *mudrās* were subsequently assigned to the passive and active groups respectively. (b) The meditation and earth-touching *mudrās* were assigned to the passive and active groups respectively becaues Māra's attack and defeat, with which they were already identified, were seen as suggesting those groups. On the basis of this classification *and* the prior association with the Māra legend, the same *mudrās* were subsequently brought into association with the thought-stream and retracing respectively.

As mentioned in Chapter VII, we consider the former possibility the more likely. It seems to us unlikely that the attack and defeat of Māra would, in themselves, have been seen as suggesting the passive and active groups respectively. Nor would the *mudrās* themselves have suggested that classification; if *mudrās* were to be chosen to represent the passive and active groups, the logical choice would have been the gift-bestowing and no-danger *mudrās*, since these point downwards and upwards respectively.

But if the meditation and earth-touching *mudrās* were associated with the thought-stream and retracing *before* being assigned to the passive and active groups, those who so assigned them must have been aware of the prior connection with meditation; they must have possessed the key to the symbolism. This hardly constitutes incontrovertible evidence of continuity in the esoteric tradition, but it does suggest the likelihood of such continuity. The Tantric tradition is claimed, by the Tantrikas themselves, to be a continuation of an esoteric tradition reaching back to Gotama. The above demonstration of possible continuity, based on analysis of the dhyāni Buddha symbolism, lends some support to this claim. The very possibility of finding, in the symbolism, such evidence of continuity in the esoteric tradition should stimulate further historical research into this question.

The Rise of the Mahāyāna

The likelihood of continuity of the esoteric tradition from the time of the early Sangha to the rise of Tantrism demands a re-examination of the evolution of the Mahāyāna. It is clear from the internal evidence of the Tipiṭaka that the meditative élite was soon relegated to a marginal position in the Sangha. The ideal of the *bhikkhu* as a 'lone rhinoceros' wandering the forest, intent only on his own spiritual development,[58] was quickly replaced by the ideal of the monk as a member of his monastic community, engrossed in a daily round of activities of which meditation was but one. Such a development would probably have been facilitated by the fact that the *ariyas*, as an élite, withdrawn group of meditators, would have had minimal involvement in the internal politics of the Sangha. The aloof withdrawal of the meditators would also have left the way clear for others to pursue intellectual discussion, minister to the lay community (popular Buddhism), and so on.

The position of meditation in the Mahāyāna also needs examining, in view of the Mahāyāna devaluing of arahantship. Of the six perfections (*pāramitā*) recognized in the Mahāyāna, the fifth is *dhyāna* (Pali *jhāna*) and the sixth and highest is *prajñā* (Pali *paññā*).[59] But the resemblance to the Theravāda scheme (*sīla, samādhi, paññā*) is perhaps misleading. The Mahāyāna *prajñā*, which appears to have been conceived as an alternative mode of cognition resulting from intuitive realization of 'emptiness' (*śūnyatā*),[60] was achieved through some higher form of knowledge rather than through introspection into the nature of the mind. The path to this cognitive breakthrough was therefore similar to the Hindu 'path of knowledge' (*jñāna-yoga*). This represents a major change of emphasis and direction in the development of Buddhism. An attempt to discover why it came about would have to take into account a complex combination of influences, especially the continued and changing influence of Hinduism. In addition, as our analysis has indicated, future historical research into the rise of the Mahāyāna must, if it is to be at all complete, take proper account of the changing nature and role of meditation, an area that has hitherto received too little attention.

It is possible that one factor affecting the rise of the Mahāyāna was a gradual change in the concept of macrocosm-microcosm parallelism, due in large part to the development of theistic Hinduism. As the Hindu concept of Brahman was developed and formalized, the idea that manipulation of the microcosm brought about corresponding changes in the macrocosm gradually declined in importance. This change would have brought with it a need for new conceptions of *nirvāṇa* and of the way to attain it. In this respect Buddhism would have been vulnerable to influence from Hinduism, which offered several different paths to 'the goal'. Thus in respect of both meditation and the Buddhist world-view, our interpretation of Buddhist symbolism appears to have important implications for the study of the origins and development of the Mahāyāna.

Historical Development of Buddhist Symbolism and the Vajrayāna

Because of the lack of solid historical evidence, any attempt at reconstructing the development of the esoteric tradition as a whole could only be highly speculative. The development of the associated symbolism can, however, be traced in broad outline, on the basis of the internal evidence now available.

The symbolic language of the Tipiṭaka as we have interpreted it was basically a statement of the microcosm-macrocosm parallelism which Gotama had discerned. It was not an intentionally constructed symbolic system. If 'recollection of former existences' provided a useful way of referring cryptically to the technique of retracing, this was an incidental benefit; the correspondence was in the first instance a statement of a recognized identity between thought processes (microcosm) and the physical world (macrocosm).

The identities recognized covered all the psychological elements that Gotama saw as relevant to the task of attaining mental-cosmic liberation. There was a quite detailed set of correspondences: the image, the arising of an image, the ceasing of an image, emotional involvement in an image, etc., each had its macrocosmic counterpart. And all of these correspondences were perceived as identities; liberation from the thought-stream *was* liberation from *saṃsāra*.

In the development from this to the Twilight Language there is a gradual replacement of macrocosm-microcosm identity by a rather artificial universal symbolic parallelism based on uniformly codified sets of three, four, and finally five members.[61] Thus two related changes came about simultaneously: (1) the old flexible, unstructured pattern of equivalences gave way to a highly formalized and regularized system; and (2) the parallelism, originally perceived as identity, came to be seen as mere symbolic correspondence. The new highly-codified system imposed serious constraints. For example, whereas the old symbolic language of the Tipiṭaka had distinguished image, arising of an image, and ceasing of an image, each with its macrocosmic counterpart, the new system required that these three all be fitted into the one 'passive' group, with no means of distinguishing them in the symbolism. The remarkable closeness of the correspondence between the five meditative stages and the five groups (defined primarily by the elements) must have seemed to the *siddhas* to validate the fivefold classification. It became the basis of the symbolism of the Twilight Language. The relationship that now existed between, say, the thought-stream and the colour blue was quite different from that which had formerly existed between the thought-stream and *saṃsāra*. A deeply-felt identity had been replaced by an explicitly symbolic relationship.

This development has implications for the origin of the Vajrayāna. The increasing codification and elaboration evident already in the earliest *tantras* indicates that for many Tantrikas the symbols were more important than the meditative practices they denoted. Well before the time of the *maṇḍala* the symbolic system had already taken on a life of its own. The connection with meditation was apparently early lost sight of (except, presumably, by a small minority),[62] and the system developed as a scholarly elaboration similar to the Abhidhamma and other digressions from the meditative path.

Symbolism plays a central role in the Vajrayāna. The symbols (elements, colours, dhyāni Buddhas, etc.) which in the esoteric tradition stood for meditative stages, served also in popular Buddhism as items of ritual worship, usually embellished with sexual symbolism appropriated from Śaivite Hinduism and the cult of Mahādevī (the Great Goddess). Given the mechanical superimposition of symbol sets evident in the *maṇḍala*, and the still worse cases of confusion and inconsistency that one finds on closely examining the literature, it seems likely that few of the authors of the *tantras* were practising meditators in the élite tradition. Indeed the emergence of the *tantras*, a millennium after the death of Gotama would seem to signal the end of the effective life of the symbolic system as a representation of meditative practices.

Survival of the Esoteric Tradition

How long the esoteric tradition survived in India and elsewhere is impossible to determine, though here again our interpretation of the symbolism sheds some light on the matter. At least two schools, the Vajrayāna and Zen, claim to be in receipt of a special transmission. In the case of Vajrayāna the claim seems well founded; in the case of Zen supporting evidence is meagre. Evidence that the esoteric tradition long survived in Tibet comes from the passages quoted in Chapter IV. These demonstrate that awareness was taught in Tibet over a long period, and was still practised there as recently as the beginning of this century (when David-Neel carried out her researches on meditative practices). In view of our interpretation of Gotama's teaching as a set of instructions for the perfecting of awareness, it seems possible that the essence of the teaching has been maintained intact in Tibet down to modern times.[63] Meditation masters in other Buddhist traditions also mention awareness, but they are isolated cases. Only in the Tibetan tradition do we find evidence that awareness has been recognized and practised throughout the centuries as a standard meditative technique.

This is not, of course, certain proof of an unbroken line of transmission from Gotama through to modern Tibetan masters.[64] It is always possible that individual meditators practising independently rediscovered ancient insight techniques and then initiated new lines of transmission. It could also be that individual meditators hit on new and different techniques for developing awareness, or even that they developed awareness directly without any form of preparatory practice, as Krishnamurti claims is possible. The Tibetan technique described in Chapter IV, in which the meditator contemplates a constructed image of a deity or a fearsome demon, does suggest an independent line of development, though as we have pointed out, this practice in fact amounts to a special case of retracing. Nevertheless, the continued Tibetan emphasis on imagery, and on awareness as the final goal, does provide evidence of continuity with Gotama's original instruction on meditation.

Tibetan Buddhism, the branch which retained an interest in awareness, also stands out as the branch that preserved the symbols of the Twilight Language. In India, Sri Lanka, China, and especially Japan, one may find occasional examples of symbolic devices; but in any Tibetan temple one comes across them at every turn. It is irrelevant that most Tibetans regard these devices as talismans or objects of worship rather than as cryptic references to meditative practices. Objects used by advanced monks to impart their secret teaching would naturally tend to be venerated in this way by superstitious lay people. Also it is likely that some of the devices in question (the *bījas*, for example) were already talismans *before* being adopted as symbols in the Twilight Language.

This geographical-cultural correlation between preservation of the meditative techniques and preservation of the symbols reinforces our interpretation. Both inside and outside Tibet it is widely believed that the Vajrayāna enshrines an esoteric transmission. Our interpretation has given that view a sounder foundation by focusing on the actual practices in question and demonstrating their connection with the symbols of the Twilight Language.

Towards a Buddhist Hermeneutic

It is widely believed that the Twilight Language was created in order to help preserve Gotama's esoteric teachings, or to conceal those teachings from the uninitiated. It seems that these explanations may be partly correct, but that the symbolic language also at different times served other purposes. Originally a statement of microcosm-macrocosm parallelism, it apparently soon became a secret code and teaching aid. The fact that the élite meditative tradition was constantly under threat of extinction (as noted in Chapter II) would have given its members good reasons for producing tangible representations of their course of practice which would help ensure that the precious knowledge was encoded for the benefit of later generations. But if this was the purpose of devices such as the set of coloured discs representing the meditative stages, then the idea has proved a failure; later generations took it that the discs were objects of concentration, and adopted various other symbols as charms, objects of worship, etc.

The details of the development of the Twilight Language will only become clear as Buddhist studies develop, and especially as a thorough textual analysis of the abundant literature is undertaken. The above study is merely a tentative attempt, based on evidence at present available, to develop a Buddhist hermeneutic drawing upon phenomenological description of meditative states, interpretation of symbols, and historical analysis. It represents no more than a hypothesis which remains open to refutation by scholars working in the field of Buddhist studies. Like any hypothesis, ours must stand or fall on the evidence which can be adduced either to support it, or to reject it in favour of an alternative hypothesis. Scholars may take issue with our conclusions, but in doing so they can no longer disregard the importance of meditation and symbolism in the history of Buddhism.

The doctrinal and historical implications discussed in this chapter have demonstrated that our analysis of Buddhist symbolism has relevance for other branches of Buddhist studies. Our interpretative methodology has led us to infer the existence of a continuous esoteric tradition in early Buddhism, and has provided a new understanding of some important aspects of Gotama's overt doctrine. Historians of Buddhism must now confront any further implications that these findings may be found to have for their particular areas of research.

CHAPTER IX

CONCLUSION

In the foregoing chapters we have addressed some fundamental problems concerning Buddhist meditation and Buddhist symbolism. In this final chapter we shall briefly review our findings and assess their relevance at the present day.

Our principal concern has been to investigate and clarify the higher stages of Buddhist meditation and the relationships between them and the symbolic language of the Tipiṭaka and the *tantras*. This we see not merely as a scholarly exercise but as a practical contribution to the growing movement toward recognition of the value of meditation. We have drawn heavily on the work of earlier researchers, but we have also developed some original methodological principles and arrived at some novel and perhaps controversial conclusions. We believe these conclusions indicate a need for certain changes of approach by both practising meditators and scholars, to which we shall now draw attention.

Regarding meditation the main point we would stress is the need for a complete 'demystification' of the subject. The air of mystery that so often surrounds meditation is due in large part to a widespread reluctance on the part of meditators to discuss their experiences and attainments. This reluctance is particularly evident in the Buddhist countries of Asia but is also found in attenuated form among Western meditators. It stems in large part from a belief that it is improper for a meditator to tell anyone but his own meditation master how far he has progressed in his practice. This view is most strongly held within the Sangha, being reinforced by certain Vinaya rules; no monk would ever announce to his fellows that he had, for example, mastered the first *jhāna* or attained the path of stream-entry. It is assumed that such open discussion would generate a sense of rivalry, thereby making for tensions in the monastic community, as well as hindering the meditator's own further progress. It is also assumed that such discussion by a meditator of his own attainments could only be motivated by conceit; and since conceit is one of the 'fetters' which meditation is supposed to eliminate, it would be, in itself, evidence that little had really been attained! (Compare the Taoist aphorism: 'Those who know do not speak; those who speak do not know.') It is unfortunate that the people most strongly bound by this prohibition are Easterners and monks in the Sangha, the very groups among whom meditative skills are mostly highly developed. Westerners are not entirely exempt, however. A Westerner who publishes an account of his meditative experiences, particularly if he is writing within a Buddhist framework, does so in the knowledge that Buddhist readers will, if only subconsciously, condemn him for his supposed conceit and devalue his account accordingly.[1]

This attitude is a major obstacle to research in meditation, and there is no good reason why anyone, least of all a Westerner with a basically scientific world-view, should feel bound by it. Meditation should be brought out into the open and freely discussed. To publish a first-person account of one's meditative experiences and attainments is, as transpersonal psychologists increasingly realize, to make a useful contribution to a poorly-documented area of study.

Another factor contributing to the mystification of meditation is the widespread use of unclear language in describing it. All too often one finds writers on meditation referring to 'higher planes', 'cosmic consciousness' or 'immutable wisdom', and describing mental states as 'ineffable', 'transcendent', etc. This practice is usually taken for granted. Many people assume that meditative states simply cannot be described in ordinary language. Language that is vague, highly metaphorical, even self-contradictory is therefore often regarded as not only permissible but virtually mandatory.

This only serves to perpetuate the mystery surrounding meditation. Admittedly, description of supernormal states of consciousness does sometimes pose linguistic problems, but that should not be made an excuse for unclear terminology. A writer on meditation must make some attempt to explain the terms he uses. A reference to 'transcending the worldly condition' is unacceptable unless accompanied by an explanation of what 'the worldly condition' is, and in what sense it is transcended.

Equally unacceptable is the practice of using Sanskrit or Pali technical terms to describe meditative states without adequately explaining their meaning. Some seek to justify this practice on the grounds that modern Western languages are inadequate for the purpose, since they lack a sufficiently rich and precise terminology. But the use of a Sanskrit or Pali term to refer to a meditative state entails the assumption that the writer knows what that term originally denoted for the master who coined it, and that an understanding of this meaning is shared by present-day readers. For example, a person who refers to 'attaining the first *jhāna*' implies that he knows what Gotama meant when he used the term 'first *jhāna*' — something he is not entitled to do unless he has first carried out an adequate analysis of the classical use of the term and demonstrated its correspondence with a certain meditative state. Again, even if Sanskrit/Pali terminology is as rich and precise as is generally supposed, this does not facilitate communication unless the speaker or writer explains with comparable precision what each term denotes.[2] Without such explanation the result is merely greater confusion. If progress is to be made in understanding meditation and making it accessible to interested people, description must be clear and straightforward, designed to clarify rather than to mystify.

To people who have no experience of it, meditation seems inherently mysterious; and to those who do have some experience, the more advanced practices are no less a cause for puzzlement and speculation. Particularly mysterious is the final goal of the practice. The Buddhist texts, if taken at face value, support the popular expectation of omniscience accompanied by supreme purity and bliss. Compared with this glorious prospect, permanent awareness, which we have argued is in fact the goal of the practice, may appear disappointingly rational and this-wordly. Awareness brings no radical transformation into something totally other. When there is awareness, the thought-stream continues flowing as usual, its content as trivial and mundane as it was before the meditator embarked on his practice. The only difference is that with awareness the meditator has unbroken insight into the true nature of the thought-stream, an unobscured view into the cluttered junk-shop that is his own consciousness. The five-stage course of practice that culminates in this attainment has been described (in Chapters III and IV) in straightforward, non-technical language, with no concealment of any detail of the method or the final goal, no assumed acceptance of Buddhist doctrines, no insistence on step-by-step guidance by a guru, and no reference to ritual practices. This is what we mean by 'demystification' of meditation.

For students of psychology whose concern is to discover the nature of mental phenomena *per se*, the five-stage course of practice should be of particular interest. In that field awareness is the ultimate research tool. Through awareness the researcher becomes his own subject, observing his own mental processes from moment to moment. There could be no better way to gain insight into the human mind.

Here conservatives will no doubt raise the old objections to introspection as a technique in psychology. One such objection is that the act of observing one's own mental processes would interfere with those processes, or conversely that the continuing mental processes would interfere with the act of observing, thus rendering the observations unreliable. Another is that inner observation of mental processes would always be incomplete, since whatever part of the mind it is that does the observing would always escape detection: just as a hand can never grasp itself, and an eye can never directly look at itself, so the introspecting part of the mind could never observe itself introspecting. These superficially plausible objections to introspection are, however, based on invalid theoretical extrapolation from everyday experience in observing events outside ourselves. As noted in Chapter IV, awareness is not at all like observing outside objects. When there is awareness, 'the observer is the observed', as Krishnamurti puts it. Any thoughts that arise do not interfere with the act of observing, but are part and parcel of that act of observing. The only interference has to do with affective states. Awareness is inherently incompatible with affective states; in the process of gaining awareness, the connection between affective states and mental content is revealed and thereby severed.

In spite of such objections, there is in Western psychology, a growing trend towards recognition of the validity of introspective observation as a technique for learning about mental phenomena, and a growing interest in Eastern techniques of meditation.[3] The day is perhaps not far off when psychologists will fully recognize the enormous value of awareness, and be humbled by the realization that the means for attaining it were discovered by a wandering sage in India twenty-five centuries ago.

For non-Buddhists the question whether the five-stage course of practice was taught by Gotama is perhaps not of great importance. The psychologist, therapist, Theosophist, or man-in-the-street with an interest in his own mind can, without reference to any established tradition, make an intellectual evaluation of the practice as described, in terms of its likely effectiveness in achieving his own particular goals — insight into the nature of the mind, resolution of inner conflict, efficiency in utilizing the mind as a worktool, etc.

For committed Buddhists, however, the question whether the five-stage course of practice was actually taught by Gotama would be a crucial factor in the decision whether or not to embark on that course. It is largely for this reason that the two chapters on meditation are followed by a further four chapters on symbolic language and doctrinal and historical points. These set out the case for affirming that this course of practice was indeed Gotama's meditative path; they can thus provide the intellectual basis (right view) for a decision to undertake the practice (right aspiration).

Committed Buddhists may, however, perceive our interpretation of *saṃsāra* and *nirvāṇa*, the three knowledges, and Gotama's enlightenment as an unacceptable devaluation of the Blessed One's achievement. Gotama's enlightenment, usually understood as nothing less than omniscience, is here equated with permanent awareness — seemingly a far less exalted attainment; and his *nirvāṇa*, for Buddhists the ultimate cosmic breakthrough, is explained as his interpretation of this meditative attainment in terms of the archaic notion of macrocosm-microcosm parallelism. But this is not really a devaluation. Once Gotama's meditative attainment (enlightenment, permanent awareness) and his culture-dependent interpretation of it (*nirvāṇa*) are distinguished from each other, his teaching acquires a present relevance that is otherwise lacking. The goal of the Buddhist path then no longer appears as something quite otherworldly, whose relevance is conditional on acceptance of the doctrine of rebirth. It is shown, instead, to be within the reach of any devoted meditator (though by no means *easy* to attain), and to be immediately relevant to all human beings regardless of cultural background.

The Tantric symbolism too may appear to have been devalued by our interpretation. Many regard the *maṇḍala* as almost sacred, and genuinely believe in the existence of the *cakras*. Such people will perhaps be dismayed at seeing these precious things demystified. But here again to demystify is not to devalue; rather the reverse. Recognizing the processes of distortion that occurred during the decadent later phases in the history of the Twilight Language reveals the beautifully simple underlying fivefold structure of the symbolism, and its remarkable correspondence with the five-stage course of meditative practice. Thus the chaotic, mutually contradictory arrangements, whose meaning could hardly be guessed at, are replaced by a coherent system in which a valuable message can be discovered.

That the symbols of the Twilight Language denote stages in the aspirant's meditative progress has long been recognized both by scholars and by Vajrayāna Buddhists themselves. In equating those symbols with the five-stage course of practice we are therefore merely refining and rendering more specific a long-accepted interpretation. Similarly, our interpretation of the symbolic language of the Tipiṭaka is merely a development of interpretations already suggested by Buddhadasa and others. As well, the meditative techniques on which our interpretations are based, have already been described by various well-known authorities — Krishnamurti, Tarthang, Humphreys, etc. What is new in our presentation is its greater thoroughness, precision, and concern for methodological rigour. We have sought to describe, analyse, and interpret fully, systematically, and critically, where others have, in our view, dealt with the subject too briefly or too loosely. Nevertheless, we recognize that our assumptions, methods, and inferences are open to question, and that serious gaps remain, especially in the historical evidence. We therefore regard our arguments and suggestions as one more contribution to the growing field of Buddhist hermeneutics, which later research by specialist workers may show to be more or less in need of revision.

The most important feature of our methodology is the bringing together of phenomenological description of meditation, and analysis of textual-historical data. Scholarly analysis of textual material is only one part of the process of interpreting symbolism. We would suggest that attempts to make sense of Buddhist symbolism, and equally of overt Buddhist doctrine, will always be incomplete as long as they disregard meditation. This is not to say that all scholars should become meditators, but rather that scholars who do not draw on the findings of meditators have little chance of penetrating beyond the symbols and technical terms to the mental realities they denote.

Gotama expressed his message in terms of the world-view that was current in his time and culture. To people in the twentieth century who subscribe, consciously or unconsciously, to a rational scientific world-view, that message remains barely intelligible unless it can be 'translated' into our modern idiom. This is what we have attempted to do: to identify the correspondences between the idiom of ancient India and that of the modern West, and translate the message accordingly. Even when thus shorn of its old cultural assumptions, the message remains an important one. It amounts to a guide for exploring consciousness, a set of instructions by following which the mind can become fully aware of its own nature. For mankind today no other message could be more important.

NOTES

Notes to Chapter I

1 On transpersonal psychology and meditation, see Roger N. Walsh and Frances Vaughan, *Beyond Ego* (Los Angeles: Tarcher, 1980), pp. 15–24; and Roger N. Walsh, 'Meditation Research: An Introduction and Review', *Journal of Transpersonal Psychology* 11 (1979), pp. 161–74. Also see Michael Murphy and Steve Donovan, 'A Bibliography of Meditation Theory and Research', *Journal of Transpersonal Psychology* 15 (1983), pp. 181–228.

2 In this book Buddhist technical terms are generally cited in Pali, less often in Sanskrit or Japanese depending on the context.

3 On awareness as the only true meditation, see J. Krishnamurti, *Freedom from the Known*, ed. Mary Lutyens (London: Gollancz, 1969), pp. 114–17.

4 On the importance of this, see Alan Richardson, *Mental Imagery* (London: Routledge and Kegan Paul, 1969), pp. 109–17; and T. Tart, 'Scientific Foundations for the Study of Altered States of Consciousness', *Journal of Transpersonal Psychology* 3 (1971), pp. 93–124. The case for recognizing inner experience, in particular imagery, as a valid object of psychological study is presented in Alan Richardson, *The Experiential Dimension of Psychology* (St Lucia: University of Queensland Press, 1984). For a very readable discussion of imagery, a topic particularly relevant to insight meditation, see Stephen M. Kosslyn, *Ghosts in the Mind's Machine* (New York: Norton, 1983); and for a more technical state-of-the-art overview of the same topic, see Anees A. Sheikh, *Imagery: Current Theory, Research, and Application* (New York: John Wiley and Sons, 1983).

5 For example Roger N. Walsh, 'Initial Meditative Experiences: Part I', and *idem* 'Part II', *Journal of Transpersonal Psychology* 9 (1977), pp. 151–92, and 10 (1978), pp. 1–28; and Rod Bucknell, 'Experiments in Insight Meditation', *Australian Journal of Transpersonal Psychology* 3 (1983), pp. 96–117.

6 Attempts have been made to determine the nature of this 'original Buddhism'; e.g. Kōgen Mizuno, *Primitive Buddhism*, transl. Kōshō Yamamoto (Ube: Karin Bunko, 1969). Other scholars, however, have questioned whether this is possible. See André Bareau, 'Recherches sur la biographie du Buddha dans les Sūtrapiṭaka et les Vinayapiṭaka anciens', vol. I (de la quête de l'éveil à la conversation de Śāriputra et de Maudgalyāyana) and vol. II (les derniers mois, le Parinirvāṇa et les funérailles). Publications de l'École Française d'Extrême-Orient vol. 53 (1963) and vol. 77, part 2 (1971). See also

David L. Snellgrove, 'Śākyamuni's Final Nirvāṇa', *Bulletin of the School of Oriental and African Studies* 36, part 2 (1973), pp. 399 – 411. And for a study of the biography of the Buddha, see Frank E. Reynolds, 'The Many Lives of Buddha', in *The Biographical Process: Essays in the History and Psychology of Religion*, ed. by Frank E. Reynolds and Donald Capps (The Hague: Mouton, 1976), pp. 37 – 61; and Edward J. Thomas, *The Life of Buddha as Legend and History*, 3rd rev. ed. (London: Routledge and Kegan Paul, 1949).

7 See e.g. D ii 311 – 313. All such references are to volume and page numbers in the Pali Text Society's edition of the Tipiṭaka; D = Dīgha, M = Majjhima, S = Saṃyutta, A = Aṅguttara. Quoted translations from the Pali Tipiṭaka are, unless otherwise stated, from the Pali Text Society's English versions.

8 Many equate right view with the final liberating insight; e.g. Nyanatiloka, *The Word of the Buddha* (Kandy: Buddhist Publication Society, 1971), pp 26 – 7. This opinion, first expressed by the nun Dhammadinnā (M i 301), assumes the Path sequence is without significance. For evidence against it see Chapter VIII, and Rod Bucknell, 'The Buddhist Path to Liberation: An Analysis of the Listing of Stages', *Journal of the International Association of Buddhist Studies* 7 (1984), no. 2, pp. 7 – 40.

9 For example, D ii 312 – 313. This path is clearly both sequential (simpler, more basic practices precede more difficult and advanced ones), and cumulative (earlier stages are maintained as later ones are taken up). See M iii 71 – 77, and our discussion in Chapter VIII.

10 D ii 217, iii 271, etc. For an analysis of the Tenfold Path and other important variations on the Eightfold Path (including the 'footprints of a Buddha', discussed below), see Bucknell, 'The Buddhist Path to Liberation'.

11 The distinction is made at D iii 273, M i 494, etc.

12 The relationship between concentration and insight is discussed at length in Phra Maha Singhathon Narasabho, *Buddhism: A Guide to a Happy Life* (Bangkok: Mahachulalongkornrajavidyalaya, 1971), which, despite its title, is an extended scholarly exposition of Buddhist methods of meditation according to the Pali canon. See also Vajirañāṇa Paravahera Mahāthera, *Buddhist Meditation in Theory and Practice* (Colombo: Gunasena 1962), pp. 341 – 3. More recently the problem has been examined by Paul Griffiths, 'Concentration or Insight: The Problematic of Theravāda Buddhist Meditation-Theory', *Journal of the American Academy of Religion* 49 (1981), pp. 605 – 24.

13 M i 175 – 84.

14 M i 16 – 24.

15 M i 22 – 3.

16 M i 182.

17 See *Visuddhi-magga* 412, transl. by Pe Maung Tin as *The Path of Purity* (London: Luzac, 1977), pp. 478 – 9.

18 The *Mahā-Satipaṭṭhāna-sutta* (D ii 290 – 315) and similar texts regarded as sources of information on insight meditation (*vipassanā*), make no reference to the three knowledges. Nowhere in the *suttas* is the relationship between insight meditation and the three knowledges explained, or even mentioned.

19 Only in the Vinaya-piṭaka (Mahāvagga I i 7) is Māra directly associated with Gotama's enlightenment, though throughout the Sutta-piṭaka he is portrayed as the Tempter; cf. the Māra *suttas* of the Saṃyutta-nikāya, S i 103 – 27. For the full later legend of the temptation by Māra before the enlightenment, see *Mahāvastu* ii 276 – 83 and 412 – 13. See also T. W. Rhys Davids, transl., *Buddhist Birth Stories or Jātaka Tales* (New York: Arno Press, 1977), no. 273, p. 101. Also on Māra, see Lowell W. Bloss, 'The Taming of Māra: Witnessing to the Buddha's Virtues', *History of Religions* 18 (1979), pp. 156 – 76.

20 Buddhadasa's position is most clearly stated in *Two Kinds of Language*, transl. Ariyananda Bhikkhu (Bangkok: Sublime Life Mission, 1974), and *Another Kind of Birth*, transl. R.B. (Bangkok: Sublime Life Mission, 1974). Portions of the former work are reprinted in Donald K. Swearer (ed.), *Toward the Truth* (Philadelphia: Westminster, 1971), pp. 56 – 86.

21 Buddhadasa, *Two Kinds of Language*, p. 14.

22 Ibid., pp. 20 – 4.

23 Wayman concludes that *saṃdhyā-bhāṣā* meaning 'twilight language', is the correct reading; Alex Wayman, 'Concerning saṃdhā-bhāṣā/saṃdhi-bhāṣā/saṃdhyā-bhāṣā', in *Mélanges d'indianisme à la mémoire de Louis Renou* (Paris: Éditions E. de Boccard, 1968), pp. 789 – 96. The following authors, however, prefer the translation 'intentional language': Vidhushekar Shastri, 'Sandhabhasa', *Indian Historical Quarterly* 4 (1928), pp. 287 – 96; Mircea Eliade, *Yoga: Immortality and Freedom*, transl. Willard R. Trask, 2nd ed. (London: Routledge and Kegan Paul, 1969), pp. 249 – 54; and Agehananda Bharati, *The Tantric Tradition* (London: Rider, 1965), pp. 164 – 84. The corresponding Tibetan terms *dgongs pa'i skad, gsang ba'i skad, ldem po, ldem por dgongs te bshad pa*, etc. appear to be used more or less interchangeably. Chinese translators have used variously *mi-i yü-yen* (Japanese *mitchi gogen*), *mi-i yen-i* (*mitchi gongi*), *sui-i so sho* (*zuigi shosetsu*), *yin-fu chih shuo* (*ombuku shi setsu*), etc. On the possibly rather different significance of the term *saṃdhā-bhāṣya* in the Lotus Sūtra (*Sanskrit Buddhist Texts*, vol. 6, p. 21; *Taishō*, vol. 9, p. 5c), see Toda Hirofumi, '*Saṃdhābhāṣya* in the *Saddharmapuṇḍarīkasūtra*', *Indogaku Bukkyōgaku*, 15 (1967), no. 2.

24 D. Snellgrove, *The Hevajra Tantra*, vol. I Introduction and Translation (London: Oxford University Press, 1959), p. 99.

25 W. Y. Evans-Wentz, *The Tibetan Book of the Dead* (New York: Oxford University Press, 1960), p. 3.

26 Benoytosh Bhattacharyya, *Introduction to Buddhist Esoterism* (London: Oxford University Press, 1932), p. 35.
27 Anagarika Govinda, *Foundations of Tibetan Mysticism* (London: Rider, 1960), p. 53.
28 Eliade, *Yoga: Immortality and Freedom*, p. 2.
29 On the purpose of the Twilight Language, see Bharati, *The Tantric Tradition*, pp. 168–72.
30 Alexandra David-Neel, *Magic and Mystery in Tibet* (London: Transworld, 1971), pp. 259–62.
31 The term *dhyāni Buddha* is of modern coinage, and its use has been criticized by some scholars; e.g. E. Dale Summers, 'A Note on Śakti and Dhyānibuddha', *History of Religions* 1 (1962), pp. 300–6. However, it is convenient and widely used, and will be adopted here.
32 These sets of symbols are listed in Shashi Bhushan Dasgupta, *An Introduction to Tantric Buddhism*, 2nd ed. (Calcutta: University of Calcutta Press, 1958), p. 110; also in Govinda, *Foundations of Tibetan Mysticism*, p. 87.
33 Govinda says: 'The maṇḍala is like a map of the inner world we want to explore and realize in the great venture of meditation.' Anagarika Govinda, *Creative Meditation and Multidimensional Consciousness* (London: Unwin Paperbacks, 1977), p. 60. See also *idem, Foundations of Tibetan Mysticism*, pp. 112–14. For other attempts to interpret the *maṇḍala* see C. G. Jung, 'Concerning Mandala Symbolism', in *Collected Works*, vol. 9, part 1 (London: Routledge and Kegan Paul, 1953–79), pp. 355–84; Giuseppe Tucci, *The Theory and Practice of the Mandala*, transl. A. H. Brodrick (London: Rider, 1969); and Grace E. Cairns, 'The Philosophy and Psychology of the Mandala', *Philosophy East and West* 11 (1962), pp. 219–29.
34 Govinda, *Foundations of Tibetan Mysticism*, p. 113.
35 Pierre Rambach, *The Art of Japanese Tantrism* (London: Skira/Macmillan, 1979), p. 105.
36 *The Tibetan Book of the Dead*, trans. by Francesca Fremantle and Chögyam Trungpa (Berkeley: Shambala, 1975), p. 46. As listed in the *Tibetan Book of the Dead*, the sequence of the *maṇḍala* cells begins at the centre then proceeds clockwise from the east. Consequently the western cell is the fourth.
37 Evans-Wentz, *The Tibetan Book of the Dead*, pp. 2–6.
38 Lama Anagarika Govinda, 'Introductory Foreword' to Evans-Wentz, *The Tibetan Book of the Dead*, p. lix. Elsewhere Govinda says that the 'intermediate state' discussed in the *Tibetan Book of the Dead* 'is not only the state between the physical death and the physical rebirth, but relates to every moment of our life.' Govinda, *Creative Meditation*, p. 192. For a discussion of some problems of interpretation of the *tantras*, see George R. Elder, 'Problems of Language in Buddhist Tantra', *History of Religions* 15 (1975), pp. 231–51.

39 Dasgupta, *An Introduction to Tantric Buddhism*, p. 150. The *bījas* (seed syllables) are variable; usually they are as in the *maṇḍala*.

40 E. Dale Saunders, *Mudrā: A Study of Symbolic Gestures in Japanese Buddhist Sculpture* (London: Routledge and Kegan Paul, 1960), p. 88.

41 Among the best is Wayman; see Alex Wayman, *The Buddhist Tantras: Light on Indo-Tibetan Esotericism* (London: Routledge and Kegan Paul, 1974).

42 Anagarika Govinda falls into this category. See Govinda, *Foundations of Tibetan Mysticism.*

43 The problem of methodology is discussed in Rod Bucknell and Martin Stuart-Fox, 'On the Methodology of Interpretation of Buddhist Symbolism', *The Journal of Religious Studies* 8, no. 2 (1980), pp. 38 – 57. A similar approach to that adopted in this book is proposed and applied in Rune E. A. Johansson, *The Psychology of Nirvāṇa* (London: George Allen and Unwin, 1969), especially pp. 13 – 14 on method.

Notes to Chapter II

1 A good study of the *śramaṇa* tradition is provided by Padmanabh S. Jaini, '*Śramaṇas*: Their conflict with Brahmanical society' in *Chapters in Indian Civilization*, vol. I, Classical and Medieval India, rev. ed., ed. by Joseph W. Elder (Dubuque, Iowa: Kendall/Hunt, 1970), pp. 40 – 81. See also A. L. Basham, 'The Rise of Buddhism in its Historical Context', *Asian Studies* 4 (1966), pp. 395 – 411; J. W. de Jong, 'The Background of Early Buddhism', *Journal of Indian and Buddhist Studies* 12 (1964), pp. 424 – 37 (34 – 47); A. K. Warder, *Indian Buddhism* (Delhi: Motilal Banarsidass, 1970), chapter 2; and Vishvanath Prasad Varma, *Early Buddhism and its Origins* (New Delhi: Munshiram Manoharlal, 1973).

2 On the importance of the guru-disciple relationship see Eliade, *Yoga: Immortality and Freedom*, p. 5, and pp. 165 – 6, where the author stresses the initiatory role of the guru in both Hindu yoga and Buddhism. For a discussion of initiation by a guru in Tantric Buddhism, see Bharati, *The Tantric Tradition*, chapter 7. See also Herbert V. Guenther, *Philosophy and Psychology in the Abhidharma* (Berkeley: Shambala, 1974), p. 191, note 1, where Guenther points out that that part of the path which deals exclusively with meditative processes 'is usually transmitted from teacher to disciple because certain exercises cannot be practised without the guidance of a teacher who himself has gone through the particular discipline.' Conze makes the same point. See Edward Conze, *Buddhism: Its Essence and Development*, 3rd ed. (Oxford: Bruno Cassirer, 1957), pp. 180, 198.

3 The account of Gotama's life story which follows is drawn almost entirely from the Pali Tipiṭaka. But, as many scholars have pointed

out, this is a sectarian compilation of the Theravādins not written down until centuries after Gotama's death. As a source for Gotama's biography, it must therefore be treated with care. There is no reason to believe, however, that the principal events recorded in the older parts of the canon are pure invention. In particular — and this is what is important for our argument — there is every reason to believe that the broad outline of Gotama's thinking, particularly in so far as it differed from then current ideas of other thinkers and ascetics, was faithfully recorded, for it was that which made Buddhism unique. But for references to the alternative view on whether it is possible to discover even in the earliest texts, Gotama the *śramaṇa* and his original teaching, see note 6 of Chapter I.

4 M i 116 – 117. 'Mental states' translates the Buddhist technical term *dhammā*, whose meaning in this context we discuss in Chapter VIII.

5 Gotama refused to discuss certain points: whether or not the world is eternal or infinite, the nature of the soul, and what happens to a Buddha after death. See M i 426, M i 484 – 485. On the reasons for Gotama's silence on these 'unexplained points', see Troy Wilson Organ, 'The Silence of the Buddha', *Philosophy East and West* 4 (1954), pp. 125 – 40; K. N. Upadhyaya, 'The Significance of the Buddha's Silence', *Philosophical Quarterly* 39 (1966), pp. 65 – 80; and Richard H. Robinson, 'Some Methodological Approaches to the Unexplained Points', *Philosophy East and West* 22 (1972), pp. 309 – 23.

6 Cf. D ii 154.

7 Ānanda is believed not to have achieved arahantship during Gotama's lifetime. His backwardness is alluded to at D ii 155. See C. P. Malalasekera (ed.), *Encyclopaedia of Buddhism* vol. I (Colombo: Government of Ceylon Press, 1961), p. 532. An extensive literature exists on the first council. See Charles S. Prebish, 'A Review of Scholarship on the Buddhist Councils', *Journal of Asian Studies* 33 (1974), pp. 239 – 54.

8 For evidence in the Tipiṭaka of these divisions, see A iii 355.

9 For developments in early Buddhist monasticism see Sukumar Dutt, *Early Buddhist Monachism 600 BC – 100 BC* (London: Kegan Paul, Trench, Trubner and Co., 1924), and *idem, The Buddha and Five After-Centuries* (London: Luzac, 1957). As Buddhism became a mass religion there arose a demand for objects of popular worship — at first symbols such as the *stūpa*, later on images of the Buddha. Little research has been done on the rise of popular Buddhism, but see Dutt, *The Buddha and Five After-Centuries*, Chapters 10, 13, and 14.

10 As Kalupahana has pointed out, since Gotama left only the Dharma as guide for the Sangha, instead of appointing a leader to succeed him, it was essential for his disciples to be sure of the nature of the doctrine. Hence the interest in the early Sangha in doctrinal exegesis. See David J. Kalupahana, *Buddhist Philosophy: A Historical Analysis* (Honolulu: The University Press of Hawaii, 1976), p. 93.

11 An example is the extension of the four *jhānas* described in the Suttapiṭaka to five in the Abhidhamma, apparently in order to accommodate more neatly the five *jhāna* factors. A discussion of this process and of relevant historical considerations is provided by Martin Stuart-Fox, '*Jhāna* and Buddhist Scholasticism', forthcoming.

12 An example of this can be found in the *Pāsādika-sutta* (D iii 127 – 8). The elaborate summaries of lists in the *Saṅgīti-sutta* (D iii 127 – 8) and *Dasuttara-sutta* (D iii 272 – 292) are both ascribed to Gotama's most advanced disciple Sāriputta. Pande has concluded that these three *suttas* were all late compilations; see Govind Chandra Pande, *Studies in the Origins of Buddhism*, 2nd ed. (Delhi: Motilal Banarsidass, 1974), pp. 115.

13 D ii 100. The same passage occurs at S v 152.

14 *The Book of the Kindred Sayings* Part V, trans. by F. L. Woodward (London: Luzac, 1956), p. 132.

15 Ibid., p. 132, note 2.

16 S v 437.

17 This is a widely held belief. Buddhaghosa distinguishes two modes of preaching, *sammutidesana* (pertaining to convention) and *paramatthadesana* (pertaining to the ultimate); see James W. Boyd, 'Symbols of Evil in Buddhism', *Journal of Asian Studies* 31 (1971), p. 74, quoting *Papañcasūdanī Majjhimanikāyaṭṭhakathā of Buddhaghosācariya* (London: Oxford University Press, 1928) I, 137. See also the *Laṅkāvatārasūtra*, 172, 17 – 18, which D. T. Suzuki translates: 'I teach the twofold truth: realization and teaching. I teach the ignorant: realization is for those who discipline themselves [in Buddhism].' Daisetz Teitaro Suzuki, *Studies in the Laṅkāvatāra Sūtra* (London: Routledge and Kegan Paul, 1930), p. 435. Sopa and Hopkins translate this passage in the following verse:

> My doctrine has two modes,
> Advice and tenets.
> To children I speak advice
> And to yogis, tenets.

Geshe Lhundup Sopa and Jeffrey Hopkins, *Practice and Theory of Tibetan Buddhism* (London: Rider, 1976), p. 53. To this can be linked the question of 'levels of understanding' in Buddhism, on which see Donald K. Swearer, 'Two Types of Saving Knowledge in the Pali *suttas*'. *Philosophy East and West* 22 (1972), pp. 355 – 72; and Herbert V. Guenther, 'The Levels of Understanding in Buddhism', *Journal of the American Oriental Society* 78 (1958), pp. 19 – 28.

18 A number of *suttas* in the Tipiṭaka are said to have been delivered by disciples of Gotama on his instructions; e.g. the *Saṅgīti-sutta* by Sāriputta (D iii 209) and the *Sekha-sutta* by Ānanda (M i 354).

19 The implausibility of this tradition does not affect our conclusion that information imparted by Gotama in private would not have found its way into the Tipiṭaka.

20 These developments are examined by Dutt, *The Buddha and Five After-Centuries*, especially chapters 7 and 8. Pande states: 'As Buddhist dogmatics grew and Buddhists came to believe in theories and speculation with a zeal paralleled only by the Master's condemnation of them, intellectual understanding came to be regarded as the primary way to the knowledge of truth'. Pande, *Studies in the Origins of Buddhism*, p. 358.

21 In the process Buddhism came to absorb certain Hindu concepts and vice versa. This is especially evident in the later Mahāyāna schools such as the Vijñānavāda, and in Advaita Vedānta. These cross-influences have been insufficiently studied, but for reference to them, see e.g., T. R. V. Murti, *The Central Philosophy of Buddhism* 2nd ed. (London: George Allen and Unwin, 1960), pp. 109 – 17; and S. Radhakrishnan, *Indian Philosophy*, vol. II (London: George Allen and Unwin, 1927), pp. 456 – 60. See also J. E. Jennings, *The Vedāntic Buddhism of the Buddha* (Delhi: Motilal Banarsidass, 1947).

22 Even in Ceylon where Buddhism was the state religion, it was apparently not easy by the fifth century A.D. to find a competent meditation master. Cf. Buddhaghosa, *Visuddhi-magga* 121.

23 Also known as the Mantrayāna. Among the best studies of the Vajrayāna are Bharati, *The Tantric Tradition*, and Wayman, *The Buddhist Tantras: Light on Indo-Tibetan Esotericism.* See also Dasgupta, *An Introduction to Tantric Buddhism.*

24 See David-Neel, *Magic and Mystery in Tibet*, pp. 221 – 2. Also see Dasgupta, *An Introduction to Tantric Buddhism*, p. 159, for the dangers of Tantric practices without the guidance of a qualified guru.

25 See Tenzin Gyatso, *The Buddhism of Tibet and the Key to the Middle Way*, trans. Jeffrey Hopkins and Lati Rimpoche (New York: Harper and Row, 1975), p. 20. Cf. W. Y. Evans-Wentz, ed., *The Tibetan Book of the Great Liberation* (London: Oxford University Press, 1954), p. 122, note 1, where the three turnings of the wheel are called the Three Secret Doctrines.

26 On the *Guhyasamāja-tantra*, see Alex Wayman, *Yoga of the Guhyasamājatantra* (Delhi: Motilal Banarsidass, 1977).

27 See, e.g., Snellgrove, *The Hevajra Tantra*, vol. I, pp. 99 – 100.

28 See the discussion of this secret transmission in Bharati, *The Tantric Tradition*, chapter 6. Cf. also Eva M. Dargyay, *The Rise of Esoteric Buddhism in Tibet* (Delhi: Motilal Banarsidass, 1979).

29 Cf. W. Y. Evans-Wentz, *Tibetan Yoga and Secret Doctrines*, 2nd ed. (Oxford: Oxford University Press, 1958), p. 101, where the important meditative practices incorporated in *The Epitome of the Great Symbol* are traced back to the first century B.C.

30 For the origins of the Buddha image see David L. Snellgrove, ed., *The Image of the Buddha* (Paris: UNESCO, 1978).

31 See D. L. Snellgrove, *Buddhist Himalaya* (Oxford: Bruno Cassirer 1957), pp. 64 – 6.

32 For speculation on reasons for the development of the Twilight Language, see Bharati, *The Tantric Tradition*, pp. 168 – 172.

33 A more detailed argument in support of an esoteric tradition in early Buddhism is presented in Rod Bucknell and Martin Stuart-Fox, 'Did the Buddha impart an esoteric teaching?', *Journal of Indian History* 61 (1983), pp. 1 – 17.

Notes to Chapter III

1 *Visuddhi-magga* 112 – 17 (*The Path of Purity*, pp. 129 – 37).

2 Vajirañāṇa, *Buddhist Meditation*, p. 227.

3 Singhathon, *Buddhism: A Guide to A Happy Life*, p. 190.

4 Ibid., p. 120.

5 M i 246 and I. B. Horner, *The Middle Length Sayings* vol. I (London: Luzac, 1967), p. 301, note 3. (Reference is to the *Papañcasūdanī* ii 291.)

6 *Papañcasūdanī Majjhimanikāyaṭṭhakathā of Buddhaghosācariya* ed. J. H. Woods and D. Kosambi, vol. I (London: Pali Text Society/Routledge and Kegan Paul, 1977), p. 124.

7 M iii 82.

8 E.g. M i 56, M i 421, *Visuddhi-magga* 266 – 93 (*The Path of Purity*, pp. 305 – 77).

9 M iii 82.

10 The following account is based on the *Visuddhi-magga*.

11 The meditative experiences described in this chapter are discussed in more detail in Rod Bucknell, 'Interpreting the *Jhānas*: Problems of Correlating Theory and Practice', forthcoming.

12 S ii 94.

13 J. Krishnamurti, *Talks: Krishnamurti in Europe, 1968* (n.p. The Netherlands: Servire/Wassenaar, 1969), pp. 132 – 3.

14 Krishnamurti, *Freedom from the Known*, p. 103.

15 Krishnamurti, *Talks: Krishnamurti in Europe, 1968*, p. 50. Krishnamurti advocates developing this image-free condition through communing with nature rather than through the systematic practice of concentration, which he regards as 'a waste of energy' (ibid., p. 73).

16 Robert S. De Ropp, *The Master Game: Pathways to Higher Consciousness Beyond the Drug Experience* (London: George Allen and Unwin, 1968), pp. 72 and 73 – 4. A similar experience following the practice of mindfulness (essentially a form of concentration) is described by Shattock: 'I became far more intensely aware of the characteristically golden-toned singing of the temple bells . . . It filled the whole of my awareness, and became a part of me.' E. H. Shattock, *An Experiment in Mindfulness* (London: Rider, 1958), p. 69.

17 Walsh, 'Initial Meditative Experiences: Part I', p. 184.

18 Krishnamurti, *Talks: Krishnamurti in Europe, 1968*, pp. 117–18.
19 De Ropp, *The Master Game*, p. 71.
20 For a discussion of *nimittas*, see Narada Maha Thera, *A Manual of Abhidhamma* (Kandy: Buddhist Publication Society, 1968), pp. 47–9.
21 Such effects, known to meditation masters as 'defilements of insight' (*vipassanupakilesa*), are generally considered to be distractions from the path to enlightenment.
22 M ii 14–15; *Visuddhi-magga* 118–77 (*The Path of Purity*, pp. 138–204).
23 For a description of the technique by its discoverer see Mahasi Sayadaw, *Practical Insight Meditation*, trans. U Pe Thin and Myanaung U Tin (Kandy: The Forest Hermitage, 1971); also Nyanaponika Thera, *The Heart of Buddhist Meditation* (London: Rider, 1972), pp. 85–107.
24 At a '*vipassanā* centre' in Bangkok, where R.B. practised for a time, the technique taught was nominally Burmese *vipassanā*. However, any resemblance to Mahasi's technique proved only superficial. The practice of observing sensations and thoughts, which figured in the earlier part of the course, was soon abandoned in favour of simple concentration, and the culmination was the same plunge into mental emptiness as may be attained through mindfulness of breathing or any other concentration exercise. The method taught at that centre (and some others) was severely criticized by certain masters whom R.B. subsequently consulted. It had, they claimed, departed widely from the originally intended course of practice, and therefore did not qualify as *vipassanā*.
25 E.g. M i 21–3.
26 *Yogaścittavṛttinirodhaḥ*. Patañjali, *Yogasūtras* i 2. On Hindu *samādhi* see K. S. Joshi, 'Is Samādhi a State of Concentration?', *Philosophical Quarterly* 38 (1965), pp. 55–9; also Ian Kesarcodi-Watson, 'Samādhi in Patañjali's Yoga Sūtras', *Philosophy East and West* 32 (1982), pp. 77–90.
27 The relationship between *samatha* and *vipassanā* is not entirely clear in the Tipiṭaka (see Chapter I, note 12, above). The four *rūpa jhānas* serve as preparation sometimes for the three knowledges and sometimes for the four *arūpa* (formless) *jhānas*, followed optionally by *nirodha* (cessation of consciousness). The latter course is pure *samatha*; yet occasionally the *arūpa jhānas*, with or without *nirodha*, are said to be followed immediately by destruction of the *āsavas* (M i 159–60, A v 204–9). This conflicts with the statement that the *arūpa jhānas* do not 'expunge' unskilful states (M i 41–2) and with the fact that Gotama became dissatisfied with his early teachers who taught only the *jhānas*. It has been suggested, originally by Friedrich Heiler and later by Winston King, that the *arūpa jhānas* and *nirodha* represent a late 'yogic imposition on Gotama's original scheme culminating in the three knowledges'. (See Winston L. King,

Theravāda Meditation: The Buddhist Transformation of Yoga (University Park and London: The Pennsylvania State University Press, 1980), p. 15.) To us this seems an extreme view. We would, however, agree that the inclusion of destruction of the *āsavas* immediately after *nirodha* represents a textual corruption. Destruction of the *āsavas* is the culmination of the path of *vipassanā* (through the three knowledges); it has no place in the path of pure *samatha* (the *arūpa jhānas* and *nirodha*).

Notes to Chapter IV

1 Quoted in Alan W. Watts, *The Way of Zen* (Harmondsworth: Pelican, 1962), p. 114.

2 Buddhadasa Bhikkhu, *Handbook for Mankind* (Bangkok: Sublime Life Mission, 1969), pp. 94 – 5. Reprinted in Jack Kornfield, *Living Buddhist Masters* (Santa Cruz: Unity Press, 1977), p. 121.

3 Ibid., p. 95. Another Thai master, Achaan Chaa, similarly says: 'Absorption [*jhāna*] is not necessary. You must establish a modicum of tranquillity and one-pointedness of mind. Then use this to examine yourself.' Quoted in Kornfield, *Living Buddhist Masters*, p. 42. Govinda makes the same point: 'We should not imagine that by the suppression of thought or of our intellectual faculties, we can attain enlightenment'. Govinda, *Creative Meditation*, p. 21.

4 Ernest E. Wood, *Mind and Memory Training* (London: Pitman, 1947), p. 89.

5 Christmas Humphreys, *Concentration and Meditation* 3rd ed. (London: Stuart and Watkins, 1968), p. 54. (Our emphasis.)

6 Donald K. Swearer, *Secrets of the Lotus* (New York: Macmillan, 1971), pp. 212 – 35

7 Ibid., p. 214.

8 Ibid., p. 215.

9 Krishnamurti, *Freedom from the Known*, p. 103.

10 The Tibetan master, Tarthang, suggests a slightly different analogy: 'Mental events — thoughts — are like a motion picture: though there is a sense of continuity, continuity itself is an illusion created by the projection of a series of similar — but actually individual images.' Tarthang Tülku, *Openness Mind* (Berkeley: Dharma, 1978), p. 104.

11 On this technique, see David-Neel, *Magic and Mystery in Tibet*, pp. 241 – 2. According to Darian, 'Since all is *śūnyatā*, the gods themselves have no real existence . . . they served as an aid to concentration.' Stephen G. Darian, 'Antecedents of Tantrism in the Saddharma-Puṇḍarīka', *Asiatische Studien* 24 (1970), pp. 121 – 2.

12 For further examples of *kōans*, see Paul Reps (ed.), *Zen Flesh, Zen Bones* (Harmondsworth: Penguin, 1971), pp. 95 – 131; also Watts, *The Way of Zen*, pp. 182 – 92.

13 Others have attempted to explain *kōan*-solving in different terms.

See, for example, D. T. Suzuki, *Zen Buddhism*, ed. by William Barrett (Garden City, New York: Doubleday, 1956), p. 138, where the purpose of the *kōan* is said to be to force the mind 'to go beyond the limits of intellection'. Reps says the Chinese masters devised *kōans* 'to stop their students' word-drunkenness and mind wandering'. Reps, *Zen Flesh, Zen Bones*, p. 91. For an interpretaion of Theravāda equivalents of the Zen *kōan* practice see Winston L. King, 'A Comparison of Theravāda and Zen Buddhist Meditational Methods and Goals', *History of Religions* 9 (1970), pp. 314–15.

14 This is demonstrated by the 'Perky effect', on which see Sydney J. Segal and Shifra Nathan, 'The Perky effect: Incorporation of an external stimulus into an imagery experience under placebo and control conditions', *Perceptual and Motor Skills* 18 (1964), pp. 385–95.

15 For a summary of work in this area, see Richardson, *Mental Imagery*, pp. 115–18.

16 Francis Galton, *Inquiries into Human Faculty and its Development* 2nd ed. (London: Dent, 1907), pp. 133–4.

17 Padma Karpo, 'Yoga of the Six Doctrines', in W. Y. Evans-Wentz, *Tibetan Yoga and Secret Doctrines*, 2nd ed. (Oxford: Oxford University Press, 1958), p. 242.

18 *The Śūraṅgama-sūtra* (*Leng Yen Ching* [Taishō 945]), trans. by Upāsaka Lu K'uan Yü (Charles Luk), (London: Rider, 1966), p. 139. Also suggestive of retracing is the following statement by the Ch'an (Zen) master Yung-chia: 'Illusory thoughts come forth in disorder; yet if we trace them back to their source, they are nothing but silence'. Quoted in Chang Chung-yuan, *Original Teachings of Ch'an Buddhism* (New York: Random House, 1971), p. 31.

19 Swearer, *Secret of the Lotus*, pp. 214–15.

20 Ibid., p. 215.

21 Humphreys, *Concentration and Meditation*, pp. 57–8.

22 J. Krishnamurti, *The Penguin Krishnamurti Reader*, ed. by Mary Lutyens, (Harmondsworth: Penguin, 1971), p. 121.

23 Krishnamurti, *Freedom from the Known*, pp. 115–16.

24 Ibid., pp. 114–16. Krishnamurti also sometimes uses the term 'choiceless awareness' with the same meaning. Less common synonyms adopted by some authorities include 'bare attention', 'watchfulness', and 'self-remembering'.

25 Quoted in Swearer, *Secrets of the Lotus*, pp. 28, 33, 36, 51.

26 Dhiravamsa, *A New Approach to Buddhism* (Lower Lake, Calif.: Dawn Horse Press, 1974), pp. 31, 39.

27 Ibid., p. 39.

28 Tarthang Tülku, *Gesture of Balance* (Emeryville, Calif.: Dharma, 1977), pp. 67, 71, 116, 120. Chögyam Trungpa, another Tibetan master teaching in the West, says much the same: 'Whenever thoughts arise, just observe them *as thoughts* . . . What usually happens when we have thoughts, is that we are not aware that they are thoughts at all . . .' Chögyam Trungpa, 'Meditation', in Virginia

Hanson (ed.), *Approaches to Meditation* (Wheaton, Ill.: Theosophical Society Publishing House, 1973), p. 136.

29 David-Neel, *Magic and Mystery in Tibet*, pp. 245 – 6.

30 Ibid., p. 245.

31 Alexandra David-Neel, *Secret Oral Teachings in Tibetan Buddhist Sects* (Calcutta: Maha Bodhi Society of India, 1964), p. 95. Cf. the following statement by Govinda, who also travelled extensively in Tibet: 'Meditation . . . means to be conscious of consciousness, to become a detached observer of the stream of changing thoughts'. Anargarika Govinda, 'The Significance of Meditation in Buddhism', in Hanson (ed.), *Approaches to Meditation*, p. 18.

32 Padmo Karpo, 'Manual of the Spontaneous Great Symbol' in Stephan Beyer, *The Buddhist Experience* (Encino, Calif.: Dickenson, 1974), pp. 158 – 60.

33 Padma Karpo, 'Epitome of the Great Symbol', in Evans-Wentz, *Tibetan Yoga and Secret Doctrines*, pp. 129, 138.

34 Dhiravamsa, *A New Approach to Buddhism*, p. 29.

35 J. Krishnamurti, *Krishnamurti in India 1970 – 71* (n.p., India: Krishnamurti Foundation, 1971), p. 50.

36 Krishnamurti, *Freedom from the Known*, p. 115.

37 See, for example, Edwin G. Boring, *A History of Experimental Psychology*, 2nd ed. (Bombay: The Times of India Press, 1969), pp. 190 – 1, 197 – 8, 217, 224 – 5, 228 – 9, 238 – 9.

38 Compare the following description by Walsh: 'It soon became apparent that the type of material which forceably erupted into awareness and disrupted concentration was most often material . . . around which there was considerable affective charge. Indeed, it seemed that the stronger the attachment or charge, the more often the material could arise.' Walsh, 'Initial Meditative Experiences: Part I', p. 162.

39 It is perhaps to this that Padma Karpo was referring when he said: 'keep your mind as if you were spinning a thread . . . keep an even tension upon your mind by alternatively tensing and relaxing it.' Quoted in Beyer, *The Buddhist Experience*, p. 158.

40 Krishnamurti, *Krishnamurti in India 1970 – 71*, p. 85.

41 Tarthang, *Gesture of Balance*, p. 117.

42 Krishnamurti, *Penguin Krishnamurti Reader*, p. 122.

43 Ibid., p. 133.

44 Krishnamurti, *Krishnamurti in India 1970 – 71*, p. 50.

45 Krishnamurti, *Freedom from the Known*, p. 103.

46 Quoted in Beyer, *The Buddhist Experience*, p. 160.

47 Tarthang, *Openness Mind*, pp. 121, 122. Also cf. Dhiravamsa: 'When you can observe closely enough how each thought presents itself, you will see that there is no thinker apart from the thinking, and there is no thinking apart from the thought.' V. R. Dhiravamsa, *The Way of Non-Attachment: The Practice of Insight Meditation* (New York: Schocken Books, 1977), p. 18. Similarly Walsh and Vaughan: 'Awareness now perceives itself as being that which it

formerly looked at'. Walsh and Vaughan, *Beyond Ego*, pp. 59–60; and Goldstein: 'The thought is the thinker. There is no-one behind it. The thought is thinking itself'. Joseph Goldstein, *The Experience of Insight: A Natural Unfolding* (Santa Cruz: Unity Press, 1976), p. 27.

48 Krishnamurti, *Freedom from the Known*, p. 98.

49 For a first-person account of this course of practice from the point of view of the meditator, see Bucknell, 'Experiments in Insight Meditation'.

50 Also not mentioned in our account is meditation on the qualities of the Buddha (*Buddhānussati*), a practice that resembles meditation in the Christian sense. Such meditation on a prescribed topic usually entails contemplating the content of thought *for the sake of that content*. Insight meditation is quite different in that attention is directed to how the mind functions: mental content is important only in so far as it illustrates mental function.

51 E.g. D ii 120, D iii 253. But cf. A ii 141, where *paññā* is omitted, and the variant listing at A iii 9 and A v 123–4.

52 M iii 82, see p. 37 above.

53 See M i 181, M i 346.

54 D ii 290–315.

Notes to Chapter V

1 The Tenfold Path is listed in several places, e.g. D ii 217, D iii 271. But where the stages are explained at all, explanation of the last two is quite inadequate. See, e.g., M iii 71–8.

2 M i 482; also S ii 213–14. On the Buddha's omniscience, see Padmanabh S. Jaini, 'On the *Sarvajñatva* (omniscience) of Mahāvīra and the Buddha', in L. Cousins, A. Kunst, and K. R. Norman (eds.), *Buddhist Studies in Honour of I. B. Horner* (Dordrecht: Reidel, 1974), pp. 71–90.

3 *Milinda-pañha* 102. The translation is from T. W. Rhys-Davids, *The Questions of King Milinda* vol. I (Oxford: Clarendon, 1890), p. 154. I. B. Horner has in her translation 'knowledge-and-vision was not constantly and continuously present to the Lord. The Lord's omniscient knowledge was dependent on the adverting [of his mind].' *Milinda's Questions*, vol. I (London: Luzac, 1969), p. 142.

4 D i 81.

5 *Visuddhi-magga* 412–13 (*The Path of Purity*, pp. 478–9).

6 Vasubandhu, *Abhidharma-kośa* vii 123, in Eliade, *Yoga: Immortality and Freedom*, p. 184.

7 Mircea Eliade, *Myths, Dreams, and Mysteries* (London: Collins, 1968), p. 50.

8 Ibid.

9 Dhiravamsa, *A New Approach to Buddhism*, p. 14.

10 Chögyam Trungpa, commentary to Freemantle and Trungpa, *The Tibetan Book of the Dead*, p. 2.
11 Anagarika Govinda, foreword to Evans-Wentz, *The Tibetan Book of the Dead*, p. lx.
12 Anagarika Govinda, *The Psychological Attitude of early Buddhist Philosophy* (London: Rider, 1969), p. 128.
13 Watts, *The Way of Zen*, p. 69.
14 Buddhadasa, *Another Kind of Birth*, pp. 2–5. (Emphasis in original.)
15 This question is discussed in detail in Rod Bucknell and Martin Stuart-Fox, 'The "Three Knowledges" of Buddhism: Implications of Buddhadasa's Interpretation of Rebirth', *Religion* 13 (1983), pp. 99–112.
16 This equation appears to be stated in the Tibetan *Phyag-rgya-chen-po'i man-ngag gi bshad-byar rgyal-ba'i gan-mdzod*: '. . . discursiveness is memory and association, memory and association are creative activity, creative activity is *saṃsāra*'. Quoted in Herbert V. Guenther, *Tibetan Buddhism in Western Perspective* (Emeryville, Calif.: Dharma, 1977), p. 40. Even more explicit is the following statement from the *Maitrī Upaniṣad*, which is probably sufficiently late to have been influenced by Buddhist ideas: 'One's own thought, indeed, is *saṃsāra*.' *Maitrī Upaniṣad* vi 34.
17 D i 83.
18 A iii 415. Cf. Johansson's discussion of *viññāṇa* and *saṅkhārā*. The latter is 'the effector of the deeds (*kamma*)', while the former, the 'dynamic stream of consciousness', is 'the accumulator of the effects'. See Johansson, *The Psychology of Nirvāṇa*, pp. 71–2.
19 T. W. Rhys Davids and William Stede, *Pali-English Dictionary* (London: Luzac, 1959), p. 271, *cetanā*.
20 On the implausibility of the *karma* doctrine, even in its Buddhist form, see Paul J. Griffiths, 'Notes Towards a Critique of Buddhist Karmic Theory', *Religious Studies* 18 (1982), pp. 277–91.
21 Phra Khantipalo, *Buddhism Explained* (Bangkok: Mahamakut Rajavidayalaya Press, 1973), p. 34.
22 Buddhadasa, *Handbook for Mankind*, pp. 40–1. Cf. *Pali-English Dictionary*, p. 191. Those items of sense data towards which there has been a strong emotional response, whether 'positive' or 'negative', are the ones most frequently re-presented to consciousness in the form of images; those towards which there has been no emotional reaction are re-presented rarely if at all. (For example, we remember best the people we love most dearly or hate most bitterly; those about whom we have neutral feelings are soon forgotten.)
23 *Abhidhammattha-saṅgaha* V ii. (Our translation).
24 Cf. Nārada Mahā Thera, *A Manual of Abhidhamma, being Abhidhammattha-Sangaha of Bhadanta Anuruddhācariya* (Kandy: Buddhist Publication Society, 1968), pp. 265–73. A similar explanation

is given in V. F. Gunaratna, *Rebirth Explained* (Wheel Publications No. 167/168/169, Kandy: Buddhist Publication Society, 1971), p. 21.

25 D i 84.

26 The difficulties in translating *āsava* are discussed in T. W. Rhys Davids, *Dialogues of the Buddha* (London: The Pali Text Society, 1973) Part I, pp. 92–3, note 3. For a full discussion of *āsavas*, see G. P. Malalasekera (ed.), *Encyclopaedia of Buddhism* vol. 2 (Colombo: Government of Ceylon, 1966), pp. 202–14.

27 See *Pali-English Dictionary*, p. 114, *āsava*.

28 Listed at M i 23, 255, etc. A fourth *āsava, diṭṭhi* (false view), is sometimes included, e.g. at D ii 98.

29 The three *lokas* are also called *avacaras* and, confusingly, *bhavas*. See *Pali-English Dictionary*, pp. 589, 499; and D ii 57.

30 See Nārada, *A Manual of Abhidhamma*, pp. 32–4, 49, etc.

31 These two categories are represented in many other sets of 'unskilful states', e.g. the familiar triad *lobha, dosa, moha* (desire, aversion, delusion) (A i 201). *Moha* respresents category (1) ignorance; *lobha* and *dosa* together represent category (2) affective states. Further examples are given in Chapter VIII.

32 Buddhadasa, *Two Kinds of Language*, pp. 3–4. Buddhadasa appears to have misinterpreted the passage from the Tipiṭaka which he cites (S i 87, A iii 48), but the point he makes is valid nevertheless.

33 This parallelism is spelled out in some detail in the Vedas (e.g. at *Ṛg Veda* x 16 3; x 59 5–7; x 58; x 161 5). It underpinned belief in the efficacy of Brahmanic sacrificial ritual as this developed in the *Atharva Veda* and the Brāhmaṇas. (Cf. the identity spelled out in the *Śatapatha Brāhmaṇa* (vi) between the fire sacrifice and the universe.) It also informed much Upaniṣadic speculation (cf. *Bṛhadāraṇyaka Up.* 2 v 1–15; 3 ii 13; *Chāndogya Up.* 3 13; 5 11–23; *Aitareya Up.* 1 i 4 etc.). The identity of ātman (the microcosmic self) with Brahman (the macrocosmic world-principle), which is the central teaching of the Upaniṣads may be seen as representing a philosophical extension of the earlier materialistic parallelism of the Brāhmaṇas. The concept of macrocosm-microcosm parallelism was not confined to Indian thought. On its appearance in Western European and Islamic, Hebrew, and Greek thought, see George Perrigo Conger, *Theories of Macrocosm and Microcosm in the History of Philosophy* (New York: Russell and Russell, 1967); also Alex Wayman, 'The Human Body as Microcosm in India, Greek cosmology, and Sixteenth Century Europe', *History of Religions* 22 (1982), pp. 172–90.

34 On the anthropomorphic universe see Narendr Nath Bhattacharyya, *Jain Philosophy: Historical Outline* (New Delhi: Munshiram Manoharlal, 1976), pp. 140–5. See also Heinrich Zimmer, *Myths and Symbols in Indian Art and Civilization*, ed. Joseph Campbell (New York: Harper and Row, 1962), p. 56, note 1.

35 Cf. Thomas J. Hopkins, *The Hindu Religious Tradition* (Encino, Calif.: Dickenson, 1971), chapter 2.

36 As Reat states: '. . . early Buddhism incorporates, in a fundamentally rational theoretical system, the basic insight of the Upaniṣadic synthesis of Vedic and Yogic thought, namely that the human being is the supreme being and that all of the mysteries of the universe are generated and resolved within the human mind.' Noble Ross Reat, 'The Origins of Buddhist Psychology', PhD thesis, University of Lancaster, 1980. That for Gotama the microcosm of mind reflects the macrocosm of the universe is evident from the following often repeated statement: 'It is in this fathom-long carcase, friend, with its impressions and its ideas that, I declare, lies the world, and the cause of the world, and the cessation of the world, and the course of action that leads to the cessation of the world' (S i 62). As Govinda has noted concerning Tantric thought, microcosm-macrocosm parallelism was all-inclusive between 'mind and universe, ritual and reality, the world of matter and the world of the spirit'. Govinda, *Foundations of Tibetan Mysticism*, p. 93.

37 Buddhadasa, *Another Kind of Birth*, p. 16.

38 Ibid.

39 On this point Tarthang says: 'As we develop more balance, our mind gravitates more easily to a deeper level of awareness. When we learn to sustain this awareness for longer and longer periods, it becomes like an internal light, always radiant'. Tarthang, *Openness Mind*, p. 106.

40 As noted in Chapter IV, retracing and observation of linking, both of which entail disrupting the flow of thought, can be practised only intermittently, while awareness, which entails no such disruption, can be practised uninterruptedly. This contrast is paralleled in Gotama's attainment of the three knowledges: the first and second were intermittent, the third was permanent. See M i 482.

41 This is hardly surprising as the two are consistently confused in the Tipiṭaka; and, as we suggest below, Gotama himself probably did not distinguish them.

Notes to Chapter VI

1 See page 20, where note is taken of the traditional association of Amitābha's meditation *mudrā* with Māra's attack on the meditating Gotama, and of Akṣobhya's earth-touching *mudrā* with Gotama's repulsing that attack. In addition, Amoghasiddhi's no-danger *mudrā* is associated with Gotama's subduing a wild elephant, and Vairocana's Dharma-wheel *mudrā* is similarly associated with Gotama's first teaching of the Dharma after his enlighenment. These and other symbolic cross-references are further discussed in the next chapter.

2 Eliade stresses that the essential characteristic of religious symbolism is its 'multivalence, its capacity to express simultaneously a number

of meanings whose continuity is not evident on the plane of immediate experience'. Mircea Eliade, 'Methodological Remarks on the Study of Religious Symbolism', in Mircea Eliade and Joseph M. Kitagawa (eds.), *The History of Religions: Essays in Methodology* (Chicago: University of Chicago Press, 1959), p. 99.

3 Both the *maṇḍala* and the *cakra* system are variable in structure. The tables represent the most widely recognized versions.

4 For a more detailed discussion of the approach adopted in this chapter, see Bucknell and Stuart-Fox, 'On the Methodology of Interpretation of Buddhist Symbolism'.

5 For the Vedic roots of this symbolic division, see J. Gonda, *Triads in the Veda* (Amsterdam: North Holland, 1976). For a discussion of their application in Tantric Buddhism, see Alex Wayman, 'Female Energy and Symbolism in the Buddhist Tantras', *History of Religions* 2 (1962), pp. 87–94.

6 This threefold classification is one of several applied to the Indian letters; however, it is the only one immediately relevant to the present case.

7 This set of 'the four great elements' (*mahābhūta*) is the one recognized throughout most of the Sutta-piṭaka, e.g. at D i 55, M i 53. The later set of five elements (see below) occurs there only rarely. On the importance of the number four, see Dipak Bhattacharya, 'The Doctrine of Four in the Early Upaniṣads and some Connected Problems', *Journal of Indian Philosophy* 6 (1978), pp. 1–34. Bhattacharya refers to macrocosm-microcosm parallelism as 'macro-micro symmetry' and emphasizes that whereas 'it does not have any immediate significant development in the Upaniṣads', it did 're-appear in the Tantras in a far more refined form' (p. 11).

8 This set is mentioned repeatedly throughout the Tipiṭaka and post-canonical works, e.g. at D i 76, M i 293, and *Visuddhimagga* 172–174.

9 These four shapes are said to be represented in the principal sections of the Tibetan *chörten* (*stūpa*), namely the square base, the globular main section, the slender conical tower, and the small crescentic top-piece. (Often a drop-shaped fifth section is included, to pair with space.) See Plate 7; also cf. Govinda, *Foundations of Tibetan Mysticism*, p. 185. They are more explicitly depicted in a form of Japanese funerary tower known as the *gorintō* (or *gorinsotoba*), literally 'five-wheel-tower', where 'wheel' is to be equated with '*cakra*'. See *Japanese-English-Buddhist Dictionary* (Tokyo: Daitō Shuppansha, 1965), p. 87, *gorinsotoba*; and Rambach, *The Art of Japanese Tantrism*, p. 57. The two-dimensional counterparts of the four shapes are represented in an early version of the Indian world-map, as a set of four continents having the shapes of a square (or sometimes a rectangle), circle, triangle, and semicircle. See Fig. 11; also cf. N. N. Bhattacharyya, 'Bramanical, Buddhist and Jain Cosmography', *Journal of Indian History* 47 (1969), p. 58.

10 In the Sutta-piṭaka *ākāsa*, as one of the elements or *mahābhūtas*, occurs only rarely, e.g. at M i 413, S iii 227. The addition of *ākāsa* to the basic set of four elements therefore appears to be relatively late. On this point see Malalasekera, *Encyclopaedia of Buddhism* vol. I, p. 341.

11 Most of the other triads (e.g. female, male, union) were similarly treated, the third member being transferred from air to space. However, in a few cases the original association with air was retained and a new fourth member was added to pair with space. (E.g. the triad moon, sun, eclipse was retained and given light as fourth member.) Other kinds of revision also took place. An interesting case is that of the Upaniṣadic triad *vāk, manas*, and *prāṇa* (speech, mind, and breath). These were originally classified thus: *vāk/manas/prāṇa* = female/male/union, thereby recognizing breath as supreme; but with the later recognition of mind as supreme, *manas* and *prāṇa* were interchanged. See *Bṛhadāraṇyaka Upaniṣad* 1 v 7 and 5 viii 1. This case is discussed by Reat in the context of the growing recognition of the importance of mind during the immediately pre-Buddhist period of Upaniṣadic thought; see Reat, 'The Origins of Buddhist Psychology', pp. 288–91. For a discussion of four- and five-membered sets in Tantric Buddhism, see Wayman, 'Female Energy and Symbolism in the Buddhist Tantras', pp. 94–100.

12 Probably also an important contributing factor was the popularity of cruciform arrangements. These defined five positions: the four cardinal points and the centre.

13 The sections of the *chörten* or *gorintō* are regarded as symbolizing the elements; in Japan they often have the names of the elements inscribed on them. See Rambach, *The Art of Japanese Tantrism*, p. 57, upper photograph.

14 In south Indian temples these symbols for the two eclipses may be seen in plaques representing the 'nine planets' (*navagraha*). The nine are arranged in three rows of three, and each row corresponds to an element as shown:

3. air:	lunar eclipse	Saturn	solar eclipse
2. fire:	Mars	Sun	Jupiter
1. water:	Moon	Venus	Mercury

15 On Vāyu and his flag emblem, see T. A. Gopinatha Rao, *Elements of Hindu Iconography* (Delhi: Motilal Banarsidass, 1968), vol. II, p. 532 and Plate cli.

16 On this classification of Amitābha, Akṣobhya, and Vairocana, see Wayman, 'Female Energy and Symbolism', pp. 89–90.

17 On the 'five Ms', see Benjamin Walker, *The Hindu World*, vol. I (New York: Praeger, 1968), p. 221; on the five 'body-fluids' see Elder, 'Problems of Language in Buddhist Tantra', pp. 241–2.

18 See Wayman, 'Female Energy and Symbolism', pp. 89–90; also Snellgrove, *The Hevajra Tantra* vol. I, p. 27.

19 For correspondences between the dhyāni Buddhas and the five

wisdoms see Snellgrove, *The Hevajra Tantra* vol. I, p. 128 – 9. For a discussion of the five wisdoms, see Wayman, *The Yoga of the Guhyasamājatantra*, pp. 213 – 15, and Alex Wayman 'The Mirror-Like Knowledge in Mahāyāna Buddhist Literature', *Asiatische Studien* 25 (1971), pp. 353 – 63; also Herbert V. Guenther, *The Life and Teaching of Naropa* (London: Oxford University Press, 1963), p. 73, note 1.

20 D iii 105. See Vishwanath Pandey, 'Early Buddhist Conception of Consciousness', *Bharatiya Vidya* 29 (1972), p. 68, note 95.

21 As quoted in Beyer, *The Buddhist Experience*, p. 157. See also Evans-Wentz, *Tibetan Yoga and Secret Doctrines*, p. 129.

22 *Calm and Clear, Mi-pham 'Jam-dbyangs rnam-gyal rgya-mtsho*, transl. by Tarthang Tülku (Emeryville, Calif.: Dharma, 1973), p. 105.

23 See Garma C. C. Chang, *Teachings of Tibetan Yoga* (New York: University Books, 1963), p. 35.

24 Tarthang, *Calm and Clear*, p. 77.

25 Tarthang, *Openness Mind*, p. 67.

26 David-Neel, *Magic and Mystery in Tibet*, p. 245.

27 William James, *The Principles of Psychology* (London: Macmillan, 1901), vol. I, p. 239. (Emphasis in original.)

28 Eliade, *Yoga: Immortality and Freedom*, p. 48.

29 The thought-stream is characterized by *passive movement*. In contrasting the thought-stream with concentration we emphasize the property *movement*; in contrasting it with retracing we emphasize the property *passive*. In each case we focus on that property of the thought-stream by virtue of which it contrasts with the other stage, and we disregard any shared or common properties. In the contrast thought-stream versus retracing, the quality *movement* is disregarded because it is irrelevant, being common to both stages; what matters is the *nature* of the movement, passive or 'downhill' in the one case, active or 'uphill' in the other.

30 Cf. Buddhadasa's statement (p. 50) that the meditator who has attained deep *jhāna* must return to shallower levels before he can develop insight. However, a meditator who has, after long practice, mastered concentration and experienced the pleasant effects that accompany it, naturally tends to regard any return to the normal condition as a backsliding. It is therefore not surprising that even in practices designed explicitly for the developing of insight (e.g. Burmese *vipassanā*), deep concentration sometimes comes to be regarded as the goal. (Cf. p. 47).

31 However, in the case of observation of linking, this sequential correspondence is not a consequence of a prior assigning to a group, but rather is the criterion for that assigning.

Notes to Chapter VII

1 For a discussion of the colours in the *maṇḍala*, see Govinda, *Foundations of Tibetan Mysticism*, pp. 115 – 122.
2 Three different lists of *kasiṇas* are given: (1) earth, water, fire, air, blue, yellow, red, white (*Dhammasaṅgaṇi* 203, 41 – 2); (2) earth, water, fire, air, blue, yellow, red, white, space, consciousness (D iii 268, M ii 14 – 15, A i 38); (3) earth, water, fire, air, blue, yellow, red, white, light, space (*Visuddhi-magga* 110).
3 *Visuddhi-magga* 118 – 77.
4 M i 57 – 8.
5 The female consorts (not dealt with in this analysis for lack of sufficient information) appear to be, like the colours/elements and the *vāhanas*, a set independent of the dhyāni Buddhas with whom they are 'associated'. See Figs, 3, 4.
6 On these associations see Snellgrove, *The Image of the Buddha*, pp. 134 – 7; and Saunders, *Mudrā, A Study of Symbolic Gestures in Japanese Buddhist Sculpture*, pp. 43, 55, 58, 81, 88. Also Benoytosh Bhattacharyya, *The Indian Buddhist Iconography* (Calcutta: Mukhopadhyay, 1968), pp. 47 – 8.
7 M iii 136. Compare the simile of the monkey, p. 39.
8 Śāntideva, *Śikṣa-samuccaya* (*Compendium of Training*), quoted in Nyanaponika, *The Heart of Buddhist Meditation*, p. 201.
9 The symbolic status of the elephant is discussed in Zimmer, *Myths and Symbols in Indian Art and Civilization*, pp. 102 – 9.
10 Cf. Śāntideva's statement, in the passage cited above, that when the mind is tied with the rope of mindfulness, 'all danger has ended'.
11 Beyer, *The Buddhist Experience*, pp. 158 – 60. (Our emphasis.)
12 Geshe Nyawang, *Tibetan Tradition of Mental Development*, p. 220.
13 On the iconographic development of the dhyāni Buddhas, see Snellgrove, *The Image of the Buddha*, pp. 134 – 7.
14 Before the introduction of Buddha icons, the principal events in Gotama's life-story were represented by various symbolic objects: his birth by a lotus, an elephant, or the goddess Śrī; his enlightenment by a Bodhi Tree or an empty throne; his first teaching by a wheel or a pair of deer; and his death by a *stūpa*. Three of these objects, the lotus, elephant, and wheel, reappear in the later dhyāni Buddha symbolism.
15 See Govinda, *Foundations of Tibetan Mysticism*, p. 121.
16 For an example of such a variant listing, see Snellgrove, *The Hevajra Tantra* vol. I, p. 129.
17 For this version, see Wayman, *Yoga of the Guhyasamājatantra*, p. 10; also Dasgupta, *An Introduction to Tantric Buddhism*, p. 87.
18 On the root *mantra* (*mūlamantra*) and *bījas* in general, see Bharati, *The Tantric Tradition*, chapter 5. The sequence *Oṃ Āḥ Hūṃ*, with the balance category (*Oṃ*) named first rather than last as expected, represents a fairly common situation. Similar to this is a variant

version of the movement through the *maṇḍala* in which the centre cell comes first rather than last. (Cf. Chapter I, note 36.)

19 For examples of attempts at interpretation, see Bharati, *The Tantric Tradition*, pp. 133–4; and Govinda, *Foundations of Tibetan Mysticism*, which purports to be an extended interpretation of this *mantra*. Also see B. Bhattacharyya, 'Scientific Background of the Buddhist Tantras', *Indian Historical Quarterly* 32 (1956), pp. 290–6.

20 In theory *padme* could represent any one of the following: locative singular masculine/neuter, vocative singular feminine, nominative/accusative/vocative dual neuter/feminine. As a simple noun *padma* is optionally either masculine or neuter. Such ambiguity is common in Sanskrit, and can usually be resolved by considering context. However, in a brief *mantra* context gives little guidance.

21 Bharati, *The Tantric Tradition*, p. 133.

22 In a *dvandva* two or more nouns combine to form a compound whose grammatical number is determined by the number of items referred to. For example, 'Rāma and Lakṣmaṇa' (the names of two Hindu heroes) become *Rāmalakṣmaṇau*, the final *au* being the dual masculine inflexion. In the case of *maṇipadme*, we take the final *e* to be the dual neuter inflexion, whence the meaning 'jewel and lotus'.

23 The odd sequence of listing the five groups, and the frequent omission of *Hrīḥ* are both discussed in note 40 below.

24 On this *mantra* see Bharati, *The Tantric Tradition*, p. 135.

25 The words *Evaṃ mayā* ('Thus by me . . .'), which introduce each *sūtra* in the Sanskrit, are often similarly broken into pseudo-*bījas*: *E, Vaṃ, Ma, Yā*. See, for example, Fig. 4 and the description of the *cakras* quoted on page 19 above; also see Dasgupta, *An Introduction to Tibetan Buddhism*, p. 150.

26 We are not aware of any actual occurrences of this *mantra*. However, Dargyay describes a close approximation to it, namely *Oṃ Ā Hūṃ Svāhā*. See Dargyay, *The Rise of Esoteric Buddhism in Tibet*, p. 19.

27 The recognizing of *Svā* and *Hā* as *bījas* is a good example of the scholastic elaboration so evident in the *tantras*.

28 That such confusions do happen is demonstrated by the existence of the further variant versions mentioned earlier in which, apparently, *Traṃ* has been misread as *Traḥ*, *Oṃ* as *Vaṃ* or *Vuṃ*, etc. *Bījas* are particularly likely to be misread because they lack meaning in the usual sense.

29 A v 33. See also I. B. Horner, *The Middle Length Sayings* vol. II (London: Luzac, 1970), p. 335, note 2. The lion is further equated with the teaching of the Dharma and the turning of the Dharma-wheel, thus reinforcing the connection with enlightenment.

30 On this incident see J. Hakin *et al., Asiatic Mythology* (London: Harrap & Co., 1932), p. 154. A rather different account of the incident is given at *Dhammapada-aṭṭhakathā* iii 241–7.

31 On the serpent symbolism, see Zimmer, *Myths and Symbols in Indian Art and Civilization*, pp. 59 – 68; also J. P. de Souza, 'The Serpent as a Symbol of Life and Immortality', *Journal of Indian History* 44 (1966), pp. 441 – 53.

32 The available descriptions of Mount Meru differ in details but all agree in emphasizing the cruciform arrangement. See, e.g. Swami Pranavananda, *Kailas-Manasarovar* (Calcutta: S P League, 1949), pp. 8 – 9.

33 One of the four Tirthaṅkaras depicted is Pārśva, identified by a *nāga* hood arching over his head. Tibetan representations of the dhyāni Buddhas frequently omit the central Vairocana, and show Amoghasiddhi with a similar *nāga* hood. (See Plate 1.) In such cases it is barely possible to distinguish Tirthaṅkaras from dhyāni Buddhas. To complete the resemblance, both Tirthaṅkaras and dhyāni Buddhas are referred to as *jinas*, 'conquerors'. Also similar to the dhyāni Buddha arrangement is a grouping described briefly at S i 182 – 3. There it is related that on one occasion the Buddha appeared in the Brahmā-world and that four of his principal disciples then appeared to the north, south, east, and west of him, but on a lower level and with Brahmā in their centre.

34 Eliade, *Yoga: Immortality and Freedom*, p. 250.

35 Govinda, *Foundations of Tibetan Mysticism*, pp. 115 – 25.

36 Wayman, 'Female Energy and Symbolism in the Buddhist Tantras', p. 90.

37 A good example of such a *maṇḍala* may be seen in the collection of the Birla Academy of Art and Culture in Calcutta.

38 The positions of the circular and semicircular continents are sometimes interchanged, perhaps because the semicircle suggested the moon and therefore the water group. (Cf. Evans-Wentz, *Tibetan Yoga and Secret Doctrines*, pp. 303 – 6.)

39 The occasional interchanging of the colours of the eastern and central cells (without any corresponding interchanging of the colours of the dhyāni Buddhas that occupy those cells), may reflect later vacillation on the part of the *siddhas* over the question whether it might be more appropriate to associate blue with space and white with water. (Cf. p. 107).

40 On the *vāhanas* in the Tibetan world-map, see Pranavananda, *Kailas-Manasarovar*, p. 14 and Plate 102. The arrangement of the *vāhanas* in the map differs from that in the *maṇḍala* as shown:

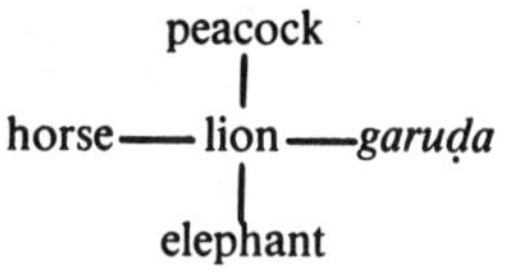

Maṇḍala

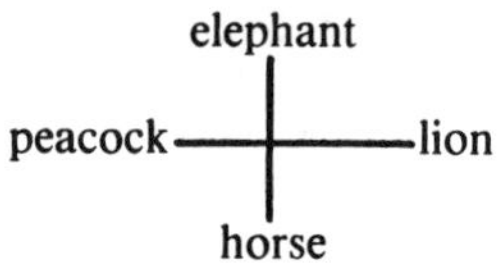

Map

Regarding the discrepancy between these two arrangements it is pertinent to consider the following variant of the *maṇḍala*, commonly seen in cases where the dhyāni Buddhas are located around a large *stūpa*. (See Plate 8.)

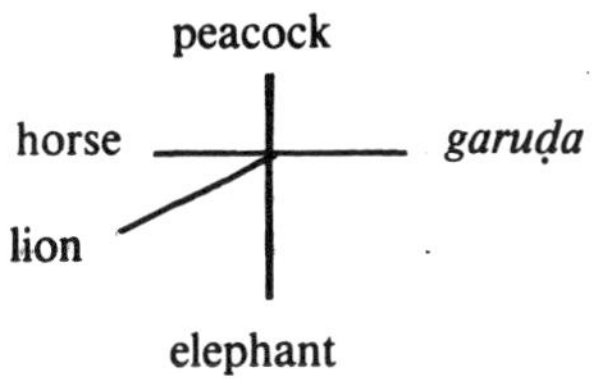

Here Vairocana (lion *vāhana*) has been moved from his proper place at the centre of the *stūpa* (where he would not be seen) to a point on the periphery between Akṣobhya (elephant) and Ratnasambhava (horse). Let us now consider speculatively the effect of deleting Amoghasiddhi (*garuḍa*) from this arrangement and moving Akṣobhya (elephant) and Vairocana (lion) around to fill the gap. The result would be the following hypothetical arrangement:

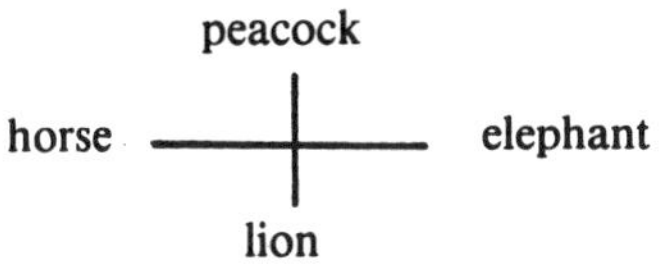

This is identical with the layout of the Tibetan map except for a ninety-degree difference in orientation. Such a difference in orientation is not surprising given that Tibet was simultaneously under the influence of two different conventions for the orienting of maps: the Indian, which placed north at the right, and the Chinese, which placed north at the top.

The above hypothetical arrangement of the dhyāni Buddhas has further explanatory value, as will now be shown. The associated *bījas* and emblems are:

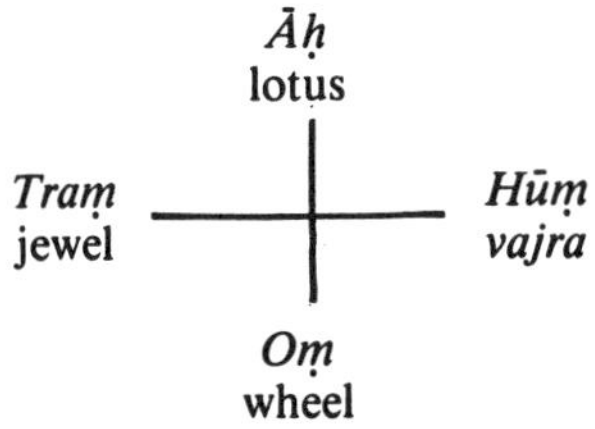

The *pradakṣiṇa* movement through this pattern, with arbitrary choice between *bīja* and emblem, yields: *Oṃ*, jewel, lotus, *Hūṃ*, that is the *mantra Oṃ maṇi-padme Hūṃ*. Here the components of the *mantra* are in the familiar illogical sequence, and, as is often the case, *Hrīḥ* is missing. Thus the frequent omission of Amoghasiddhi's *bīja* from the *mantra* correlates with the omission of his *vāhana* from the Tibetan world-map. This, together with the above ready explanation for the sequence *Oṃ maṇi-padme Hūṃ*, indicates that the postulated deletion of Amoghasiddhi (the last dhyāni Buddha encountered on circumambulating the *stūpa*) is in fact likely to have taken place.

41 Some doctrinal sets often included in the *maṇḍala* (the five *skandhas*, sense spheres, wisdoms, etc., see Fig. 3) have not been dealt with. Of these the wisdoms would seem to be directly relevant to our study; however, comparison reveals no evident pattern of correspondence.

42 The four-*cakra* version is very variable. See Dasgupta, *An Introduction to Tantric Buddhism*, pp. 146 – 53; and Snellgrove, *The Hevajra Tantra* vol. I, pp. 38 – 9. The alternative *bījas E Vaṃ Ma Yā* shown in Fig. 4 are discussed in note 25 above.

43 Govinda, *Foundations of Tibetan Mysticism*, p. 184. This version of the *cakra* system (for which Govinda gives no textual authority) serves to bridge the gap between the usually cited Buddhist version with four *cakras* (Table 5) and the Hindu version with six or seven, described in the *Saccakranirūpaṇa* (translated in Arthur Avalon, *The Serpent Power* (New York: Dover, 1974)). The Hindu version has an extra *cakra* at the genitals and another between the eyes, probably as a result of superimposing the *nāḍi* system. The addition of the new genital *cakra* necessitated a further rearrangement of the elements: water, fire, air, and space all had to be moved down one place to fill the gap.

44 See Govinda, *Foundations of Tibetan Mysticism*, pp. 173 – 85; and Eliade, *Yoga: Immortality and Freedom*, pp. 236 – 49. For a remarkably detailed account of the *cakras* allegedly based on introspective observation, see C. W. Leadbeater, *The Chakras — A Monograph*, (Adyar: Theosophical Society, 1968).

Notes to Chapter VIII

1 D i 156, D iii 107, S iii 168, etc.

2 On the *saṃyojanas* and the discarding of them by the different grades of *ariya*, see D i 156 – 7, and *Encyclopaedia of Buddhism*, vol. I, pp. 506 – 7.

3 *Vimutti-magga* of Upatissa (Taishō 1648), trans. by N. R. M. Ehara, Soma Thera, and Kheminda Thera as *The Path of Freedom* (Colombo: D Roland D Weerasuria, 1961), p. 222.

4 *Dhammapada* 277 – 9. Cf. also D iii 143, S iii 67, A i 285 – 6. Impermanence is often mentioned alone, e.g. at D ii 198, S i 200. Great importance is attached to the three characteristics at the present day.

Many Theravāda monks chant the three-line formula every morning and evening.

5 Cf. *Pali-English Dictionary*, pp. 335 – 8, where *dhamma* as a term in Buddhist psychology, is defined as 'that which is presented as "object" to the imagination and as such has an effect of its own'. It is 'a presentation, . . . idea, or purely mental phenomenon as distinguished from a psychological phenomenon, or sensation.' 'The mind deals with ideas as the eye deals with forms: it [*dhamma*] is the abstraction formed by *mano*, or mind proper, from the object of sense presented by the sense-organ when reacting to external objects.' The *Abhidhamma* mentions analytic knowledge of *dhammas* as a means of insight into causal antecedents (*Vibhaṅga* 263); *dhamma* is 'an object of ideation' (*Dhammasaṅgaṇi* 146, 157, 365); and *dhamma-dhātu* is 'the mental object considered as irreducible element' (*Dhammasaṅgaṇi*, 58, 67, 147 etc.; *Vibhaṅga* 87, 89).

6 D i 70, D iii 103, etc.

7 E.g. T. W. Rhys Davids, I. B. Horner. However, occasionally Rhys Davids translated *dhamma* as 'image' in this context, e.g. in his *Dialogues of the Buddha* Part II, p. 336. As the fourth object of mindfulness, *dhamma* appears to have a broader reference (See below).

8 M i 116 – 17. See pp. 24 – 5 above, where we quoted Horner's translation, in which *dhammā* is rendered 'mental states'.

9 See *Pali-English Dictionary*, pp. 324 – 6. On the difficulty of translating the term *dukkha*, see Rhys Davids, *Dialogues of the Buddha* Part I, p. 249, note 1.

10 D ii 305 – 7.

11 Cf. D iii 209.

12 See *Pali-English Dictionary*, pp. 664 – 5. Also cf. Rhys Davids, *Dialogues of the Buddha* Part II, p. 196; and Horner, *The Middle Length Sayings* vol. I, pp. xxiv – xxv.

13 The five *khandhas* are *rūpa, vedanā, saññā, saṅkhārā, viññāṇa* (body, feelings, perceptions, affective states, consciousness). Horner translates *saṅkhārā* in this context as 'habitual tendencies', but in the *paṭicca-samuppāda* as 'karma formations'. See *The Middle Length Sayings* vol. I, pp. xxiv – xxv. Rhys Davids prefers 'volitional complexes' (in his translation of D iii 233). Cf. also *Pali-English Dictionary*, pp. 664 – 5, where *sabbe saṅkhārā* is translated 'everything, all physical and visible life, all creation', 'the world of phenomena'. Compare this macrocosmic meaning with the microcosmic definition given in the *Dhammasaṅgaṇi* : *saṅkhāras* are 'the mental concomitants, or adjustments which come, or tend to come, into consciousness at the uprising of a *citta*, or unit of cognition' (Dhs 1, cf. M iii 25). Much of the confusion over the meaning of this term stems from a failure to recognize its simultaneous macrocosmic and microcosmic reference. Gotama was faced with the need to invent a psychological vocabulary; he did so by giving an additional microcosmic reference to existing macrocosmic terms.

14 Cf. S iv 156 for *anicca* as referring to mental phenomena.
15 One of the best expositions is at D ii 305–14.
16 D ii 308–9.
17 D ii 310–11.
18 D ii 61, 388. The three kinds of *taṇhā* are also (rarely) given as *kāma-*, *rūpa-*, and *arūpa-* (D iii 216); or as *rūpa-*, *arūpa-*, and *nirodha-* (D iii 216).
19 See A i 201, D i 71, 156–157. The full sets are as follows. *Nīvaraṇas: kāmacchanda, vyāpāda, thīna-middha* (drowsiness), *uddhacca-kukkucca* (distraction), *vicikicchā; saṃyojanas: kāmacchanda, vyāpāda, rūparāga* (attachment to the *rūpa jhānas*), *arūparāga* (attachment to the *arūpa jhānas*), *māna* (conceit), *uddhacca-kukkucca, avijjā*. But the list of *saṃyojanas* is very variable; often three others are added at the beginning: *sakkāyadiṭṭhi* (mistaken view that there is a self), *vicikicchā*, and *sīlabbataparāmāsa* (belief in the efficacy of precepts and vows).
20 This fact is recognized in the *paṭicca-samuppāda*, the chain of conditioned arising: the first link, *avijjā* (ignorance) is the condition for the second, *saṅkhāras* (affective states). (See S ii 7.) But whereas the presence of affective states implies the presence of ignorance, absence of affective states does *not* necessarily imply absence of ignorance. Affective states can be temporarily suppressed (as in the first *jhāna*) without insight being present.
21 E.g. at D ii 98.
22 M i 23. The translation is Horner's, as quoted earlier on p. 8, but with the Pali terms *dukkha* and *āsava* retained.
23 Thus the macrocosm-microcosm parallelism to which we drew attention in the case of the third knowledge also applies in the case of the third Noble Truth: the macrocosmic liberation from *saṃsāra* is effected through a microcosmic (mental, meditative) attainment.
24 A more complete discussion is given in Bucknell, 'The Buddhist Path to Liberation'.
25 M i 301. According to Pande, the *Cūḷa-Vedalla* is relatively late among the Majjhima *suttas*, and 'shows very clearly the tendencies of scholastic systematization'. Pande, *Studies in the Origins of Buddhism*, pp. 134, 179.
26 *Dukkhe ñāṇaṃ, dukkhasamudaye ñāṇaṃ*, . . . D ii 312.
27 M iii 74–76 (Our translation).
28 M iii 71 (Our translation). Beginning from *jhāna 1*, the Path becomes substitutive rather than cumulative.
29 D ii 122, iii 229, A ii 1, 78, 141.
30 The grouping of stages mentioned at D i 171 and 206 indicates that *sīla* may include stages 1 and 2 as well as 3–5.
31 *So idaṃ dukkhan ti yathābhūtaṃ pajānāti, ayaṃ dukkhasamudayo ti yathābhūtaṃ pajānāti*, . . . M i 183; and cf. note 26 above.
32 The footprint series occurs at M i 179–84, 344–8, ii 38–9.
33 For a detailed discussion of these correspondences, see Bucknell,

'The Buddhist Path to Liberation', pp. 11 – 16.

34 Some scholars have alleged that Theravāda Buddhist morality is essentially selfish. On this debate see Richard H. Jones, 'Theravāda Buddhism and Morality', *Journal of the American Academy of Religion* 48 (1979), pp. 371 – 81; and N. Ross Reat, ' "Theravāda Buddhism and Morality": Objections and Corrections', ibid., pp. 433 – 40.

35 The wisdom of this suppressing of emotions would be questioned by most Western psychologists. However, it is only in this early stage of the Path that suppression is advocated. In more advanced stages emotions are diminished through detached observation (Stage 7), or completely dissipated through the practice of insight (Stage 9).

36 Krishnamurti made this comment during a public address at Madras, India, in 1973.

37 D ii 312 – 13.

38 M i 180 – 1.

39 On the *brahma-vihāras* see D i 249 – 51.

40 Mindfulness is described in detail in the *Mahā-satipaṭṭhāna-sutta* (D ii 290 – 315) and the *Satipaṭṭhāna-sutta* (M i 56 – 63). These differ only in that the former includes an expanded explanation of the four Noble Truths.

41 D ii 299 – 300.

42 D ii 300 – 3.

43 The seven are: *sati, dhamma-vicaya, viriya, pīti, passaddhi, samādhi, upekkhā* (mindfulness, investigation of the Teaching, energy, joy, tranquillity, concentration, equanimity) (D ii 303 – 4). The second item raises again the problem of the meaning of *dhamma*; but translators consistently take it as referring to truth or the Teaching, and we follow this interpretation. Cf. Rhys Davids, *Dialogues of the Buddha* Part II, p. 336; and *Pali-English Dictionary*, p. 490.

44 Cf. Note 13 above.

45 D ii 304, M i 62 (Our translation). In the former case the quoted section is followed by a long explanation of the Truths.

46 M i 183, and above, pp. 166 – 7.

47 See Taishō 26 (98) (vol. I, pp. 582 – 4), corresponding to the *Satipaṭṭhāna-sutta*. The *Mahā-Satipaṭṭhāna-sutta* has no Chinese counterpart — naturally, since it differs from the *Satipaṭṭhāna* only in the section on the four Noble Truths. This situation indicates that the Pali versions represent stages in a progressive elaboration from an earlier version which did not mention the *khandhas* and Truths. First the *khandhas* and Truths were added, giving the *Satipaṭṭhāna*; then to this was added the nine-page discussion of the Truths, yielding the *Mahā-Satipaṭṭhāna*. Cf. Thich Minh Chau, *The Chinese Madhyama-Āgama and the Pali Majjhima-Nikāya (A Comparative Study)* (Saigon: Institute of Higher Buddhist Studies, 1964), p. 94; and Warder, *Indian Buddhism*, pp. 86, 87.

48 The Sutta version occurs, e.g., at D i 182 – 4, the Abhidhamma at Vibhaṅga 263 – 6.

49 This fact is demonstrated in Stuart-Fox, '*Jhāna* and Buddhist Scholasticism'.

50 See, e.g., Henepola Gunaratana, *A Critical Analysis of the Jhānas in Buddhist Meditation*, PhD dissertation, The American University, Washington, 1980, pp. 112 – 13, 142 – 3; and Nārada, *A Manual of Abhidhamma*, pp. 47 – 55, 58 – 9. The confusion appears to have arisen out of the Abhidhamma statement that *cittass' ekaggatā* (mental onepointedness) is present in the first *jhāna*. This led to an assumption that *jhāna* is a state of deep concentration, and hence to a reinterpretation of *vitakka-vicāra* (discursive thought) as an attentive focusing on the meditation object. It also necessitated the setting up of a subsidiary series of stages passed through on the way to this revised 'first *jhāna*' — whence the series *parikamma-samādhi*, etc., each with its corresponding object: *parikamma-nimitta*, etc.

51 This summary is abstracted from Bucknell, 'Interpreting the *Jhānas*'. It parallels the description given in Chapter III.

52 The term 'space' (*ākāsa*) is apparently being used to signify the absence of the elements earth, water, fire, and air. This is appropriate since in this *jhāna* the object is a mental image; all perception of external objects and of one's own body has ceased.

53 In fact the *uggaha nimitta is* experienced with tactile objects; however, it is masked by the original tactile sensation — hence the apparent skipping of a stage.

54 M i 22. The full quotation is given on pp. 7 – 8 above.

55 M iii 230.

56 J. W. de Jong, 'The Background of Early Buddhism', p. 426(45). Cf. Jacobson: The path of the Buddha is 'an arduous type of spiritual experimentation'. Nolan Pliny Jacobson, *Buddhism: The Religion of Analysis* (Carbondale, Ill.: Southern Illinois University Press, 1970), p. 49; or Dutt: Sambodhi 'was no intuitive experience; it was one strenuously reached through ascending stages of meditation'. Dutt, *The Buddha and Five After-Centuries*, p. 39.

57 S i 103 – 27. Cf. Chapter I note 19 above.

58 Cf. the *Khaggavisāna-sutta* of the *Sutta-nipāta*, each verse of which ends with 'let him [the meditator, monk] wander alone like a rhinoceros'.

59 The six *pāramitās* are *dāna, śīla, kṣānti, vīrya, dhyāna, prajñā* (charity, moral conduct, patience, energy, concentration, insight).

60 This is the goal of the Mādhyamika. See Nāgārjuna, *Madhyamaka-śāstra*.

61 The analysis of the world into its five constituent elements (Cf. *Taittirīya Up.* 1.7) became the basis for a universal classification in which 'identities' were purely symbolic.

62 An early emphasis on meditation is indicated by the Vajrayāna concern with achieving *prajñā*, not in some distant future existence, but

here and now. Practice (the Tantric search for awareness) replaced the sterile intellectualism of the Mahāyāna schools. Unfortunately the practice all too often degenerated into a mystifying ritualism — but there was nevertheless a renewed interest in meditation.

63 Such continuity is strongly suggested by the emphasis on awareness in the teachings of Tarthang Tülku and other present-day Tibetan masters.

64 Nor is such proof provided by the lists of early Buddhist patriarchs found in *Taranatha's History of Buddhism in India*, trans. Lama Chimpa and Alaka Chattopadhyaya (Simla: Indian Institute of Advanced Studies, 1970), pp. 355–61; or in the chronology of Tantric *siddhas* given by L. M. Joshi, *Studies in the Buddhistic Culture of India* (Delhi: Motilal Banarsidass, 1967), appendix 5, pp. 449–58.

Notes to Chapter IX

1 King dismisses this condemnatory attitude with the following comment: 'One may suspect a degenerate-age psychology which seeks to cover up its own embarrassment at its paucity of arahatship with appropriate warnings against pride.' King, 'A Comparison of Theravāda and Zen Meditational Methods and Goals', p. 313.

2 As the compilers of the *Pali-English Dictionary* freely acknowledge, the meanings of many key Buddhist psychological terms are far from clear.

3 See, e.g., recent papers in the *Journal of Transpersonal Psychology, Journal of Altered States of Consciousness*, etc.

INDEX